Praise for Charting the Unknown

"*Charting the Unknown* shows what is possible when you are prepared to step out of the imagined security of a suburban existence. Confronting her fears to sail the Atlantic, Kim Petersen enriches her life with the spirit of adventure and discovers that an ordinary existence can be made extraordinary. Along the way, she reconnects with her family and her innermost self. This is not only a journey of the oceans, but a journey of the heart."
~**Suzanna Clarke** – author of *A House in Fez*

"Kim Petersen's *Charting the Unknown* tells a story that has been told many times before—a tale of loss, grief, and the slow, uncertain mysteries of healing. What sets it apart is that, like all the best memoirs, it grounds that story in the lives of particular people the reader comes to care about and root for. There is also plenty of adventure in this tale, but perhaps the most daring feat of all is that behind every word we feel the sustained force of Petersen's intrepid honesty and unflagging compassion."
~ **Gregory Wolfe**, Editor, *Image* journal, founder and director of the Master in Fine Arts in Creative Writing at Seattle Pacific University

"It's not very often in life that you meet a family with a dream. Even less frequently you meet a family that will take a big risk to follow their dreams! This is that family and there is an important message for all of us in the story of their adventure, risk and reward!"
~**Dave Phillips,** coach of Canada's national freestyle ski team, holder of two World Records for Duration Skiing, motivational speaker and life/business mentor/coach.

A joyful and heartfelt account of getting into the cruising life! Enchanting stories and reminiscences of all aspects of the process of getting out and living your dream. We get to know the whole family and live with them as they master the cruising life. A great read for anyone who is a little hesitant about getting out there! "

~ **Paul & Sheryl Shard,** Authors of - *Sail Away! A Guide to Outfitting and Provisioning for Cruising,* and hosts for *Distant Shores Sailing* TV Show

"This is so much more than the surface story of a couple and their two teenagers who spend several years facing the challenges of living together aboard a 65-foot catamaran. The book begins with the author's inner journey as she copes with the loss of a child. Once we have lived with her through the worst, we are caught in her vivid and colorful images of the following years. As the challenges come her way, she brings us again and again into her inner search for meaning and connectedness. Right from the start we care about this family and its journey. The intimacy--and the camaraderie--of the book and the family are captivating."

~ **Rita Golden Gelman,** author of *Tales of a Female Nomad: Living at Large in the World*

Charting the Unknown

Family, Fear, and One Long Boat Ride

by
Kim Petersen

Behler™
PUBLICATIONS

California
USA

Behler Publications
California

Charting the Unknown
A Behler Publications Book

Copyright © 2010 by Kim Petersen
Cover design by Cathy Scott – www.mbcdesigns.com

Library of Congress Cataloging-in-Publication Data

Petersen, Kim.
  Charting the unknown : family, fear, and one long boat ride / by Kim Petersen.
    p. cm.
  ISBN-13: 978-1-933016-63-4 (trade pbk.)
  ISBN-10: 1-933016-63-9 (trade pbk.)
  1. Boat living--Atlantic Ocean. 2. Yachting--Atlantic Ocean. 3. Petersen, Kim--Travel-
-Atlantic Ocean. 4. Petersen, Kim--Family. 5. Atlantic Ocean--Description and travel. 6.
Family recreation--Atlantic Ocean. I. Title.
  GV777.7.P48 2010
  797.109163--dc22
                        2010010621

FIRST PRINTING

ISBN13: 978-1-93301694-8 (e-book)

Published by Behler Publications, LLC
Lake Forest, California
www.behlerpublications.com

Manufactured in the United States of America

For Lauren and Stefan.
Finer crewmates, teachers, friends, I cannot imagine.

For Bethany, whose short life compelled us to explore outside the lines.

And for Mike, fellow dreamer, navigator, vagabond and stand-up comic.

It's been worth the climb. The view from here is spectacular.

The Sound of the Sea

The sea awoke at midnight from its sleep,
And round the pebbly beaches far and wide
I heard the first wave of the rising tide
Rush onward with uninterrupted sweep;

A voice out of the silence of the deep,
A sound mysteriously multiplied
As of a cataract from the mountain's side,
Or roar of winds upon a wooded steep.

So comes to us at times, from the unknown
And inaccessible solitudes of being,
The rushing of the sea-tides of the soul;

And inspirations, that we deem our own,
Are some divine foreshadowing and foreseeing
Of things beyond our reason or control.

~ *Henry Wadsworth Longfellow*

Introduction

When I was in my twenties, I began to have my suspicions. The future, it seemed, rarely worked out the way I planned it. You would think this idea simple enough, but it took several metaphorical whaps on the noggin in the form of lost jobs, fires, break-ups, and blown out tires, to make me wonder how much control I really maintained over my life. It didn't help that early on I had picked up the notion that if I just minded my own business and strode confidently along with my five-year plan and seven highly effective habits, I could cajole life into doing what I wanted and what I wanted was no sudden movements. No unexplained phenomenon. What I wanted was a life submissive to my will with a benign, uneventful future that included copious amounts of coffee, books, and overstuffed LazyBoy. I wouldn't object to a sleek, red, byte-endowed laptop with which to write all the lofty thoughts I was having while reading about other people's lives. Surely the Universe could see that it was all so practical, convenient and comfortable, and would align itself with my path of least resistance.

But Life, that lackey of the Universe, obviously had other plans because it was inevitably handing me an unforeseen event cloaked in a grenade, the resulting "Ka POW" creating a reality far different than the one I had anticipated. The plot twisted. The landscape changed. I found myself in an alternate universe with no charts and no compass. Here, like everyone else, I was expected to survive using what little wit, wisdom, and provisions remained. Although previously incomprehensible, the unexpected became my home.

I didn't always have Lazy Boy aspirations. As a kid, I was encouraged to dream big. America, after all, had been built through the aspirations of many a profitable dreamer. The right to dream, I assumed growing up, must be listed somewhere in the Charters of Freedom. All the way through elementary school and even as a college student, I dreamed of a triumphant future and not only believed it a virtue but that, a la Disney, if I wished hard enough, my dreams would come true. By the time I was in my thirties, I had just enough life experience behind me to realize that things weren't always that simple.

Around that time, I was sitting in a trendy coffee shop and imagined meeting the person I was back in university. I was pretty sure she would have been a little perturbed to find that my life had become increasingly conventional, and through dogged busyness, devoid of ambition. After listening to my harried description of life, she would say,

"Look, I don't mind that you are married and have kids and are living in suburbia. But you seem so frazzled. Check it out-"

Here she would point to my white button down shirt, "You missed a button."

Then she would study my face closely, before adding, "And did you forget to put mascara on both eyes? Geez!" She would throw up her hands. "You see, this is exactly what I am trying to point out. You don't seem to have time for anything anymore! When did you last read a book? Or go skinny dipping? Have you played any foosball lately, and if so, are we still able to beat Mike? These things are important. And, say, whatever happened to that list of dreams we wrote up with Mike in college? You know, the ten things we hoped to accomplish before we died? Did you ever accomplish anything on that list? Hey!" She would stop and reach over to grab my arm enthusiastically, "Did you ever live on a boat like we planned? Because that was our favorite!"

Glancing around while discreetly re-buttoning my shirt, I would have to tell her that I hadn't read a book in ages, but I did read magazine articles while waiting for the dentist. And no, I hadn't played foosball, but maybe I would go to the arcade with the kids one of these days and show them a thing or two. Skinny dipping…well honestly, who did that at my age? And living on a boat? I had forgotten about writing it down on that dream list of long ago. I remembered that Mike and I had intended to read it every now and again in order to keep ourselves inspired, but then we had kids and got jobs and life shifted into 5th gear. I had no idea where that list ended up.

Then I would go on and on about how things were actually going great and yes, I was busy, but busy, once you got used to it, wasn't all that bad. After all, everyone was doing it and getting along just fine. And then my past self would roll her eyes and that would really tick me off. On the drive home from the coffee shop, I would consider how young and naïve I was back then. Too young to understand the demands of surviving in a hectic culture that required making ends meet and running the kids to clubs, sporting events, and music lessons, and playing catch up on the weekends with chores and housework. She had no knowledge of the emotional energy involved in relating to teenagers living under the same roof. I found her know-it-all attitude condescending. But I did envy her freedom and the unappreciated gift of believing anything was possible. I thought again of that dream-list and wondered if I would ever regret not being able to cross one or two things off of it.

What I barely recognized in the eyes of my younger self was hope. I wondered where along my journey I had tossed aside this kernel from which, upon germination, the green shoots of dreams begin to grow. Perhaps it wasn't that I had tossed the kernel aside as it had become buried under the hectic pace of years, the grief of losing someone dear to me, and the further thought of, "so what if I dream or set goals, life can come along at any time with its volcanic interruptions and ruin my plans anyway." I realized, then, that it had been several years since I had given my future a consideration outside of what to make for dinner and what warm locale I might live in when I retired. What I was missing, I recognized, were the grains of hope and their eventual growth into acres of tall, leafy stalks that swayed in the winds of my soul.

Acknowledging my position in life put me at risk. In the quiet recesses, the hard, pale green skin of my soul softened. Without recognizing it, I ripened. One day while cleaning, I unexpectedly happened upon that dream-list. When I showed it to Mike, I had no idea of the residual power it still retained. Like a stick of dynamite, it spontaneously ignited and blew a hole in the safety deposit boxes that had held our imaginations for so long. That list sparked a chain of events that led to a future whose storyline I could never have predicted, one that included Mike, our two teenagers, a 65 foot power catamaran yacht, and crossing the Atlantic Ocean.

If I had to name the chapters for this season of my life, the titles might have centered around building a boat and crossing the ocean, but things are never as simple as they seem. Behind the meta-narrative of our lives exists an intricately woven tale, one whose details are pertinent to the bigger picture. During that season, the outside events of my life combined with the reflections of my soul to gradually reveal a hesitant, mid-life dream, one whose texture reminded me of the dreams I had in childhood, when my mind was a vast open space, before it became cluttered, and all that laid before it was verdant potential, waiting to be grasped. The dream was further fueled by an intense desire to recapture time, live simply, and reconnect with myself, my kids, the environment, and even God. All this brought about an intense desire for change, which created its own combustible energy with enough propulsion to push my whole world right out into the unknown.

I look forward to running into my university self again one day. She will be pleased to hear that we built a boat, lived on it with our kids, and crossed the Atlantic Ocean. I will try to explain to her that it is one thing to write down your dreams on a scrap piece of paper, quite another to live them out, but I don't think she will understand. You have to live it to understand it, and she had yet to accomplish that dream. Reaching over to take her hand, I will look into her eyes and tell her that despite the hardships along the way, Goethe was right. There is power and magic in boldness. In following a dream.

Prelude

I was sitting on the soft, dimpled leather seats inside a black limousine, one of several in a somber lineup, and thinking that although I was twenty-four years old, it was only the second time I had ever been in limo. The first time was for my friend Jody Spencer's 13th birthday when I was in the 7th grade. Her parents rented a white limo and, as a surprise, went around and picked up about ten girls at their homes. I remembered that when the limo pulled up into my driveway there were a bunch of pastel colored balloons floating out through the sunroof along with several squealing girls beckoning me to join them. The limo took us to a fancy Italian restaurant where we stuffed ourselves with chicken scaloppini and, feeling sophisticated and chic, raised our apple juice filled wine glasses to toast the birthday girl.

The memory of my previous limo ride was a pleasant diversion, maybe even a coping mechanism, in what was otherwise a horrific day. Aptly, it was raining, and as the limo pulled further into the bucolic cemetery with its manicured lawn and tall oak and maple trees, I found the natural beauty, normally inspirational, a queer juxtaposition to my devastation. On a low lying hill under a tree, I caught sight of the pastor, our good friend, looking doleful in his dark suit. At his feet, a small casket rested on poles over a hole in the ground. A few people had arrived ahead of us, but they blended together in a monochromatic wash of black and grey. I kept my eyes on the casket. I thought how there was bone of my bone, flesh of my flesh, inside that box. A memory presented itself: my cheek against the softness of hers. The thought made my breath come in short, rapid bursts, and I felt like I might begin to hyperventilate. I clutched the armrest on the door and searched my mental files for a life-ring. Whether Divine or simply an effort at self preservation, a phrase from the past presented itself: "Why do you look for the living in the place of the dead?" I instantly began to relax. 'You've got to remember that,' I told myself. 'She isn't in that box. She isn't here anymore at all.'

And then, Mike and I got out of the limo and were ushered to a place of prominence, close to the shiny, white casket, and despite the fact that I loved our pastor friend, who was, quite honorably, talking about questions and doubt, my mind began to wander. I thought what a stupid cultural tradition this was, standing there dressed up in front of all those people, when what I really wanted was to escape to a remote cave in the Himalayan Mountains and hide out for the rest of my life. I began to dread the reception after the burial. I imagined it would be similar to the visitation we'd had at the funeral home the night before, with awkward conversations and meaningless chit chat, both annoying under the best of circumstances. I got mad at myself for being a spineless wimp and allowing events to be carried along by the masses instead of saying "STOP! We are not having a traditional funeral. We are going to deal with this in our own way." This was just another example, I thought, of what happened when you were a people pleaser like me.

Most surprising, was how I had come to be here at all when four days ago life was going along just as normal as ever. I had been master of my domain then, a queen presiding over two young daughters, running to the mall, making homemade lasagna for dinner, folding stacks of laundry, and kissing Mike when he came in the door after work. Life was going along exactly as I had scripted, and why shouldn't it? I loved God, my neighbor, and myself, but was careful not to love myself too much so as to be selfish. I went to church and volunteered in the nursery. I thought of myself as a good person with a good heart.

The God of the universe was apparently fond of my church denomination, or so I had been taught, and he had my back. I lived in one of the wealthiest countries in the world and up to that point in my life, had little personal experience with sickness and death. The fact that death and grief should interrupt my life-plans was galling.

For how long, I wondered, had I clomped over the crust of the earth heedlessly believing myself above reality? Standing in the rain that day, I felt a keen sense of loss, not only for my daughter, but for the loss of my youthful innocence when my life was less complicated. Now, the future seemed uncertain, and each step I made was one that took me further into the unknown. As I stared at the white casket, I could practically feel the cellular structures in my brain transforming to include fear and doubt, and I knew that from that point on I would be a different person. The freedom and invincibility of my childhood receded and was replaced by a dread of future events. Now that I knew the truth, that control did not exclusively belong to me, would I ever be free to dream again?

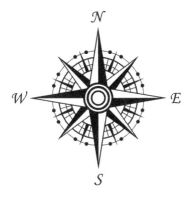

~Part One~

True course: a nautical term used to describe a course corrected for variation and deviation; one that is referenced to geographic north.

1

I try to remember what it was like to have the heroic, uninhibited, completely impractical dreams of a child. Now that I am over 40, searching the cranial hard drive that far back is like trying to catch a piglet in a corral. I played a game of this once at a summer fair, and just before the starter's whistle blew I wondered what the big deal was. Once the ten greased piglets were released into the corral, how hard could it be to grab the one piglet that had a ring in its nose? I studied my competition, five teenage boys, lined up against the gate next to me. They gazed intently across the broad corral that was full of mud and ringed with spectators in cowboy hats, and had little regard for a scrawny girl wearing a backwards baseball cap. None of it mattered to me. The pig was small and not nearly as smart as I was at thirteen.

While the rest of the contestants bolted into the corral at the whistle, I hung back, intending to let them chase the little beasts right to me. The piglets ran in a large arc close to the fence, mud spattering against the paint-crackled two-by-fours, my cohorts in hot pursuit of their curly tails. The herd, moving as one, made a fluid turn, and continued to make tracks down the middle of the pen directly toward me. Not much in life is more daunting than ten stampeding, squealing piglets, followed by a company of teenage boys, both groups careening through the mud right for you as if you were a bull's eye.

In my terror, I almost forgot to look for the pig with the ring but, at the last second, spotted him leading the pack. As he raced past, I made the lunge of my life, head first through the mud and slime. Pete Rose would have been proud. Amidst the trampling of swine hooves, I grasped a sleek, pink, torso for all of two seconds, before he slipped through my grimy hands. I looked up to see my rivals put on their brakes and change directions, resulting in a whirling of cartoon-like legs and a pandemonium of bodies attempting to avoid collision with my own. The spray of mud, similar to a school bus plowing through a gutter after a hard rain, hit me head on. Drenched, dripping, and dazed, I managed to stand. My attempt pleased the crowd, who burst into applause and laughter.

By the time I was mobile again, some young buck in a cowboy hat was holding a shrieking, wiggling, prize with hardly a smudge on him. He won a cake and a hot air balloon ride. Memories are like that. You see a bunch speeding in your direction and try to nab one. Just when you think you have captured it, it slips away into the darkness. The whole endeavor is mucky business and you attempt it at your own risk.

As a kid your greatest asset is that you lack the significant experiences that might cause you to pause in your dreaming. Through the mental mire, I have a vague memory of a now fuzzy faced adult asking if I wanted to be an astronaut. I examined the idea like a Rubik's cube, turning it over in my mind. Such occupations required helmets and space suits which reminded me of a man I had seen shot out of a canon at the circus. Exploding bodily from a plume of smoke to fly through the air was certainly something to admire.

"Why yes," I said, "I think I will be an astronaut and fly to the moon."

Or, on a different day, a pilot. Years of schooling, risks, and relocation, are not computed by youthful innocence which walks by the buffet table of life and says, "I'll have some of this and some of that." The future is an Aladdin's lamp which you rub and receive three wishes. I knew nothing of Ernest Shakleton or the Titanic. I did know Luke Skywalker and Superman. Things seemed to work out just fine for them.

Back then, I didn't mind that in superhero storylines there was always a life threatening battle to be fought. A hell bent Medusa to foil. Evil may loom around the corner waiting to take over the world, but that isn't a problem for a kid who routinely plans to rescue it in one gallant swipe of a cut-out cardboard sword. The universe awaits your glory when you are five and wearing a red towel for a cape. Your mother may tell you, as she rolls her eyes, that the neighborhood absolutely needs saving. It's a good thing you're around. Please go out and rescue it in time for supper.

On the first day of kindergarten, you quickly learn that a cape is not appropriate and certainly does no good in saving you from the numerous snide comments that will be hurled in your direction should you choose to wear one. From that day forward, you begin to compartmentalize. Things you can do. Things you can't. The pain versus reward ratio reveals itself to you in botched attempts at skateboarding down the stairs. The elders of the community regurgitate the dangers of a world gone mad on the six o'clock news, which confirms your fears, and you become a skeptic at age 7. Unknown to you, a sleeping giant has been roused in your brain who may shake her head doubtfully and mutter for the rest of your days, "I'm not so sure you can do that." If you are one of the lucky ones, you can ideally transfer your imaginary superpowers to your father, who will remain invincible until he loses his job, sees your first bad report card, or turns out to be Darth Vader.

With considerable clarity, I do recall wanting desperately to be quarterback of the Denver Bronco football team. In my elementary years I watched the lanky quarterback, Craig Morton, throw bomb after bomb to the lithe and quick Rick Upchurch. I loved the drama of watching a play begin in a huddle of desperados who whispered to each other in code, nodded in agreement, patted each other's butts, and clapped in confirmation. Strategy came to life in a Napoleonic effort to claim turf. Wars of this magnitude would be nothing without the world looking on, cheering or groaning, and spilling beer on their neighbor. From my own seat on the couch in the family room, I watched every Bronco game religiously. I knew all the players and stats. On the days I wasn't wearing the team colors of orange and blue, I drank the teams carbonated beverage, Orange Crush, by the barrelful. In 1978, the Broncos lost to the Dallas Cowboys in Superbowl XII, and I lay on the same couch and sobbed. Upon expressing my quarterback dreams, certain significant others, seeking to spare me disappointment, asked if I might want to be a cheerleader instead. Perhaps it was natural as I was blonde and leggy even as a child. I was mortified. Who would want to stand on the sidelines when you could be in the game?

I was nine years old when I learned the hard truth that women could not play in the NFL. I learned it from Avery Adams, youngest member of the "Adams Family" who lived in an unkempt, dilapidated rancher on the corner. Jokes abounded. During a schoolyard game, I stood on the line of scrimmage, my hands ready to receive the hike, and told Avery where to stand. He refused. I was furious. I told him I was the quarterback and he would do what I said or I'd bench him. He yelled back at me, "Whatever boss lady, it's not like you're ever going to play in the NFL!" I stuck my tongue out at him and subsequently threw the ball 10 yards to my wide receiver, who ran across the goal line for a touchdown.

Later, I considered his comment. I worked systemically through all the teams in the NFL. Sure enough, not a woman in the lot. It was the first time I realized that there were certain things I could not do because I was a girl. Frustrated, I all but gave up on my gender that day. After all, what fun did they have? While women took care of the food and the cleaning, not at all thrilling, men watched football, a highly valued pastime in my opinion. True, they may be in charge of the barbeque, but that was outside and near the croquet set or volleyball net and there was always time for a game in between flipping burgers. I admired this work/play strategy and aligned myself with it whenever possible.

As I neared adolescence, I found myself on the opposite side of a growing chasm from my girlish contemporaries. I could not relate to their annoying giggles or their frequent and dramatic spats. While they seemed content to huddle on sidelines, I wanted in on whatever game was being played that recess. To influence certain boys holding the keys to the forbidden city of male dominated sports, I distanced myself from my playground sisters. I practiced throwing a football through a tire hanging from a tree branch on the weekends. This did little to eliminate the grumbling of several boys every time I tried to get in on the action. After several successful attempts at proving myself, classmate Greg Tanner, keeper of the keys, called my name relatively early in the picking of teams and from then on I was a normal addition to recess sports.

Since I believe in a life after this one, it is my hope that there might be opportunities to fulfill unrequited dreams. You can be sure that I will look up Craig Morton, assuming he is post mortem, and get him to give me some pointers. We'll track down Rick Upchurch and Haven Moses and have ourselves a Denver Bronco-Dallas Cowboy rematch. I will be quarterback. There will be a stadium filled with fans eating hot dogs and doing the wave. In the last 10 seconds, with our team down by three, I will hurtle a Hail-Mary cannonball from our own 30 yard line which Upchurch will catch while diving into the end zone. He'll hold the ball up and wiggle his knees back and forth. After the game, I will run into Tom Landry, coach of the Cowboys during that fateful Bronco-Cowboy Super Bowl game. He will want to congratulate me on my success, and although I have the utmost respect for him, I will probably have to cross over to the other side of the street.

My fourth grade math teacher's name was Miss Kahn. I also had her for social studies. She was young, I thought, for a teacher. She had a thin, willowy, frame, long dark hair and, my mother said with some aplomb, was Jewish. We were Christians and from what I had picked up at Sunday school, Jews were practically kin. A religious grandparent of sorts. For this reason, I had an affinity for Miss Kahn, but also because she sighed. Voluminous breaths were slowly expelled from her small frame whenever we misbehaved or wrote a wrong answer at the blackboard. Mostly she sighed in math class and this I could relate to.

One day we were reviewing multiple digit subtraction and she said, "Class, I'd like all of you to take out a blank sheet of paper." There was a pause and a rustling of wide ruled sheets. "On the top I'd like you to write the number two thousand."

Another pause.

"Now, directly below this I want you to write the year in which you were born...everyone have that? All right, now I want you to subtract it from the two thousand."

A lengthier pause and the sound of pencils scratching.

"Paul, what number do you have?" she asked. Paul wore thick glasses and was quick in math, not so good in football.

"Thirty two," he said.

"Good. Anyone else have anything different?"

A few kids had thirty three, but most, including myself, had thirty two.

Right there at the front of Room 8 where nothing exciting ever happened, Miss Kahn morphed into an enchantress. She stood up from her desk and walked to the doorway, lifted her small hand to the light switch and flicked off the light. I turned around in my desk to look at the wide eyed girl who sat behind me. We shrugged our shoulders. The air was tingly. This, I thought, was the best kind of math. I glanced at my classmates through the dimness of light let in through thinly curtained windows. For the first time all year the class was completely absorbed.

"Now, I want you to close your eyes and imagine that you are in the year 2000.…think hard…what might life be like so many years into the future? "

Into my mind came a picture of the space age cartoon The Jetsons. Simultaneously I heard the theme song: "Meet George Jetson….his boy Elroy…."

Interrupting the chorus in my head, Miss Kahn continued in a soft voice, "What do you think it will be like in the year 2000? Raise your hand if you have an idea."

I raised my hand and said, "We'll travel in flying cars." Hands shot up across the room. I was peeking. Someone else said, "We'll live on the moon." "We'll eat instant food." "Travel by teleporting from one place to another." "Maybe we'll have our own robots and they'll do all our chores for us!" This got us going. "Maybe there won't be any school!" a boy from the back row shouted out without raising his hand. There were numerous shouts of "hurray!" at this answer.

Miss Kahn, leery of the boy in the back row, steered the conversation along by saying, "Class, I want you to open your eyes and look at your sheet of paper….The number you have written down on the paper in front of you is how old you will be when we leave this century, the nineteen hundreds, and enter into a new one, the two thousands. I want you to close your eyes again and imagine yourself at thirty two or thirty three. What will your life be like? Who will you be?" This time, there was a lengthier pause.

In my mind emerged a vision of me in biggie size, the face obscured. I was wearing a long, straight, blue skirt and was busy getting ready to leave the house for an important job like taste testing ice cream flavors for Baskin Robbins. On second thought, I would likely be a double agent and secretly packing heat around my waist. It appeared I was married to a man with dark hair who wore a blue pin stripe suit and a red tie around his neck. He sat at the kitchen table eating Fruit Loops. I was shooing two (or three?) children out the door with bag lunches: peanut butter and jelly sandwiches, apples, and Ding Dongs for dessert. I watched the kids board a yellow school bus and then the future me went down the front steps carrying a black leather briefcase, jumped into a car, and sped off in a hurry.

I was surprised to find that the future me was a stranger. A stranger driving in an unknown car. I didn't recognize her hair or her body or her shoes. I imagined my fourth grade self walking down the sidewalk carrying a load of school books and my grown up version pulling over to the curb next to me.

Rolling down the car window, she would ask, "You need a ride there, hon?"

Peering skeptically inside, fourth grade Me would quicken her pace, frown, and say, "I'm not supposed to get in the car with strangers."

Future Me would say something like, "Okay then. Your loss," and drive away. Later I would try to shake the curious feeling that I'd seen her someplace before. All too soon, Miss Kahn turned on the light and the moment was gone. I was left grasping at something I could not quite put my finger on, but felt like it was important and I had missed it. Through a dissipating mental fog I heard her say, "Children, you can open your eyes now. I wanted you to stretch your imaginations and learn that numbers are important. Remember that."

2

After high school graduation, I decided I agreed with Miss Kahn. Numbers were important. For instance, eighteen years was far too long to live in the same city, the same house, with the same people. I had zero tolerance for any numbers that happened to make up a curfew or the amount of chores needing to be completed on a Saturday. What I needed were fresh numbers in my life. Like the telephone digits of new friends who didn't insist on recounting all my embarrassing moments at every party. And it was definitely time to live at a new house number on what was preferably an avenue or a boulevard. Better yet, a Rue Le something-or- other. Going to university provided the opportunity to mix up the numbers in my life. To eliminate any possibility of running into people from my past at the mall, I decided to go to someplace outside the United States. I wanted something foreign, exotic, but not third world. Nothing too crazy. Canada, I thought, could be just the place. I applied to a university and got accepted. When friends asked where I was going for university, I told them British Columbia. Several of them asked why I was going to school in South America.

My preconceived ideas of Canada came largely from watching the fictional characters Bob and Doug McKenzie on SCTV, and later, the movie *Strange Brew*. I had further instruction from them in a tape cassette possessed by a friend called, *The Great White North*. I wasn't much of a beer drinker at that time, but I figured jelly doughnuts, if truly as prevalent as implied, would help ease my culture shock into Canadian society. I found the interjection of "eh" to be a quaint locution, much better than the American "huh." The summer before I left for school, I practiced calling my younger brother a "hoser" and found it to be a more than adequate insult. I told him to "take off eh" when he tried to tag along to the mall. Yes, it would seem to be cold in Canada, as evidenced by Bob and Doug's toques, but I figured I would keep warm by singing, with friends in a round, the catchy, "Coo Roo coo coo coo coo coo."

On a more educated level, I had heard of Canadian political giant Pierre Trudeau. If his antics, including mouthing the euphemism "fuddle duddle" to opposition MPs and performing a pirouette behind the back of Queen Elizabeth II, were any indication of the passion and humor of Canadians, I figured I was in for a rousing four years.

I was shocked to find that life in Canada was less than shocking.

Even without the help of jelly donuts, no more numerous than other doughnuts, I settled into a similar culture whose subtle nuances were initially lost to me. I was at university to get educated, not to get the famous MRS. degree. The first week of school I told my roommate I was not interested in boys or dating. She smiled and gave me two weeks before I succumbed like a wuss to having a boyfriend. I told her in no uncertain terms that I had my life all worked out and a boyfriend was not in the plan. I wanted to graduate and get a good job. It was important to me to be able to provide for myself without being dependent on some guy. She grinned.

The second week of school, I walked through one of the guys' dorms and found a foosball table. It was not my intention to set myself up as a foosball hustler, but when I asked the guy running the table if I could play and he smirked, nudged his buddy, and said something like, "next thing you know some girl is gonna want to be Prime Minister" I had no choice.

Sidling up to grab the handles, I said things like, "What a cute little ball," and "I think I'll name this little man here in the front row, Hank. Go Hank GO!"

The foosball junkies who had been hanging around dispersed in disgust until I got quiet and scored several goals in rapid succession. My burly opponent began to look nervous. A vein started to bulge in his neck, and beads of sweat formed on his forehead. His friend clapped him on the back and said jovially, "Dude! You're getting smoked by a chick!" If I didn't find the moment so savory, I would have felt sorry for him. How could he have known I spent my Saturdays playing the neighborhood on the foosball table in our basement? I decided to stop toying with him and end his misery, sliding the score counters to 10 on my side and 1 on his. By that time, a lineup of testosterone hopefuls, unable to bear the thought of a woman ruling what was so obviously a guy's domain, had formed to play me. At the end of this line, I noticed a shorter, robust guy in jeans and an untucked, blue, button down shirt. His eyes crinkled when he smiled reminding me of pictures I had seen of Santa Claus.

When it was finally his turn, he sauntered up to the table and said with cocky confidence, "Care to make it interesting?"

"Don't see that there's much need of that…" I stated, grinning wryly.

"How about if I win, you buy me dinner, if you win, I buy you dinner."

"Looks like you win no matter what," I said shrugging nonchalantly.

"How's that?"

"Either way you get to have dinner with me."

"Exactly," he said, making the first shot on goal.

Later that evening, he bought me take-out pizza. We ate it in the girls lounge because neither of us had a car.

Foosball aside, Mike reminded me of Evil Knievel without the white leather outfit. He jumped his motorcycle over flaming piles of bush, and raced around dirt bike trails. When he wasn't doing that, he climbed rocks and snuck around campus with a posse of guys wreaking havoc. Subsequent impressions led me to imagine him standing in the middle of life like a young Clint Eastwood saying, "Go ahead, make my day." When he was not climbing, jumping, or shooting things, he was betting.

"See that boulder down there? The one about 100 yards over this ledge?" he'd ask me as we hiked around Golden Ears in Lower Mainland, BC.

"A buck says I can peg it with this pebble."

Unfamiliar with his impeccable aim, but always up for a bet or two, I countered, "You're on, but then I get a chance to throw." His pebble would fly gracefully through the air and hit the center of the boulder most every time. Mine would land close. I was incensed but intrigued and continually out a couple of bucks.

Over the course of years, my childhood love of adventure had largely been tamed. As I neared my twentieth birthday, it was achieved from an overstuffed Lazy Boy. While the snow floated unnoticed across a large picture window, I would sit curled up under a goose down duvet sipping a cup of hot cocoa and allow myself to be transported via the written word through time, circumstance, and geography. It took little effort to superimpose my own image in place of the hero. It was sufficient enough stimulation and created within me the idea that thrill seeking was still part of my nature.

But backseat gun slinging is quite a stretch from actually grabbing a vine in the middle of a dank, scorching jungle and hurtling yourself over a precipice to elude oncoming tribal head hunters. When I first met Mike, I was unaware of this distinction. I was smitten by his motorcycle riding, skydiving, and rock climbing. It all reminded me of a character in one of my books.

In a favorite coffee shop one morning, I told Mike with sparkly eyes that I was an adventurer too. He believed me. I said it with such conviction that even I believed me.

"That's great news," he said with a mouth full of muffin. "How about going rock climbing with me this Saturday?"

I had never gone rock climbing in my life, but I figured how bad could it be?

Half way up a dry waterfall, I looked down 30 feet below and experienced my first bout of vertigo. My head reeled and my toes began to shake. The shaking traveled all the way up my body and reminded me of the cartoon character Wile E Coyote after he had eaten earthquake pills. Even my hands started shaking and I found it difficult to grasp the rocks. I thought I would fall with less fortunate results than the Coyote, who always managed to sit up holding an "oh drat" sign.

It took all of my reserve control to look over my shoulder and shout down, "I can't move!"

"How come?" he shouted back up, shielding the sunlight from his eyes with his left hand.

The jig was up and I would have to admit it. "I guess I'm afraid!"

"Good!" he yelled back, "that's what adventure is all about! Don't you feel alive?"

"Yes, but it's because I'm going to die!"

Mike patiently coached me earthward, and once superglued to terra firma again, my heart thumping in my chest, I nodded meekly as he told me what a great job I did and hadn't this been a fun day? Later I considered that rock climbing was not one of my dreams and told him so. It wasn't that I didn't enjoy rock climbing, it was that I hated the feeling of being out of control. As mile markers proceeded along the highway of our relationship, I noticed that Mike thrived outside his comfort zone and sought out situations that would test the fabric of his endurance. Perhaps this was why he was dating me.

One Monday night, several months later, we sat in the university cafeteria eating Sunday's leftover roast beef dinner slung together and topped with mashed potatoes quaintly labeled "Shepherd's Pie." We were discussing dreams of greatness and goals we hoped to accomplish in our lifetime. Every once in awhile, one of us would wave our arms wildly in the air, while the other nodded vigorously. We were invincible Rambos with a million lives. Old enough to think we had the qualities and resources to make life happen with zero responsibilities. The concoction made us bold. In a burst of inspiration, I ripped out a piece notebook paper and offered to write down the top 10 things we hoped to accomplish in our lifetime.

We gave ourselves complete permission to disregard any constraints, mainly time and money, and to be open to any idea no matter how cockamamie it seemed. The compilation was largely the result of watching too much CNN and Xtreme Sports Videos. Discussed in detail were the fears we had of becoming cogs in a globalized, industrial world. Running around all bug-eyed and stressed. No time for each other, family, life. For what? For money? We scoffed at the thought, which was ironic since earlier we had given ourselves a blank check upon which to dream, and where that money would come from was anyone's guess. Like most youth we were addicted somewhat to experience. Mike suggested bungee jumping in New Zealand.

"Why go bungee jumping?" I asked.

"Because it will keep us awake and alive to life. We can do it, say, five years into our marriage, just about the time we get comfortable and it will shock us awake again. Like throwing cold water on someone who has passed out."

His unconscious use of the "M" word aside, I considered it. By that time, I was just self actualized enough to suspect that I was a fireside daredevil, but not enough to say "forget it that's not who I am." I had no desire to go bungee jumping, but I wondered if I could change. He made a good point about "waking up," and since I still wanted to impress him with my openness to wild ideas, I wrote it down.

Seeing the seven natural and manmade wonders of the world made the list as well as *canoe down the Amazon.* We recognized that some of those goals were a little self absorbed and lacking in substance, so out of duty we added: *working as peacekeepers in a third world country.* As people who cared about the environment, or at least should, we decided that while canoeing in the Amazon we would *tie ourselves to some trees and help save the rain forest.* After that we could make a *pilgrimage to meet Pope John Paul,* if possible, *and Mother Teresa.* Good, we said, pleased with the list so far, we needed to be people of principle.

At the time, we were reading a book together about a young couple who lived aboard a sailboat and cruised the Hawaiian Islands. One of us brought it up as a potential dream. Here was a lifestyle where you could be free. Free to travel and live creatively. Connect with ourselves and each other. We could write books to earn a living and eat fish cooked over the fire on the beach of a deserted island. Even as the more cautious one in our relationship, I had to admit the idea appealed to me.

"Look," I said, "you could live for next to nothing on a boat. We would be living outside of conventional society, and how cool would that be?" Mike thought it was a grand idea.

"Wouldn't it be amazing if we could cross the ocean?" he said. Enchanted, number 6 became *Live on a boat and cross an ocean.*

To round out the list, we added: *learn to scuba dive,* which, Mike said excitedly, could be combined with the sailboat idea. Moving on, I mentioned Thoreau, and we decided *building our own log cabin in the woods next to a pond* should be on the list. Simplicity was important. We could live there for a year or two, maybe more. Grow our own organic food. We could eat walleye pike from the pond and I would make stew from the rabbits Mike shot in the forest. Nice. One of us, probably Mike, brought up having a family, and we enthusiastically agreed that *having a family and staying together* were of the utmost importance and became the last entry.

As our discussion wound its way to a conclusion, one thing concerned us. How would we remind ourselves of the importance of these goals, these dreams? Didn't life have the potential to drug us and make us forget? We thought of adult workaholic zombies and shuddered. Several options were considered, including tattoos, but in the end Mike suggested that we read our list every year on the anniversary of our first date. Great idea, I said, and so we agreed.

We looked at each other shyly and beamed. Mike stuck out his hand. I shook it. It was a great list, we said. We knocked our Coke bottles together and said, "Cheers." I opened my Abnormal Psychology textbook, the class for which I was now running late, unceremoniously folded our now gravy stained manifesto, and stuck it inside the front cover.

Despite the ensuing differences, our hearts were bound. In a smoke filled shabby diner, we began to speak openly of marriage. Contrarians even then, if the rest of the world said "wait to get married," we figured it would be wise to do the opposite. What did the world know anyway? We were familiar with the current marital statistics which suggested the stakes were high and the risks great. Just what Mike needed to hear. Plus, we said, marriage would be what we made it. We imagined it similar to climbing Mt. Everest. A fair bit of uphill trudging, but when you got to the top 50 or 60 years later, man, what a view!

We discussed strategy. Marriage must always be first, we said. If other things took priority, a spouse would become an adversary. A prison warden. At the time, the freshness of our friendship made it impossible to imagine being "trapped" or confined by our relationship, but it might be possible down the road. We wondered if we could craft a marriage in which we were both habitually aware of the freedom such a relationship offered. A marriage would be complete and total freedom to explore the other person, like a country, over the course of a lifetime, in turn allowing a partner, a friend most dear and true, to explore our own depths and heights with absolute trust that they had our very best interests at the foremost of their thoughts.

We speculated: to be explored in this way, known for who you are and loved unconditionally, wouldn't that bring the greatest peace and joy? How could we ever be bored when there would be some other peak to explore?

Against the better judgment of numerous elders who believed we should finish school first, we married after our second year of university. I was 20, Mike 21. Everyone said with breathy skepticism that we were young. In between university classes, we held down two jobs each and played house in our tiny nearby apartment. We were interested in building a solid marriage foundation so naturally I bought silly string. I hid two cans away and was patient. While Mike was in the shower, I cracked the curtain aside and opened fire with double barrels. Several days later, while singing in the shower, a bowlful of ice water spilled over the curtain rod rudely interrupting my near perfect interpretation of Whitney Houston's, "I Will Always Love You." Once I awoke in bed to find myself cocooned like a fly in a silly string web. We packed up club sandwiches and went to the park to study for our World Politics exam. When that got boring we read poetry while sitting on the grass with our backs up against a favorite oak tree. I gave Mike, a high school running back, largely unappreciated pointers in how to throw a football.

Around that time, a friend asked me how I found married life. I had dreamed of marriage. Once I had dreamed about it in Miss Kahn's math class. The man in the blue suit had turned out to be Mike, who was not keen on Fruit Loops. Real life was better than the dream, and I said so.

3

The August before our senior year we rented a basement suite close to the university and began preparations to finish our last year of school. Before classes were to begin, I began to feel sluggish. After throwing up for the third time in one week and oddly craving broccoli, I went to the local pharmacy, and bought a pregnancy test. A white-haired checkout lady, now privy to my most intimate secrets, eyed me speculatively as she waved the test in front of the scanner.

Back at home, Mike and I bent our faces over the small but omnipotent wand whose half inch square window held the key to our future. Gradually, two neon blue parallel lines emerged, indicating a positive result. The lines continued to increase in intensity until the rays were so powerful we were forced to look away.

Mother is a common enough word but one I had not thought to associate with myself, at least not before I graduated from university. The word had always been in reference to someone older: my own mother, grandmother, my mother in law. I was only 21. I took the last few days of summer vacation to consider the implications. I had a friend, Ruth, who was several years older than I, and had two small children. She was a Resident Director at the university. I asked her to lunch.

In between bites of Caesar salad, I told her I was pregnant. She was thrilled for me. It was as if I had won a new car.

I told her, "Honestly, I'm not sure how to feel. I don't know if I am ready to be a mother. I'm not even through university. We were supposed to go backpacking through Europe next summer."

She got quiet and sighed. Then she brightened. "Okay," she said, "here's how it is. Being a mother is no different than being a super hero."

"Oh brother," I said, throwing up my hands, "you can do better than that. I have serious problems. I'm not kidding around here, Ruth."

"No no, I am serious. Who's that Marvel Comic book guy? Stan Lee, right? He should have animated motherhood. Just like that spider in *Spider Man*, LIFE has bit you and your very cellular structure is changing. Once the baby comes you'll find you have three superpowers that you didn't have before: super-hearing, super-eyesight, and super-quick reflexes. In addition," (she sounded like a game show host. I started imagining Bob Barker on *The Price is Right* saying, "Come stand right over here and take a look and THIS!") "as time progresses you'll receive the gift of discerning truth from your kids and you don't even need a magic lasso."

She saw that I was doubtful. She took my hand in both of hers and said, "Being a mom is the best thing going. I guess I can't describe it in a way that you can relate to; you have to experience it for yourself. Raising them is the most difficult and rewarding thing I've ever done. It is not what I imagined, but it's better in so many ways, and it has made me better person. I know right now you don't think it's possible, but you can do this. The universe has given you nine months to get ready. Listen to yourself. To God. Once you hold that baby in your arms, you'll be blown away by the amount of strength you have."

Back at home, I told Mike I was warming up to the idea of being a mother. While making me pancakes he said, "Hey I thought of something. Remember our list of dreams we wrote down in the cafeteria? We are fulfilling number 10--having a family. One down, nine to go! Where is that list anyway?"

I told him it was true that we were fulfilling the dream, but it was not how I had planned it. Then I said I didn't really feel like pancakes so we walked to Dairy Queen, and I ordered two foot long chili cheese dogs. Mike eyed me suspiciously. "So it's come to this, then, has it?"

"Well," I said taking a huge bite and continuing with my mouth full, "I am eating for two now."

Maybe being pregnant and having a kid would work out okay after all.

Strangely, for the next two weeks, I seemed to have a violent case of the stomach flu. Friends told me it was morning sickness, but the book I was reading described a morning sickness far easier than what I was experiencing. To be safe, I saw my doctor who told me I might be "one of those women" who goes through a more violent morning sickness.

"Nothing to worry about," he said. "It should lessen by the end of the first trimester."

I came home depressed thinking I had two more months of throwing up. I told Mike I was likely "one of those women," a fact which didn't surprise him.

In the weeks that followed, my body became the host for an extraterrestrial life form that was intent on taking over. I recalled the movie *Alien* and the disturbing scene of a reptilian-like head pushing its way out the stomach of its human host. My whole system received some subversive message in my recollection and revolted. I was so ill I couldn't even keep down water. I threw up so many times a day I got tired of making the trek back and forth from the bed to the toilet and set up camp in the form of a blanket and pillow right on the tile floor so I could be close to my porcelain altar. Here, I thought, my very life was being sacrificed. I dropped out of classes. I dropped out of life.

Experienced, well meaning friends came by and offered me ginger cookies. They brought over meals like "tuna surprise," which looked curiously similar to something I offered up in my altar earlier that morning. A few women from church who dropped by had been pregnant themselves, so I listened to all of their hints. Hopeful, I ate a whole box of saltine crackers and waited. It was not long before they reappeared for an encore. Tonic water, one said. Dry toast for sure, said another. Nothing worked. By the time I was into the 3rd month I had lost 11 pounds. The doctor was concerned, as I was thin to begin with. He admitted me to the hospital for hydration and prescribed medication to calm my nausea.

True to the doctor's prediction, by the end of the first trimester, I rebounded. I was ravenous. I made up for three months of no food in one sitting. I leaned back in the chair, patted my distended belly with satisfaction, smacked my lips, and asked what was around for dessert.

Nearing the due date, we had friends with no children tell us they were pretty sure that having a baby was like having a puppy. They had recently purchased a 10 week old yellow lab, and boy had life changed dramatically. The wee thing howled all night and wasn't housebroken, so made messes all over the place. To top it all off, she chewed on everything. Ruined a pair of Dolce & Gabbana heels, could you believe it? Sighing and shaking their heads, they described the responsibility which, by the way, was daunting: You had to make sure she got enough exercise, food (the right kind of food), and discipline because there was no such thing as a bad dog, only bad owners. How much different could a baby be, they asked?

The only thing similar between giving birth and acquiring a puppy, I thought as I lay on a bed in the delivery room like an overturned turtle, was that every time I had a contraction I felt like howling. Or barking. Maybe even biting. I was 2½ weeks late with no signs that the baby intended to do any sort of passage-making. In an attempt to encourage an exit, I had spent those weeks jumping on the bed, jogging, and eating tacos with hot sauce. The jogging in particular seemed to entertain the small town we lived in who insisted on making such comments as "you still around?" and "boy are you ever huge" as I pounded by on the sidewalk. It was fortunate for them that I owned neither a mallet, nor a gun.

Lying in the hospital, imagining what was to come, I wished there was some way to avoid the inevitable. Some ejection button I had missed all those months. It didn't help to hear the screams of the woman giving birth down the hall who kept yelling out things in Portuguese. Each time she would explode in verbiage, Mike would offer a translation like: "Oh! Giving birth is SO much FUN!" and "PLEASE, stay inside me little longer!" It helped as a distraction, but I knew there was no getting off the delivery train. My course was set with no emergency exits.

After 24 hours of various measures, including forceps and me pushing for almost two hours, I heard things whispered like "failure to progress" and "C-section." With considerable pomp and circumstance I was rushed to the operating room and minutes later, had instant baby girl. They placed her briefly on my chest, serene and swaddled tightly in a white blanket. Her eyes were shut. I reached out to touch her cheek, but barely had time to hug her to me before she was scooped up and placed in Mike's arms. I launched a weak protest, but they explained that they would take me into the recovery room for observation.

I was exhausted, but steamed. I was thinking how typical this was of my life lately. I got sick for three months, gave up my body, gained a kazillion pounds, and every one of my orifices had been poked and prodded. I then spent 24 hours in pain and pushing only to see the end result for about 30 seconds before she was handed over to Mike, who had just enjoyed a nice hospital breakfast complete with coffee and sausage. I was allowed ice chips. While I had to be in the recovery room, he would get to enjoy her for the rest of the day.

Before the drowsiness engulfed me, I reached out my hand and weakly grabbed the collar of the nurse who was taking my blood pressure and twisted it up in my fist. I pulled her face down close to mine and hissed, "You can be sure I intend to take this up with management. It is completely unfair. Someone will pay." Then I slept.

Later on that day, the same nurse came in and after checking my vitals, told me what I said. It had amused her and the other nurses. I didn't recall saying it. All of it was forgotten as Mike and I bent over the bassinette and gazed at the alien we called Lauren. We were co-conspirators in creation and heady with the drug of happiness. I tried to sculpt the moment into a monument on the pathway of my brain so that every time I walked by I would remember its texture. Its smell. The weighty moment of euphoria.

Growing up, I do not remember dreaming about being a mother. I didn't even like little kids. In high school, I was desperate for cash so I tried babysitting, which would have worked out great if there weren't any kids. Kids, I realized, were the obstacle between me and what I really wanted to do: house sit. An empty house with no parents and nothing between me, cable TV, and a well stocked refrigerator, was a dream. Kids complicated that dream. They put spaghetti in their hair, wouldn't go to bed when I told them to, and asked me to play checkers while I was watching *Charlie's Angels*. They spilled their milk and messed their diapers right after I had changed them. The whole experience was unpleasant and an inconvenience hardly worth the pittance I was paid at the end of the evening. While pregnant, I remembered my forays into babysitting. If motherhood was similar, I thought with apprehension, I was in for a long 18 years.

In the days following Lauren's birth, I discovered that being a mother was similar to babysitting, only worse. No one drove me home when the evening was through and I was eternally employed for free. I was puked on, peed on, my hair was pulled out by the roots. I ate small bits of food here and there in a sleep deprived stupor. There were piles of reeking diapers, dirty clothes, screams in the middle of the night, and no escape.

What I had not counted on was falling in love with my tormenter. This happens sometimes in hostage situations and is known unofficially as the Stockholm Syndrome, named after the Norrmalmstorg robbery of the Kreditbanken in Stockholm, Sweden, in which bank robbers held employees hostage for six days. During that time the victims became attached to their victimizers going so far as to defend them in court. Psychologists explain it as a defense mechanism. A hostage will begin to identify with her kidnapper. The victim senses that their survival depends on the connection they forge between themselves and their captor. Feelings of pity and empathy emerge until when faced with a choice to leave, they voluntarily stay.

It did not take days or weeks for it to happen to me. One look at the cherubic face gazing trustingly up at me, fluttering Bambi-like eyelashes, and I would have been happy to defend her actions, criminal as they were, in a court of law. No one had to tell me I would willingly lay down my life for my daughter, I knew it. Not only that, but I started doing it every day without even thinking about it.

In the interest of the continuation of the species, I'm pretty sure Mother Nature has created an elixir that causes women who have experienced childbirth to generally forget its intensity. This elixir is released inside the brain every time we remember the first moment our child is placed in our arms. Or the first time tiny arms reached out to us. It makes us smile and tell fellow sojourners, their bellies swollen with child, "Oh Hon, it's not so bad, really." It creates a selective amnesia that propelled me two years later, to look deeply into my love's eyes and whisper, "Let's have another one."

It was late at night and we were sitting with our backs up against the headboard reading. "Okay," Mike said, putting his book down as if he had expected it. "But you remember what happened last time? The puking, the moaning, the hospital?"

"Oh come on, it wasn't so bad. It was probably a fluke. This time will be different," I said confidently.

So we PLANNED to have a baby. We consulted a book on my monthly cycle that I just happened to have sitting on the night table. We determined that next Thursday looked good.

"Do you think you can pencil me into your schedule?" I asked playfully.

"Oh, I'll be there," he said with a wicked grin, leaning toward me.

We were having fun with the planning (what a great idea) and decided to celebrate. We were both as fertile as Carla Tortelli on the sitcom "Cheers" and regardless of what the experts in my book determined as good timing, I got pregnant a week early.

In the words of Celine Dion: "It's all coming back to me now." The puking, the moaning, the hospital. My life was a bad rerun. The days ran together in a blur between the couch and the bathroom. I ended up in the hospital again for rehydration. Many long months later, I gave birth to a girl. We named her Bethany Joy. I was into nicknames and thought how much I liked the short form "Beth." Perhaps she would be similar in nature to Louisa May Alcott's "Beth" in Little Women. If she turned out to be a tomboy instead, we could call her "BJ." She was fair and lean, placid in the first days, like her sister.

Mike, having managed to graduate from university just after Lauren's birth, was working as Project Manager at a construction company. In a mutual decision, we had decided I would remain at home with the kids for the first few years. We were up to our necks in life: kids, cars, house, a mortgage, job, meetings, and late nights. For several weeks I was seeing double. Two girls, two sets of dirty diapers, two diaper bags, two mouths to feed, two blankets, two pacifiers which continuously lost, and two car seats. I rubbed my eyes to correct my vision but it didn't help. Just going to the grocery store required as much planning and gear as climbing K2. I fell into bed around 8 p.m. and occasionally slept through Bethany's cries in the night. Mike would shake me awake for the midnight feeding.

4

By the time Bethany was six weeks old, I felt like was getting used to the whole routine. I went to the thrift store. I was excited because the next day was Halloween and I was looking forward to dressing the girls up in costumes. Walking the aisles, I came upon a bright yellow raincoat with a hood that had been made into a duck head and found yellow galoshes with orange duck feet to complete an outfit for Lauren. In the infant section, I found a pink bunny sleeper for Bethany with long ears and a white cottontail. Back at home we dressed with fanfare. It was a mild night and the streets were full. I watched my little duck waddle into the throng of tiny vampires, ghouls, and ghosts. We made our way up one side of the street and back down the other. It took longer than I anticipated as we stopped to talk with neighbors and Lauren played tag with a witch and a kid dressed up like a red crayon.

When we returned home, we spread Lauren's candy out on the floor and took stock.

"Not a bad haul for a little kid," I said.

"I'm not widdle anymore," she said with knit brows.

"True," I lied. "Care to swap college tuition for a couple of Snickers bars?"

I fed Bethany and laid her down. Lauren fell asleep on top of her candy mountain. Mike scooped her up, a Tootsie Roll sticking to her face, and put her to bed. Then the two of us curled up on the couch to watch a rented movie that happened to be about a couple trying to deal with the loss of their son. The wife couldn't let go and it ended their marriage. I was little irked at the storyline, as it was a downer and kind of wrecked the happy mood I had felt earlier after trick or treating.

While climbing into bed afterward, I said to Mike, "I can understand her heartache. If anything ever happened to you or the girls you would have to put me in some kind of asylum. There is no way I could deal with it."

I snuggled up next to him and tried not to think about it. In the fog of a deep sleep, I heard Bethany's faint cries. We had recently moved her white crib from the end of our bed to the room directly across the hall from ours. Mike stirred.

"I'll feed her a bottle," he said huskily, sliding out of bed.

"You're the greatest," I said and then was instantly asleep.

Vaguely I sensed daylight. My eyes opened and I was looking directly at the digital alarm clock on the night table. Its numbers read 7 a.m. I bolted upright and said out loud, "She slept through the rest of the night!"

Mike shifted next to me.

"What time were you up with her?" I asked urgently, shaking his arm.

"Around 1 a.m.," he mumbled.

"Fantastic!" I said.

Past experience with Lauren had indicated that once infants started sleeping more than five or six hours a night there was a good chance it would became a habit. I was elated. I walked happily out to the kitchen to make coffee. Lauren followed a few minutes later. We sat together on a chair and enjoyed a bowl of Cheerios. I told her it was Sunday and she would have to put on a dress for church. This came as good news, and she immediately slid from my lap and returned to her room to make a selection.

I walked past Bethany's room and paused to listen for stirring noises, but she slept on. No sense in waking her. I continued down the short hallway and poked my head into Lauren's room to tell that I was going to take a shower.

"If you need anything, wake Daddy," I told her.

I enjoyed a luxurious and lengthy shower for the first time in weeks. With Bethany sleeping through the night, we were entering a new stage. More sleep equaled more sanity, which equaled a healthier, less crazy me. While the water gently pelted my skin, I sang a robust rendition of the Hallelujah Chorus. I got dressed. Mike was now up, eating breakfast, and admiring Lauren's choice of outfit. There was still no evidence that Bethany was waking up, so I went ahead and dried my hair and put on makeup. Mike hopped in the shower.

I checked the clock in the kitchen and realized it was getting late. I still had to feed Beth before church, so I pushed open the door of her room. There was a slight gush of cool air. I hoped she had been warm enough. I approached her crib. Her small body came into view. She was lying on her stomach, face down on the mattress. My insides constricted. I hung back, my hands clutching the crib railing, and studied her back for breathing movement. I told myself to be calm. She was still. I extended both hands and placed them flat on her torso and waited. There was no movement. I gently picked her up and as I looked into her face, experienced a dreadful knowing. Oh God.

Instinct kicked in. While choking back sobs, my lifeguard training took over and I checked for vitals, lifted her chin, yelled for Mike, and began CPR. I had never given an infant CPR, and was concerned in my desperation not to push too hard or that all my air would end up in her stomach. Mike appeared in the doorway, dripping, with a towel around him, and ran to call 911. He returned to hover next to me, holding her small wrist to catch a pulse. After several minutes, I looked up from her into Mikes eyes.

"There are no signs of life...she's not breathing," I said.

I kept on giving CPR. Tears streamed down both our faces cheeks. I heard the wail of the ambulance and for the first time, it stopped at my house.

5

I remember swimming in a brown lake in Wisconsin. I was 12 or 13 and we were visiting extended family. Second cousins who I didn't know shouted and splashed in the water around me. To avoid their antics, I swam out into deeper, cooler water. Diving like a whale, my feet rising slowly upward, breaking the surface, my frame perpendicular to the muddy bottom below, I sunk down and let the silence engulf me. Back then I didn't like to open my eyes underwater, so I swam blindly into the deep, relishing the sensation, going deeper and deeper, until I remembered I had lungs and put myself in reverse. I opened my eyes, squinting through murky water, to find that the surface was further away than I had anticipated. Panicked, I swam as fast as I could, struggling and thrashing as my chest began to burn, but there was no way to go faster than slow motion.

In the moment of realization that Bethany was gone, I swam in the miry sea of time and frantically searched for reverse, my lungs burning. If I could just get to last night, to yesterday, find the surface somehow so I could catch my breath. I opened my eyes wide, and through the murkiness, saw my life in relation to hers. Scenes flashed forward revealing all the moments I had dreamed of so clearly in my mind it was almost as if I lived them. Her first steps. Opening presents at Christmas. Blowing out candles on her birthdays. A scraped knee, scoring a goal in soccer, borrowing the car, blonde hair in a ponytail, shopping at the mall, walking down the aisle at her wedding. An older Bethany waving goodbye after dropping her kids off for me to babysit. All these stripped, like a Band-Aid, fast, unsympathetically, off my future.

On a drippy, grey, November morning, a few days after Bethany's funeral, I sat on a black, wrought iron bench in the children's section of the cemetery and wondered how I never knew there was a children's section of a cemetery. The results of Bethany's autopsy had come in earlier that day. It was what the doctor suspected. Sudden Infant Death Syndrome. I was thinking how words like grief, torment, hopelessness and even acronyms like SIDS, could in one instant go from being words I talked about to words I owned. As if the librarian of life, sitting at her desk in some pillared hall filled with ancient volumes, opened the book of SIDS, picked up a large stamp, rolled it on a pad of red ink, and thumped it down. On the page were these words, "This volume: Sudden Infant Death Syndrome is now the property of Kim Petersen... if found please return to..."

From my bench, I looked out on a pastoral scene sprinkled with headstones and for some reason Karl Wallenda popped into my brain. While at the library weeks ago, I had read an article on this famous high wire circus performer. It took him years of practice to be a tightrope walker. He started when he was six. He believed tightrope walking to be serious business. You had to keep your wits about you when you were 30-40 feet up with no net below you. Perfect your sense of balance. Concentrate, he said.

Through the wrought iron cemetery gates and beyond the large oak and maple trees now stripped of their leaves, I could see our small town square. People were hurrying across it from all directions. A man in a dark suit was talking on his cell phone, striding confidently across the cement sidewalk. This simple gesture was part of his fragile plan for the day. It was clear that he was unaware of his high wire routine. At any moment he might misstep and fall headlong. I had a frantic desire to wave and yell out at him, "Hey buddy! Watch out!"

Circus music blared in my mind. Miraculously the businessman carried on across the street and disappeared into a

Beemer. Shortly after, a small girl entered the same square. She skipped lackadaisically beside her mother. For the girl there were many distractions. She ran to gaze at the fountain. Walked along its sculpted edge, toe to heel. Grabbed her mother's hand and pointed at a nearby ice cream store. Both seemed to be oblivious of the fact that at any second, life as they knew it might cease to exist. Not far from them, an old woman sat on a concrete bench and fed some pigeons. I imagined the bench balancing precariously on two legs high above the circus ring.

Everyone, I thought, is on high wires and completely unaware. The occasional person teetered off, arms waving, as the band played and the Master of Ceremonies cheerfully said, "Ladies and Gentleman for out next attraction..."

Despite watching several family members fall to their death, Karl Wallenda had this to say, "Life is being on a highwire, everything else is just waiting."

Some years before, while hiking with friends near a lake in Colorado, I stepped in thick mud up to my shins and couldn't get out. Everyone thought I was kidding around and left me. Noticing my absence some minutes later, they returned and a large stick was extended in my direction which eventually aided in my release, but not before I lost one of my running shoes. I had to hike back down the mountain, like the nursery rhyme, with one shoe off and one shoe on.

The memory of this incident led me research "Quicksand" in the library and in one book under "What To Do if You Step in Quicksand" I read something like: quicksand usually isn't more than a couple feet deep, but if you happen to come across a particularly deep spot, you could very well sink quite quickly down to your waist or chest. If you panic and thrash around you can sink further, but if you relax, your body's buoyancy will cause you to float. Breathe deeply. Not only will deep breathing help you remain calm, it will also make you more buoyant. Keep as much air in your lungs as possible. It is impossible to 'go under' altogether if your lungs are full of air.

In the days following Bethany's death, I recalled the movie Mike and I had watched the night before she had passed away. I remembered the words I had uttered just before falling asleep and was stunned. Life, I thought, was going to force me to deal with what I had previously thought unbearable. I decided the best way to deal with her death was to remember to keep air in my lungs. Breathe. In…and out. In…and out. I became obsessed with breathing, especially in the middle of the night. I would wake up, my eyelids flipping open, and see Mike's horizontal form next to me. Squinting through the darkness, I would study his back for breathing motion. Making out nothing, my gut in wrenching spasms, I would stretch out a tentative hand and place it on his shoulder. Oh God…Oh God…his bare skin seemed unnaturally cold and reminded me of when I bent over to kiss Bethany a final goodbye as she lay lifeless on a guerney in the ER.

Despite the coolness of Mike's skin, my fingers detected movement. The faint rise and fall of his chest. He was breathing. I realized I had been holding my own breath which I consciously released, expelling air in an audible gush through my nose. Unable to sleep, I quietly made my way to the kitchen and poured myself a glass of wine. I was wary of using wine as a relaxant, but more wary of the sleeping pills that had been prescribed to me by my doctor. It only took a scant glass of chardonnay to put me to sleep.

On my way back to bed, I crossed the tile floor and into the hall where I paused at the threshold of Lauren's room. I listened. I slowly pushed on the white paneled door which opened with a whispered whoosh. I placed my glass of wine on her dresser and knelt down beside her bed. My hand knew what to do, but before I could make contact, she sensed my presence and stirred, emitting a small sigh. She was still alive. Relieved, I made my way out of her room, climbed back into bed, and with my back against the headboard, hugged a pillow and drank my wine in the shadows. When I had sucked the last drop, I lay down and listened to the sound of my own breathing. In…and out.

If I kept enough air in my lungs, I'd remain buoyant and float.

Scientists use the word "Panagea" to describe the landmass that existed millions of years ago, when all the continents as we know them were one. Today, if you travel into space, or trust your atlas, you can trace their outline and, like pieces of a mammoth, terrestrial puzzle, can see how they might have fit together. Over the course of fifty million years (give or take a million), volcanic activity forced tectonic plates to deepen along fault lines causing colossal oceanic trenches and ridges to push bodies of land away from each other. It still goes on to this day. In another one hundred and fifty million years, Africa will have been pushed northeast, slowly eliminating the Mediterranean Sea. Two hundred and fifty million years from now folks in Tunisia will be able to walk to Naples for a slice of pizza.

While my daily life flowed in slow motion, the tectonic shifting of my soul went in fast forward. The earth shook, continents cracked apart and began drifting away. The trusting woman with all the answers stepped out of my body, a ghostly hologram, and walked across a small crack in my soul's crust. She turned to look at me, regretfully, while the crack grew into an abyss. The slab she was on broke apart from mine and I watched in silence as she floated away. I immediately mourned her and have been looking for her ever since.

I didn't recognize the new person that was me. I didn't recognize my own heart's landscape or the vacant look in the woman's eye who stared back at me in the mirror. The world itself with its vibrant colors, its people hurrying by on the sidewalk outside my window, the cold fall wind, was as vague to me as the moon. On the news, I watched in reverent horror the portrayal of a Middle Eastern woman in anguish over losing her son in a car bomb. She knelt in the dirt in the middle of a road, her covered head thrown back. What I did recognize was the look on her face. Her howl was identical to the one I heard in my own head right before I fell asleep at night. I kept thinking, if I could just find that woman, we could howl together in the dirt and maybe I wouldn't feel like I was an extraterrestrial living on an alien planet.

Friends from church and family, with the best of intentions, tried to walk me through the grief. There were many, I was surprised to learn, who had suffered great loss themselves. They were the ones who seemed to know what to do. They showed up and simply held my hand or pushed the hair from my face and didn't say a word. This was because, and I learned this, there really is nothing to say. They brought over meals and then stayed to clean up. Took Lauren to play at the park near our house.

There were a few, as there are in any fundamental bunch, who wanted to turn the ordeal into an object lesson. Mostly they were church leaders, who came with their Bibles in their hands and hop-scotched over my holy ground offering platitudes like, "all things work together for good," and "you can trust God. He will be there for you." The fact that God had not been there for me the night Bethany died had somehow escaped them. While listening to one such man ramble on about God's sovereignty, his plan for my life, I had an acute vision of me grabbing him by the shoulders and shaking him until his teeth rattled. Strange feelings coming from the newborn being that was now me.

A neighbor, an older woman with short salt and pepper hair, rang my doorbell and offered me a plate of Nanaimo bars.

"Nanaimo bars are my favorite," I whispered to her, blinking rapidly through tears. Spontaneously and slightly out of character, I asked, "Do you want to come in?"

She eyed me reticently before accepting my offer. I made a pot of tea and we sat at the kitchen table. I knew her remotely from several neighborhood parties. She was sad to hear of my loss. She hadn't known what to do but felt she had to do something, so had made the bars.

"I know what it is to experience loss," she said quietly. "When my first husband and I were a month into our marriage, my husband went out to get groceries, and died of a brain aneurysm right in the store next to his grocery cart. I loved him very much."

I studied her. Here was this woman who I had seen planting flowers in her yard, laughing with a glass of wine at a neighbor's house, and run into at the grocery store. Who knew she carried such a secret? Who else, I wondered, had secret identities?

"How did you ever make sense of it?" I asked her.

"I never made any sense of it. But I made peace with it."

She was a lapsed Buddhist, she said, or maybe an agnostic, so I shouldn't expect any answers or philosophical help from her. I told her I used to be a conservative Christian, but I wasn't sure about anything anymore. She nodded, unfazed. It happens, she said. After an amiable silence, she stood up to leave. She shouldn't keep me. If I needed any help. Any help at all….

Then she looked around at the stacks of dirty dishes and the pile of laundry in the middle of the room. She said, "I don't want to appear forward, but.. Hon, why don't you take a nap? I'll take care of these dishes, then let myself out."

Her kind gesture overwhelmed me and made me do the unthinkable, accept a stranger's offer. I went to my bedroom and fell asleep. When I woke up, I found the dishes done and the laundry folded. Everything was tidy. A note had been left on the table: "Glad you could sleep. Call me for anything." So I did.

In the next couple of weeks she came over regularly. Some days she just showed up. She watched Lauren, scrubbed my floor, washed the windows. My past self might have been mortified by the fact that she was witness to all the dust bunnies under my bed, but the new me didn't seem to care anymore. I needed help, and I knew it. It occurred to me that my church friends wouldn't have termed my neighbor a "Christian" but there she was doing the dishes again with no ulterior motive of trying to convert me. In fact, her presence seemed to convert me without her saying a word. I found the holy in her overwhelming, and wondered, if she wasn't a "Christian" per se, than where was all this goodness coming from?

I stood outside myself, an onlooker in a white lab coat, and watched my response to different stimuli. I was having conflicting responses to life. One day, I came to the conclusion that life was a charlatan. A con man who wheeled his cart into my village and put out rows of glass bottles with nifty-looking labels. He might offer me one wrapped in a cheery box, tied up in a red bow, but I now recognized the ticking I heard inside it. I put the box in a corner of my mind and tried to camouflage it with a pretty red checked tablecloth and a candle. But every day I walked by it, I heard the ticking and waited for the inevitable earth shattering ka-boom. Life was a loose cannon. I watched my back. Peeked around corners. A foreign foreboding set up camp in my soul. I told Mike to drive carefully on his ten-minute commute to work, then waited for a call from the police.

On another day, life became too precious to look at. Midway through the 6th Century BC, Archilochus the Greek poet said, in reference to a solar eclipse, "Zeus, the father of the Olympic gods, turned midday into night, hiding the light of the dazzling sun, and a sore fear came upon men." I thought that life after the death of a loved one was an eternal solar eclipse.

Running errands, shoveling snow, touching Lauren's face, dazzled with their brilliance. I wanted desperately to watch, to study the details so much clearer now than before. But to open my eyes, to look, was to open my heart. To open my heart was to risk loss all over again. "A sore fear came upon men…."

I remember my sixth grade teacher telling the class that to look directly into a solar eclipse might damage your retinas. Your eyeballs would feel no pain while they were being fried to a crisp and hours later you'd be blind. I turned my face toward life to take a peek for as long as I dared and then turned away. It was a mortal game of chance. Look too long and be burned. Longing and dread piled in opposite heaps on a scale, swaying one way then the next.

What was becoming clear to me was that I knew far less than I previously assumed. I began to have serious doubts. I tried to pray through the grief, but my prayers sounded hauntingly heathen. When I wasn't paying attention, and sometimes when I was, I said things like, "Who are you? Do you even exist? How could you let such suffering happen all over the world and not act to change things? Why are you silent? How can I ever trust you again?" God, who used to be containable, knowable, predictable, confidante, wish granter, friend (at least in my terms), had turned out to be someone I didn't recognize. Someone unknown, who might hear my prayers, but for the most part chose to ignore them. Nothing was certain anymore. I had the unfamiliar feeling of having been pushed off the edge of a theological cliff and free falling.

It would be nice to say that during this time I grieved patiently, graciously, listening and hopeful, but I didn't. I wrestled and writhed through every slow-ticking second. I stomped around and shook my fist brazenly in the face of God, which I figured would damn me to hell. God, to his credit, seemed to take my ranting surprisingly well. I wasn't struck by lightning. There were no earthquakes. I didn't break out in boils.

No one got sick or died. No one was raised from the dead either, not that I tried. Eventually, God and I developed a sort of truce. I didn't bother him (was he even a "him"?), whoever he was, and he didn't bother me, although I hardly anticipated he'd keep his end of the bargain for long. Out of a sense of duty, I decided to keep going to church, but since God had turned out to be someone other than what I had been taught at church, I separated church and theology from the person of God. For the first time, God existed outside of the lines I had unknowingly drawn in my head.

6

By day, Mike seemed to be dealing with Bethany's death quite well. He was coming off as the proverbial tower of strength. He shook hands with people at the funeral and made small talk. He tenderly held my hand and made meals. He shed a few tears at the appropriate times. One afternoon, when we were going through her things, we sat together on the floor and sobbed. But the day after her funeral he had chuckled at a story told by a friend who had flown in to attend the services. I wasn't sure how I felt about this. Despite the fact that he seemed unusually tired, a week and a half after the funeral, he went back to work.

Shortly after that, our paths crossed at 3am one early morning. I had come into the kitchen for a glass of water and was surprised to find him sitting alone in the dark in our favorite rocking chair. His face was turned toward the open window. I knelt down beside him, took his hand, and asked if he was okay. For awhile, he didn't acknowledge my presence.

Finally, he said, "I can't sleep anymore." Then he sighed and shifted his position in the chair. Still looking out the window, he whispered, "I don't think I have had more than two or three consecutive hours of sleep since she died. I can't let go of this feeling that if I had just laid her down on her back or had brought her to you for the feeding, she would be still be alive. It was only days ago. Why? Why can't I go back to that moment and change things?"

I let a few seconds go by before saying, "I don't know. I do know that I have asked myself the same questions. Why didn't I go feed her? How selfish was I to desire my own sleep over feeding her myself? But, Mike, we couldn't have known that this was going to happen."

He leaned close to me then, his eyes filled with tears, and looked earnestly into my face before saying, "I need to know that you don't blame me. After all, I was the last one to see her."

I said honestly, "The thought has never even crossed my mind. I blame myself. We are going to have to forgive ourselves, even though I don't think there is anything really to forgive."

He looked down while nodding. "It's just that, I am not sure what to do now. It's like I am lost in some unknown world."

"I feel the same," I said. Then I took his hand and led him back to bed. I held him and told him it was going to be okay even though I wasn't sure of that at all. In a sleepy voice, he said to me, "I know you are having a hard time finding God in all of this. That you feel abandoned. But right at this moment, you are the closest thing to God that I've got, and it is what's keeping me alive." It didn't take long before I heard his rhythmic breathing slow and deepen. I listened to his breathing for a long time. I thought maybe he was right. When you are lost it is good to have someone else to be lost with.

It had been awhile and there were expectations. Interruptions to my sackcloth and ashes. A woman from the children's Sunday School at our church called to see if I could help out in the second grade class. The library called to tell me I had five overdue books. I had missed four weekly committee meetings. The refrigerator had goat cheese and beer, a satisfying meal for Mike and me, not so good for a two-year-old. On my mental daily "to do" list, which only had one item on it for the past month: "breathe," I added "get out of bed." Surprisingly I survived that, and a few days later I added, "go to the market," and by the end of the week I made my way to the Sunday morning service.

Walking into the church foyer was like a sad and awkward version of a debutante "coming out" event. It was my reintroduction into society as a new person. I walked deliberately down a wide staircase into a foyer full of people who looked up to assess my evolution. They studied my face for indications of meltdown. Upon greeting me, they chose their words carefully. They hesitantly asked how I was holding up. They told me I was looking good. Some hugged me and averted their eyes.

Except for the slight tremor in my voice I felt like the new me was coming off as fairly composed. Across the foyer, I watched a friend glance in my direction and then turn away, pretending not to have seen me. She went in the opposite direction, across the sanctuary, and sat down. I thought nothing of it. I hardly knew what to say to myself and often wished I could leave me on the other side of the room.

I sat in a pew and looked around at all the lives that had been lived out the past month. Everything was oddly the same and I wondered how this could be when only a month ago a wrecking ball passed through my life with a crash, the reverberations of which must have registered on the Richter Scale. Hadn't they felt it? Wasn't anyone concerned with all this rubble? Shouldn't we be searching for survivors? Looking for building plans? Surely there were architectural blueprints kicking around somewhere with which we could rebuild?

The service began with a hymn, Be Still and Know. It was a simple chorus. One I knew by heart. "Be still and know that I am God. Be still and know that I am God." Repeat twice. I closed my eyes and begged for an oozing comfort. It would be nice to manufacture it with this song that I had sung a thousand times. I realized I was looking desperately for a painkiller. I couldn't be still. And I couldn't know. The song, the whole service, lacked the usual anesthesia. Maybe, I thought, this was why people who had lost a loved one left the church and ended up drunk and divorced.

En masse the congregation sat down and after announcements, the sermon began. The pastor was speaking on miracles. Healings. Faith. We must have faith. Faith of a mustard seed would move mountains. Mountains, he said, when I would have settled for moving the much smaller-by-comparison frame of my daughter back into this world.

The pastor then related several stories of those who had experienced healing. It was obvious that he had the faith required to produce miracles because many healings had happened through him.

"What was wrong with my faith?" I wondered.

He invited a woman up to the podium who proceeded to give her testimony. She had prayed recently and her cancer was gone. The doctors couldn't explain it. She had figured out the magic recipe. I found myself squirming uncharacteristically in my seat. I broke out into a cold sweat. I saw myself standing over Bethany's small form in the ER. Leaning over her I had whispered this prayer in what I thought to be utter faithfulness: "Even now, God, you could change this. Bring her back to life. You did it with Lazarus, why not Bethany?"

But the exact measurements of will and faith, shaken not stirred, eluded me. Sitting in the pew, I felt my stomach lurch. I put my hand to my mouth, stood up and made my way down the aisle and out the swinging doors into the foyer where I kept right on walking, past the ushers and out the front doors into the cold December air, which I sucked in like a bellows.

During all that time, I watched the channel 8 evening news. I only watched the news on channel 8 for two reasons. For starters they had a segment on good news. Usually it was local happenings: "Boy rescues puppy from sewer drain," or "Local woman raises funds for homeless shelter." After reports of death, famine, war, and rapes, I was hungry for good news. I let the events soak into my dry, crumbling, soul, and felt some relief.

The second reason was that the guy who did the sports on Sundays and Wednesdays always had a "blooper of the week" at the end of the broadcast. I would tough out the whole news hour for the bloopers alone. A guy tumbling end over end during a football game, or getting smashed into the boards playing hockey, was a tonic for my soul. Sometimes, a tall basketball player careened out of control and nailed a photographer. There was something cleansing, something purgative, about watching a local kid get confused during the pandemonium of a soccer game and run, kicking the ball in the wrong direction toward his own goal line, oblivious to people yelling at him and his coach in stitches, waving, at the sideline.

One night, I watched two outfielders collide and found myself smiling an authentic, instinctual smile. The muscles I used to smile had atrophied. They were weak from lack of use, so it came out tentatively, tottering, like a baby's first steps. I was not sure how to feel about this amused betrayal of my grief. Had I moved on without knowing it? Was it okay to do so? Despite my hesitations, the next day I found myself smiling at a kid in the grocery line. Little more than a year later, I smiled after giving birth to a son.

7

Over the course of the next six years, I pulled myself up by the bootstraps and hunkered down. Life, I realized, was a lot easier when I was busy. I wondered why I had ever scoffed at the idea. When our son, Stefan, was in the first grade and Lauren in the fourth, Mike got promoted at the money management company he was working for. We bought a big house on a hill just outside of town in a prestigious area. A two minute drive from the main road took us through rolling green farmland complete with grazing sheep. The house was a large colonial with four white pillars at the front and a long, wide front porch with a porch swing. Imperceptibly, we allowed ourselves to be drawn in by the enormous gravity emitted from the core of our pulsing culture. There were cars whose seats warmed up. Lengthy vacations in sandy countries. We filled our days with Kodak moments. Everything was okay, I thought to myself. A thick layer of dust formed on the porch swing.

For the next four years, I took on the role of soccer mom, only this was Canada where hockey was king. At 6am, I sat on the hard, cold bleachers of the ice arena sipping hot steaming coffee watching 15 would-be NHLer's bump into each other à la The Three Stooges. I considered the future of my current Saturday: return home from present practice and subsequent game by 9:30, drop Lauren off and remind her to do her homework, pick up my own hockey bag and return to the rink for my weekly Beginning Adult Hockey class, afterwards, catch a quick shower, change, and attempt to make the kids' school fundraising event at noon at which I was manning the froggy ring toss booth. If all went well, the event would be over by 4 p.m., whereupon I would race home to make supper. Re-dress for about the 4th time. Inform the babysitter of rules and regs. Hold Mike's hand as we left for a dinner party. Stay later than anticipated. Maybe kiss Mike goodnight. Maybe not. Fall into bed.

Every day was a repeat performance of rotating events. To combat it, Mike and I dusted off the porch swing, sat down, and held hands, but the extent of our conversations centered around where to have dinner, what chores needed to be accomplished on the weekend, and who was picking up what kid at which club. Our relationship entered survival mode. Instead of feeling like we were lost together, I began to feel lost and alone. We discussed this. Mike felt it too. We blamed it on the busy stage of life and planned a date night to combat it, but at the last minute we had to cancel it due to an impromptu business meeting for Mike.

In the southwestern United States there is a rest area off Hwy 160 called Four Corners. It is the only place in the US where you can technically place an appendage in four different states at one time. An arm in Colorado, one in New Mexico, a leg in Arizona, and, now looking like you are doing the bear walk in a childhood relay race, a leg in Utah. In this spot, you are in the magical world of in between marked first back in 1868 by E.N. Darling. In 1992 a more permanent granite marker was placed, a tribute to our cultures interest in the novelty of being several places at once; pieces of the body in four states but not fully existing anywhere.

In the middle of a four corners day in May, I met a friend for coffee. While sipping lattes she declared with some satisfaction that she was "simplifying" her life. She had spent the morning going through all her cupboards and closets, getting rid of junk and organizing.

"Too much clutter creates stress…when in doubt, throw it out," she said with conviction.

Simplifying, I thought. What a novel idea. I could use some simplicity. I was inspired. Back at home, I put on old clothes, tied my hair back with a pink scarf and decided to tackle the basement. 'Go big, or go home,' I thought as I descended the stairs.

In an unfinished storage room we had boxes as old as the pyramids. I was Indiana Jones in the Well of Souls blowing away years of dust. I was curious as any good archaeologist should be. I cut open the tape on a box whose contents were vaguely identified with faded black magic marker, opened the flaps and found old maternity clothes. I divided the room into two sections: stuff to keep and stuff to give away. I placed the maternity clothes in the "give away" section. There were a couple boxes of toys the kids played with when they were younger and they followed. Several mundane boxes later, I found a stash of old yearbooks. While reading through one, the kids came home from school and wondered where I was. I yelled up to them that I was downstairs cleaning the basement.

"What are you doing that for?" Lauren wondered aloud at the top of the stairs.

"I am simplifying," I announced.

"Ohhh kaaaay," she said, and in my mind I saw her shrug her shoulders at her brother.

Seeking to place as much distance from themselves and such a task, they told me they were going down the street to play with friends, which was just as well because "Simplifying is hard work and I don't need any distractions!" I yelled up.

Sensing an opportunity, Lauren said, "Maybe we should order pizza tonight since you've been working so hard?"

"Great idea," I said. If Indiana Jones got the Ark of the Covenant, I should at least get a pizza.

As they left I heard Stefan say, "Whoohooo, pizza for dinner! Hey, Mom, you should clean the basement more often."

By early evening, the side of the room stacked with things to give away was decidedly smaller than anticipated, but I had swept up all the dust, dead spiders and other bugs that were dried and crumbled like old leaves on contact with my broom. There remained one large box at the back. It was heavy and unmarked. I examined the outside but had no recollection of packing it or moving it there. With considerable effort, I half-hauled and half-shoved it into the middle of the room. Under a hanging light bulb, I cut open the tape, yellowed and frayed at the edges, and pulled back the flaps.

On top was Norton's Anthology of Literature, and just below it several spiral notebooks, mine and Mike's, full of class notes from university. I remembered this box of books. It had been packed by some other woman, a younger version of me, right after university on her way to a new apartment. I thumbed through my notebook from Philosophy 101. Despite the fact that the class was at 9a.m., it had been a favorite course. Mike and I, having recently begun dating, had sat together yawning. On the corner of one page containing notes on Plato's theory of dualism I made out in Mike's handwriting, "Care for a Plate-O muffins after class?" Directly under that was written in my own script, "A sad attempt, but yes" and after that, a smiley face. I was into smiley faces then.

I set the notebooks aside and lifted away several textbooks. At the bottom I recognized another favorite text, Abnormal Psychology, and heaved it into the lamplight. Upon lifting the cover, a folded piece of spiral notebook paper fell out, and landed on the newly swept floor. Its memory was initially lost to me. The edges were jagged on one side and it was spotted with what looked like grease. I bent over to pick it up and even as I turned it over, I began remembering my younger self sitting in the cafeteria discussing dreams with Mike.

I read through it, smiling, and then on impulse, I brought the paper up to my nose and breathed in. I sniffed the grease spots left by the Shepherd's Pie, but there was only the musty smell of aged paper. I remembered that we had meant to read this list every year on the anniversary of our first date, but we never had. Somewhere along the way, we had forgotten all about it.

Later, over pizza at the kitchen table, I said to Mike smiling, "Check out what I found while cleaning the basement today."

"You cleaned the basement?" he said in shock.

"Yes, but that's not the point. Look at this." I handed Mike the piece of paper.

He flipped open the page with little reverence, like he would a bill or the front page of a newspaper. I was watching. Waiting for the moment. It was coming.

"Hey...What is this? Where did you find this?" He was incredulous and had started rubbing the tip of the page softly with his thumb. "This is our list!" he said, exuberant, eyebrows raised. "Do you remember this? Sitting in the cafeteria! Boy, were we young then. Check it out," he said pointing and grinning up at me: "Bungee jump, are you kidding me?" He harrumphed in mockery.

"I know," I said, "and tie ourselves to trees in the Amazon? What the heck is that?"

He was suddenly earnest, "But look here, some of these are good. Like, have a family. CHECK. See the seven wonders. Meet the Pope and Mother Teresa. Build our own cabin in the woods and live there. That doesn't sound half bad. Check out this one: live on a boat and cross the ocean. You know...we could actually do that someday. Maybe when we retire."

"I know. Seeing that list after, what, 15 years? It moved me."

"I love who we are now, and in many ways, I do not have any desire to go back and be that person I was so long ago. But I love the passion of those early days, when we believed that we could make anything happen."

"I think we should keep that list around for awhile. Who knows, maybe our former selves will inspire us to do something wild and crazy?" I said grinning, patting his shoulder affectionately.

"Hmmm," he said, but I could tell he hadn't really heard me. He had refolded the paper and inadvertently raised it to his nose and was breathing in.

8

Dreams come full circle when we gaze at our own children and wonder what the future will hold for them. One day during the hot summer Stefan was four, we sat together on the back porch reading a Richard Scarry book on careers. The book covered all the usual professions that might capture a child's imagination: policeman, fireman, astronaut.

"What do you think you'd like to be when you grow up?" I asked.

He shrugged his shoulders. I looked deep into his eyes like they were crystal balls, with a heart full of a million hopes, trying to decipher his future. After discussing the pros and cons of several honorable choices and receiving little enthusiasm from him, I assumed he wasn't interested and we moved on to other books. Unknown to me was that he had taken the question seriously.

Several nights later, I learned of this firsthand at a rather formal dinner party we hosted with some of Mike's co-workers and their spouses. When Stefan came in to say goodnight, our friends made much of him. One of them asked, "So young man, what would you like to be when you grow up?"

Without hesitating, he smiled broadly and said decidedly, "I want to be a garbage man when I grow up!"

Fortunately, he took their laughter and applause as approval, made a gallant bow, and tumbled off to bed. While grinning at some good natured ribbing, I thought about his response and tried to figure out where it had come from.

The next morning, he climbed into my lap, and I asked him why he wanted to be a garbage man. He had it all worked out:

"For one thing they drive the coolest truck. It is loud and you can hear it coming from a long way off. I would be the guy hanging off the back of the truck. The one who hops off the end and grabs the garbage cans. That guy always has big muscles. I think it would be the greatest to hang off the back of that truck and go fast and loud down the street."

In a moment of comprehension, I remembered that anytime the garbage was being picked up, Stefan was at the window watching with envious eyes. I wondered how those men would have felt to know that someone was watching and admiring them. I told him it was a fantastic dream and that I would do anything in my power to help him accomplish it.

Years later, I supportively told him as he trudged out the door to take out the trash, "Just think, you're only nine years old and already you have accomplished your dream of being a garbage man."

He was not amused. He told me it certainly wasn't what he expected, nor did he think a career as a garbage man was in his future.

~*Part Two*~

Come about : to tack, to change direction relative to the wind.

9

The dream list I had excavated in our basement floated around the family room for a few weeks before Mike brought home several boating magazines. At first, I read them with casual interest, but the idea of living on a boat was subversive. It morphed into a small, brown field mouse that left droppings all over my mind when I wasn't looking. Of course, I set traps. I put an aromatic havarti on the small trigger plate, and carefully laid the traps in every nook and cranny I could think of. The mouse was clever, I'll give him that. Not only did he eat the cheese, he avoided being snapped under the bar. After some time, he became comfortable in his new digs, and I saw him brazenly cross the hearth of my brain. He looked right at me, his little nose wriggling, his whiskers shaking, brown eyes alert and mischievous, and I thought how cute he was. I agreed to let him stay if he didn't wreak too much havoc. Never make a deal with a mouse.

While I toyed with a couple of boating articles on exotic ports, I kept a wary eye on Mike, who was gulping down several periodicals in a single sitting. In between bites of verbiage, he would cast furtive sideline glances in my direction as if sizing up prey. After fifteen years of marriage, we were well familiar with each other's subtle techniques in the ways of manipulation. In a mental ballroom, we clasped hands, the music started, and we danced: he tried to hide the fact that the idea of living on a boat had captured him. I told him I was not interested in living on a boat, although secretly I was, at least from an armchair perspective. He purposefully came across as nonchalant even while he lobbed this grenade into the middle of the family room, "Hon? Living on a boat would be a great adventure, don't you think? Maybe after we're retired we could pick up a little something and cruise around the Caribbean together? You know, just island hop. Nothing too serious."

I knew he was trying to get me comfortable with the idea of boating without having to immediately commit. Sly. Even when we visited a boat show for the first time, he shrugged his shoulders and said, "Maybe someday." I was on to him from the beginning.

One morning after the kids went off to school, I pondered free will. For the first time in many years, I did some dead reckoning on my position in life. I discovered that I had been paddling down a fast moving stream, the scenery passing by in a blur. Most of the time I didn't even bother to steer my ship, I let the current take me where it willed. I was too exhausted to care. I had been lulled by errands, traffic, and beer commercials. Reading about living on a boat reminded me that there were options. This was both enlightening and unnerving. If there were options, then what was I doing here?

I went to the library and checked out books. I read about living aboard as if I was a voyeur, sitting on a tree branch looking with binoculars in a window, captivated. Right then, there were families with kids sailing around the world. They were visiting Istanbul, Tokyo, Dubai, and the lesser known Dalap-Uliga-Darrit in the Marshall Islands. Some wrote books for a living, but most saved up funds in their landlubbing years, then sailed around until the money ran out. At that point, the siren song captured them and they became addicted. They returned to land only long enough to work in order to save up for the next offshore journey. They home-schooled their children and climbed volcanoes. Swam with dolphins. They didn't watch television and played a lot of Monopoly. In their spare time, which was plentiful, their kids read books on Sir Edmund Hillary and went spear fishing.

Sailing yachts were a liveaboard's primary means of transportation. I learned that there were varying types of yachts including monohulls (boats with one hull), catamarans (boats with two hulls), and the less popular trimaran (boats with three hulls). A catamaran was a new idea to me although I had seen a few larger versions used as car ferries while living in British Columbia. My interest was heightened one afternoon by Stefan who picked up a magazine that had a catamaran on the cover and said, "That's one munchin boat, man!" I thought he was on to something and decided to look into it. In several magazines, I read that these long range power and sailing catamarans were able to travel great distances at a decent speed, with a safe, smooth ride and lots of room in which to enjoy life aboard. The phrases: "travel great distances," "decent speed," "safe, smooth, ride," and "lots of room," spoke to me like Confucius' words of wisdom. One catamaran builder even touted their yacht as "unsinkable." This, I thought, was brazen. Wasn't a similar claim made by another boat builder whose yacht subsequently sunk in the North Atlantic after striking an iceberg?

There was a burgeoning debate developing that I had been previously unaware of. A new movement of boaters had begun to extol the virtues of power boating. Many sailors, tending toward tradition, scoffed at noisy, smelly, expensive diesel engines upon which power boats depended, but other sailors said they spent most of their time motoring anyway. One such sailor turned power boater, Robert Beebe, wrote extensively about passagemaking under power, describing the advantage in weather watching as a key element in a safe journey. In offshore passagemaking, sailors participated in a tricky wind dance. They wanted just enough wind to fill their sails to get them where they wanted to go. Too little wind and they would be forced to motor. Too much wind and they could find themselves in a gale. With a powerboat, there was no question about wind. You avoided the dance altogether. The dead calm, the horse latitudes and doldrums, these were your holy grail. No wind for days on end meant smooth seas, great fuel mileage, and a happy crew. This, I learned, slightly made up for what you paid in fuel.

Vivid descriptions of the romance of living aboard captured me: quiet anchorages in deserted bays, nights filled with a million stars, the ability to hear yourself think, and travel to exotic destinations. I let my guard down and allowed myself to be seduced. I decided that living on a boat, when we were retired, might be a viable option. Mike was thrilled. The very night I pronounced it, he went to the library and checked out more books. When he returned, he said, "I have been thinking lately that living on a boat with the kids, even for a short time, might be a good idea. You know, we could reconnect as a family. Explore together."

I had anticipated his response. I told him, "Let's just deal with retirement for a few minutes and see what happens."

On a rare, quiet evening, Mike and I sat close together on the couch reading the same book. It was an anthology of sorts, containing small chapters about people's boating experiences. I had just been enjoying a bit about one couple's journey in Australia, when Mike, a good page ahead of me and into the next chapter, suddenly snatched the book out of my hands, closed it with a thump, and moved to the other end of the couch.

"Hey, what's the big idea?" I said annoyed.

"I'm pretty sure you shouldn't read this next page," he responded gravely.

"Why not?"

"Because you have an imagination. A vivid imagination. If you read this next chapter, you'll have all sorts of negative thoughts about boating and, in reality, these kind of things hardly ever happen."

"What things hardly ever happen?"

"You sure you want to know?"

"I'm sure," I lied.

He handed me back the book. I read silently.

A family with three adults and two kids were in the middle of the Atlantic when their sailboat was rammed by a whale, which tore a huge hole in the bow. Water began to flood their staterooms. The galley. Within two minutes they realized that the boat was sinking. They grabbed what they could and got into their little life raft before their sailboat turned belly up and sunk below the surface. They spent several weeks adrift at sea, eating fish and drinking the blood of turtles, surviving several storms, and wasting away to almost nothing, before finally being picked up by a tanker.

"You might as well read this, too. You'll happen upon stories like this sooner or later. I'm surprised you haven't come upon these stories yet in your reading," Mike said and he handed me a different book open to the page and pointed to a line. "Start here."

I read something like: Despite a fair weather prediction, clouds began to form on the horizon and within four hours we were in midst of a strong squall. The seas went from calm to upwards of 20 feet. The boat heaved and we were worried about capsizing. Green water poured over the bow and into the cockpit. Things spilled out of cupboards. The inside of the boat was a mess. Sometime around midnight, while I tried to rest, my husband must have been swept overboard. In the middle of the Atlantic, I awoke to find I was alone.

Horrified, I closed the book and slowly pushed it away.

That night I lay on my back in the darkness and stared wide-eyed at the ceiling. I pictured the four of us in a boat during a storm. It was dark. We were in waves of hurricane proportion--thirty feet, maybe more. The boat was vertical and water was pouring in through shattered portholes. Lightning flashed. I could see the kids, crying and afraid. The boat began to sink. Maybe, while attempting to leap into the life raft, I would be thrown over the side and lost at sea. Worse yet, it might be Mike or one of the kids. A sheer and razor like panic seized me. I wondered what it would be like to drown, the moment of knowing, sucking in burning gulps of water for air, followed by an oozing blackness.

Or it was not storming at all. We were simply traveling along in calm seas and clear skies. I would look for one of the children to help me set the table, but would not be able to find them. Frantically, we would search, opening hatches and calling their name. I would scan the miles of bluish grey water behind us looking for a tiny head bobbing, arms reaching, voice calling out. We would attempt to retrace our path. I would try not to think that the longer it takes for someone to notice a crewmate has fallen overboard the more impossible it is to find them. The current would take them at a different speed and direction than the boat. They would be swimming somewhere, alone, crying, trying to fend off sharks. Oh god.

At breakfast the next morning, I arrived bleary eyed in the kitchen and told Mike there was no way I could live on boat with the kids. He nodded as if he had been expecting my pronouncement and didn't look up from his eggs.

10

It was nice to be in such voluminous company. According to the Anxiety Disorders Association of America, forty million Americans, 18% of the population, are afflicted by some kind of anxiety disorder, which can be defined as a prolonged, irrational, and debilitating anxiety. Nineteen million have a specific phobia that might include things like bugs, heights, water, storms, and closed spaces. I realize that for most of my life, I have not been keen on all five. It has only been debilitating insofar as it has limited, without regret on my part, my interactions with each. At the root of each phobia is fear. Fear, I am told by numerous written authorities, is a natural part of life. Without it, we would all walk the concrete edge of a city building twenty nine floors up or play water polo in the Niagara River.

Over the course of several years, I had given fear a little more leeway in my life. I had become a little phobic in this area. I still flew in airplanes, but I didn't like it one bit. Each time the plane sped along the runway, I prepared myself for the worst. While clutching the armrests, I would lean over to Mike and tell him that since he had been such a devoted and kind husband, (aside from the small fact that he had made me board this aircraft which would now result in my unfortunate demise), I would pass on to him the secret location of my stash of chocolate which had plagued him for some time. He was to use this knowledge wisely and guard its contents until their use was absolutely necessary. By all means, never tell the children. He could have it all except the block of Godiva which could be buried with me or the parts left of me after the crash.

In reality, and there's a relevant term, I was fairly certain that Fate would take someone I loved, and leave me alive to deal with the fall out. In light of this, it could be said that at times I was a mite overprotective of the children. But in my defense, this was only in relation to a husband who thought walking the concrete edge of a city building on the twenty ninth floor to be a grand idea. Why not push kids outside their comfort zone? Get them to try new things? Expand their horizons? Fly, little birds, fly!

I was forced to be the voice of reason. This meant I was continually saying things like, "No you may put the Slip and Slide on the roof so you can coast off it into the swimming pool. I don't care if all the kids in the neighborhood are doing it," and "No, you may not play in that abandoned condemned warehouse even if dad told you it was okay." I was constantly reminding them to "look both ways," and "don't talk to strangers."

Unwise ideas aside, while I appreciated the fact that my fear might "save" us in the short term, I wondered if I could be passing on my fear to my kids. Would they shrink at life's challenges, or would they rise like their dad, albeit rather foolishly at times, to face them? Did I want to be the kind of person who shrank from life's challenges? And if ever Mike and the kids wanted to spend time on a boat, could I live with myself for holding them back?

While reading a book on lessons learned from legendary adventurers, I came upon a section called: "Animals that Can Eat You." It was important, I learned, that if you were trekking through Africa, as Livingston did, to be aware that there are many unseen dangers. You must be alert. Pay attention to the small details. Study the tall grass. Lions love to hide there. If you notice a group of water buffalos or gazelles watching a clump of grass there could very well be a lion hiding there. If you do come across a lion it is best not to run. This will be difficult because when you are afraid, instinct takes over, and you will want desperately to get away. However, this will only cause the lion to chase you, and you can be sure he is much faster than you are. It is best to muster all your courage and stand still, face him, and try to look aggressive. Defiant. Stare him full in the face even as he charges at you. He is testing you. He may run at you several times, stopping a feet few away, growling, but if you stand your ground, he will often turn away in the end.

I was more than a little irked that Fear had been calling the shots in my life. I decided to stand my ground. I met Fear on a bleak battlefield in the desert of my thoughts. There were two camps, mine and the enemy's. They sat at opposite ends of a dry, rocky valley. Fear was a giant woman. An older woman, surprisingly well dressed in a tan Donna Karan suit. Every day I went about my business, she called across the valley, taunting me, saying things like:

"Hey! Hey you there! Just what do you think you're doing?"

"I'm considering living on a boat," I muttered under my breath, avoiding her gaze.

"What? I can't hear you! Speak up over there."

"I'm considering living on a boat, OKAY?!" I yelled loudly attempting to sound confident.

"You can't be serious? Oh that's rich! What a laugh! Do you have any idea how dangerous that is? Ever watch a little movie called *The Perfect Storm*?"

"Yes, yes, I have seen it. Let me point out to you that those types of things hardly ever happen," I said, wincing. It was weak.

"Yes, but those things happen more frequently to people who have no experience! Let's see… how many times have you and Mike been boating on a yacht larger than 20 ft. in a body of water bigger than a swimming hole? None! How do you ever expect to survive living on a boat out on the ocean with no experience?" she scoffed.

I was irritated. "Look," I shouted in her direction, "can we at least call a truce and talk like grownups?"

"Fine," she said.

A small tent was erected in the middle of the valley, and a folding table with chairs were set up inside. Upon sitting, I requested some wine from the waiter, but Fear said she didn't drink and probably I shouldn't either. Typical. Fear had the advantage and she knew it, but I had a few weapons of my own.

I intended to reason with Fear. I would blow her away with my logic. My self awareness.

"Here's the thing," I said quietly leaning toward her. "I know Bethany's death woke you up. It doesn't take a Ph.D. in Psychology to figure out that I am afraid someone else I love will die and I'll be forced to suffer through grief again. This is why I am afraid of situations that are outside my control, like flying, for instance. I get that. What you are is a coping mechanism I have developed to protect myself and, while I really appreciate your efforts, I'm fairly certain that when I haven't been looking, you have developed a power hungry ego. I need you to let up. Besides, I don't think I need you so much anymore. I'm a lot stronger now."

Fear leaned forward and looked directly into my eyes as if sympathetic to my wretchedness. "Sweetie," she said calmly, "you need me now more than ever. You don't know what you're getting into here. There are forces at work beyond what you're capable of dealing with. I am the voice of reason that will save you, and I am telling you it would be prudent, wise, if you could keep life manageable. Why stir up trouble by living on a boat if you don't have to?"

At this point, she reached forward to gently take my hands in hers. "Look how upset you are just considering it! I don't have to tell you that there is a probability that if you do this, somewhere along the way you will run into a huge storm on the open water. Someone is bound to get hurt. Maybe die. Why willfully subject yourself to such suffering? It is not worth the risk. You are far safer doing what you know. I am just trying to protect you after all."

Pulling my hands away, I said, "I have no doubt that you have your own perceived idea of what you think is best for me, but I'm not so sure that what you have in mind is truly what is best for me. And I think you forget that just because something is comfortable doesn't mean it is safe. I feel pretty comfortable driving seventy miles per hour on the interstate or carrying laundry down the stairs, but that does not make it safe. Besides, don't you think it is far more dangerous to keep drifting downstream in my life with no thought as to my whereabouts or destination?"

Fear, confident as ever, changed the subject, "What about the children? Will it be good for them to be separated from their friends? Won't they miss out on all the opportunities that school can give them?"

"I don't know," I said. I was frustrated. Things weren't going the way I had hoped. I stood up to leave.

Fear shook her head sympathetically. "And another thing. How can you give up a financially secure future? You would be risking everything. For what? Some crazy, out of control dream? You must reconsider."

What I really needed, I decided, was bigger guns and better ammunition with which to fight fear. Knowledge would be my weapon of choice. With it, I would shatter Fear's objections into shards of meaningless drivel.

11

I figured that I might as well begin with what scared me the most: storms at sea. In a boating store, I found Lin and Larry Pardey's book, *Storm Tactics*. Here was a couple who, having voyaged for 26 years in their sailboat, covering 5 ½ circumnavigations, seemed knowledgeable about what to do in a storm in the open water. I felt relieved to learn that storms at sea were rarely a part of the cruising experience. During a stretch of eleven years of cruising they had only encountered one serious storm at the end of the season, and because their ship was well prepared, they made it through with little inconvenience. I also learned that in addition to the soundness of your ship and the overall preparedness on board to face certain scenarios as they arose, weather was one of the deciding factors for success and comfort on the water. Recognizing weather patterns and waiting for optimal conditions greatly increased your chances of a positive experience on the water.

I started watching the Weather Channel, which proved to be almost as addictive as chocolate. I watched as a meteorologist stood in front of a giant map and pointed to a series of low or high pressure systems as they marched east across North America. There was a lot of talk about barometric pressure. This I researched. I gathered that generally low pressure systems ushered in less stable weather and often involved storms. High pressure air masses typically brought warmer, stable conditions. A weather "front" involved the colliding of two opposite air pressure systems resulting in changes in the weather, sometimes violent, wherever the two happened to meet.

When the 7 o'clock news came on and a perky, blonde meteorologist said, "Tomorrow we'll see a drop in the barometer as low pressure moves in from the north bringing higher winds and shower or two," I felt like I was finally comprehending a foreign language. I translated for the kids, who sat on the couch opposite me: "This is because low pressure air is colliding with higher pressure air, causing moisture to rise, condense, and be released as rain." This resulted in blank stares and a thrown pillow aimed at my head.

On the way to the grocery store, I noticed a wall of heavy, dark, clouds, and said to Lauren, "Check it out, cumulonimbus clouds. We're in for some rain."

"What kind of clouds?" she asked.

"Cumulonimbus. Cool word eh?" We tried saying it fast over and over again until we laughed.

I learned about something called the Beaufort Wind Scale. Developed in 1805 by Admiral Sir Francis Beaufort of the British Royal Navy, the original scale was based on the effect of wind speeds on the amount of canvas a full rigged frigate of the period could carry. It began at zero and rated winds in increasing knots up to twelve, twelve being a hurricane. I decided that if I ever lived on a boat, it would be in my best interest to avoid weather higher than a Force 4, which was described as: winds "moderate" and its effects observed on the water: small waves of .5-1.25 meters becoming longer; numerous whitecaps. This, I thought, I could handle.

The more I learned about weather, the more I came to realize that weather patterns, far from being a mysterious entity beyond my comprehension, was a subject I could grasp, at least rudimentarily. I was not at the whim of a world that directly dropped Force 5 hurricanes from the sky in the middle of October. In fact, if I went out into the Atlantic in the middle of February, I was guaranteed not to run into one. And even if I was traveling by boat during hurricane season, June through to

November, meteorologists had the technology to provide ample warning enabling people to get to safety. By keeping abreast of the local weather patterns and up-to-date forecasts our chances of running into bad weather were slim. But even if we did run into a squall, keeping a well prepared boat would greatly increase our ability to come through it just fine.

The knowledge I was acquiring on storms and weather, as well as reading other peoples boating experiences, which were mainly positive, was proving to be formidable artillery against Fear. She had become less yappy. Less sure of herself. Intent on silencing her for good, I thought it would be a good idea to understand the nature of Fear. I read a lot of books like, "Three Easy Steps to Overcoming Your Fears," and "Fear Today, Gone Tomorrow." These I purchased or checked out of the library with great hope and practiced with little success.

A breakthrough happened while reading a book called *Feel the Fear and Do It Anyway* by Susan Jeffers. Here she promoted the idea that while we might be able to reason somewhat with the fear in our lives, there was a good chance we would never get rid of it altogether. All this time I had been trying to get rid of Fear, waiting until that happened, before making a decision. Instead, I needed to accept that Fear might be around for a long time. Those who accomplished their dreams, according to Jeffers, did so with Fear as their companion.

It didn't take long for Mike to figure out there was a battle going on in my brain. Seeking to up the ante in his favor, he attempted to persuade me of the values of living on a boat with Lauren and Stefan. He approached me in the same manner I approached the giant woman Fear. He had stats and research. Pie charts, graphs, and probability distributions as to why doing it now with the kids would be a good idea. When that didn't work, he used words like simplicity, solitude, and togetherness.

"Don't you feel like our lives have been so busy lately that we have become disconnected with ourselves and each other?

Living on a boat, say, for a year or two, would give us a chance to get to know our kids in the teenage years, when it is probably most important. We have some experience homeschooling, so we know we can handle that aspect. We can expose the kids to a broader reality. A reality outside of the mall. And don't you think it would be good for our relationship as well?"

It was a card well played. When I asked him how we would survive financially, he said, "We could sell everything, bank most of it, and attempt to make a living from home. You could write. I would continue to trade stocks online. As long as I have internet, I can do that anywhere. I know we would be giving up a financially secure future, but what we really have to ask ourselves is: how much is enough? We may return with considerably less cash, but with a legacy of memories and a relationship with each other and the kids. How much is that worth? Isn't that worth everything?"

There are moments in life when you are keenly aware that you stand at the vortex of two paths diverging. Choosing one over the other will affect not only your own destiny, but the future of your children and even their children. I weighed the two paths. I could ignore the dream Mike and I had written down back in college. Perhaps I could construct a different, less drastic, dream. But I had the feeling whatever I chose outside my comfort zone, Fear was going to be there citing all the reasons why I should keep life safe and comfortable. I also knew that should I decide against living on a boat, it would be the decision that would forever haunt me.

Life, I thought, was one big game of *Let's Make a Deal*. I could hear the host, Monty, saying, "You can keep this perfectly good life with all its benefits: security, comfort, and predictability or....you can choose what's behind door number three." The crowd yelled for door number three. They always did. They had nothing invested and loved the drama. There I stood in my chicken costume, plumes of feathers going in all directions, looking back and forth with the same conflicted countenance I had seen on a hundred contestants.

I was wary of what seemed like greener grass over there, but the unknown behind door number three was attractive. If I chose it, I would be banking on the fact that growing past my fears, living a simpler lifestyle, giving the kids a broad perspective of the world and the memories created on such a journey, would be worth the risks of storms, seasickness, sharks, giving up a financially secure future, and living with two hormonal teenagers and a risk- happy husband. The potential for growth, painful as it might be, was tempting.

And, for me, God was mixed in there somewhere. I wondered if I could, outside the normal confines of religiosity, find God again, or perhaps allow myself to be found. I felt pretty cautious bringing God into the equation of a big decision. I knew that God could be used to justify any cockamamie scheme. But let's be honest here, I told myself. I wasn't about to set off with a sword intending to convert or slay. I was interested in paying attention to what my journey, the journey of others, and the world around me might teach me through a season of pilgrimage.

In recent years I had tended toward a sort of theistic agnosticism. I believed it was impossible to prove the existence of God, or for that matter most of the Bible, but was inclined toward belief in a Divine Being anyway. There wasn't enough evidence to demand a verdict in my opinion, but there was evidence to *suggest*, and for the time being it was enough. I had patiently investigated atheism, but believed that altruistic acts were more than instinctual impulses designed to further the good of society under the umbrella of evolution. There was a spirit involved I couldn't bring myself to discount.

Time had gone a long way toward healing the initial shock of loss I had experienced in losing a child. I had yet to comprehend the need for suffering, and in this regard, found myself in good company. I had begun to make peace with the idea that there were not many answers to my questions, and that the questions themselves were, at least in some ways, part of the point. Releasing the confidence I placed in many of my previously held beliefs had initially freaked me out. When you spend your whole life with the idea that believing the right things will eternally save you, letting go of some of them is terrifying. It required that I throw myself at the Divine and beg for mercy in a way that I never had when I thought I had all the answers. I had come to believe that faith centered a great deal on the simple message: love God, love your neighbor, and love yourself. I clung to the vestige and figured I could spend a lifetime, let alone a season of pilgrimage, plumbing its depths. Living on a boat, I hoped, would provide a season of simpler living in which I could reconnect with God, myself, and my family.

"I choose door number 3," I told Monty hesitantly. The crowd went wild, but I knew I was a sucker. I was rolling the dice and the stakes were high. I was messing around with chance and probabilities. Starting up a game of pipe bomb blackjack. Unlike the game show *Lets Make a Deal*, with its instant gratification or disappointment upon lifting the lid or sliding open the doors, whether or not I had actually won anything of value would likely take years to reveal itself.

12

Mike and I discussed the best way to tell Lauren and Stefan that we had decided to sell everything we had, the house, cars, their bedroom furniture, the television set, and move onto a boat. The problem would not lie with Stefan, who was ten and found walking down to the river to fish an adventure. Our concern was with Lauren, who was twelve and up to her eyeballs in the seventh grade. Over the course of raising her thus far, I had thought numerous times how unlike each other we were in the realm of social aptitude. While I had been self conscious, awkward, and a people-pleaser at her age, she had a devil-may-care attitude, oozed confidence, and questioned authority. She lived for the telephone, IM, and weekend trips to the mall. Just the kind of kid who likes being uprooted from interpersonal connectedness.

"We have a couple things going for us," I told Mike privately. "She loves adventure and dislikes convention. I wonder where she gets that from?" I continued, looking in Mike's direction.

The reason, I believe, that thousands of people flock to boat shows every year is that many of us have the secret desire to become a turtle. Pushing off from shore to swim lackadaisically through the water any time you please captures our imagination. It is travel at its finest: no luggage to pack and you can take all the comforts and familiarity of home to any number of exotic locations.

Mike and I decided the best way to get Lauren to consider living on a boat was to give her a taste of the potential by taking her to the Toronto Boat Show. Even as an amateur boater, I figured boat shows were about as close to an amusement park and as far from reality in the nautical world as you were likely to get. In a cavernous, carpeted convention center, we found different types of boats: powerboats, sailboats, and catamarans, in varying lengths. There wasn't a speck of dirt anywhere. There were no dents or scrapes from botched docking attempts; all the hulls were smooth and shiny. The numerous systems were in prime working order as displayed by the suit-and-tie salesman who handed me a sheet listing about $125,000 worth of extras. The engine rooms smelled strangely of lavender, and since there wasn't a drop of slime or oil to be seen, I could actually see chrome and stainless. The polished galley tables were set with fine bone china, crystal wine goblets, and decoratively folded napkins. The whole thing smacked of the *Love Boat*, and I expected Captain Stubing to walk out of a pilothouse at any moment and ask me to join him at the captain's table for dinner.

For the kids, stepping on board a sixty-eight-foot power monohull was similar to shoving their way through fur coats in a wardrobe and finding themselves in a sort of Narnian parallel universe. They emitted small shrieks of pleasure upon finding life lived out in miniature: dishwasher, sink, bathroom, barbeque, washer and dryer, and tiny odd-shaped latching cupboards. The winding, circular stairways reminded them of secret passageways. These led to hideaway staterooms with low ceilings and enchanting portholes.

When Lauren, Stefan and I found ourselves together at the bow, I worked my magic. "Imagine this boat in the water, bobbing up and down, taking us to a faraway, deserted island."

"Wouldn't that be amazing?" Lauren whispered breathless.

I felt kind of bad about this. Like Mike and I were manipulating our kid's impressions which, if I am honest, is so much a part of what it means to be a parent. I made their favorite dinner a few nights later: angel hair pasta with chicken, sundried tomatoes, and Alfredo sauce. It had been a busy day and it was the first night all week that we had been able to sit down together.

Mike introduced the idea of living on a boat casually, as if it was no big deal. He said, something like, "Can you believe we got snow so early in the year, and how about those MapleLeafs, eh? They lost again last night... and oh hey by the way Hon, what would you think about living on a boat for a year?"

Without hesitation, I said in my best June Cleaver voice, "Well that is just a terrific idea! I think it would be kind of fun, dear."

"You know," he continued, wiping his mouth with a napkin, "we could travel to some pretty interesting places. We could go to the Bahamas. There is great fishing there I hear. We could get our scuba diving certificates. Or maybe learn to spear fish. Swim and snorkel. What would you think of that?"

"I think it is a fabulous idea," I said, but I was a little nervous about that spear fishing.

There was a bit of a lull.

"Are you serious?" Stefan finally said looking back and forth between Mike and me. "Because you guys shouldn't joke around about something like that."

Lauren kept silently shoveling noodles into her mouth, but I knew the electrical synapses going off in her brain would be similar to a fireworks display on July fourth.

"We are serious," I said quietly.

Lauren opened her mouth to say something, but before she could, Stefan interrupted with, "So what you are telling me is that we could move onto a boat, for a whole year, and I could learn to snorkel and spear fish in the Bahamas, AND get out of school? You guys are the best, man, the best," he said shaking his head back and forth.

I countered with, "You won't get out of school. You would have to do school at home. Dad and I have looked into several good correspondence curriculums and found one we think would be great. This online correspondence high school would send you all of your supplies and you could take classes over the Internet. You could study at your own pace and we could learn about the different places we visit while living on the boat. This school will keep track of all your records so that if you need to transfer back into regular school, it would be no problem."

"Where would we go on the boat?" Stefan asked.

Mike said, "Well, we could go to the Bahamas for sure. Then maybe head up the Eastern Seaboard and visit Norfolk, Boston, maybe even New York City. We might be able to cross the Atlantic Ocean and go to the Mediterranean. Visit cities like Rome and," here Mike looked in Lauren's direction, "Paris."

"What about leaving all my friends?" Lauren interjected suddenly, keeping her eyes on her plate.

I said quietly, sincerely, "Dad and I have thought about this and we know how important your friends are, Lauren. You can keep up with them over the internet, which is so great these days. And you can go to camp in the summertime. If you and your friends save up their money you could have some of them down for a visit. I imagine it would be pretty exciting for your friends to visit you on a boat."

She raised her eyebrows, interested, and nodded. After a time, she said, "What about the fact that we don't know anything about boating?"

"We will have to learn together, how to use charts, navigate, anchor. Weather will be important. But we can learn together," I said trying to sound confident.

"I do like the idea of traveling," Lauren offered.

"The thing is," Mike continued, "In any decision you make in life you will be giving up one thing for another. Mom and I have tried to weigh the good and the bad with this decision and we think the good outweighs the bad. It is true we all will miss out on some social stuff, but I think we will gain in other areas. Important areas like reconnecting with family and the environment. Learning about the world we live in and living simply. Mom and I think it will be worth giving up some things that are important to us, for a time, in order to experience what living on a boat might have to teach us."

Surprisingly, Lauren didn't flip out. She didn't think she would hate living on a boat. She told us she was interested and open to the idea, but not ready to commit. We told her to take some time and give it some thought.

In the following days, Mike and I gave her space and tried not to discuss the issue when she was around. I noticed that boating magazines ended up in her bedroom on the night table. She spent a whole Saturday on the couch reading a book about a Canadian family who lived on a sailboat for four years and circumnavigated the globe.

Several weeks later, we were having a picnic at a park. Lauren took a break from Frisbee and came to sit with us at the picnic table.

"I have decided," she said, smiling. "I want to give it a try. I'm actually pretty excited about it. "

Mike called Stefan over to the table. Without saying a word, Mike put his hand out, palm down, into the middle of the table. Stefan, grinning, immediately thrust his hand out and placed it on top of Mike's. Lauren confidently put her hand on top of Stefan's. I looked each of them in the eye, and put my hand on top of the pile.

"Well," I said, "there's no turning back now."

That night, after the kids were in bed, Mike and I pulled out a recently purchased Oxford Atlas. We thumbed through it and ended up looking at the Atlantic Ocean as it stretched from the East Coast of the US across one page, crossing over the crack in the binding, and continuing to stretch across the other page all the way to Africa and the mouth of the Mediterranean.

"Look how far it is from one side to another," I pointed out quietly.

"Yeah. It would be amazing to cross, wouldn't it? Start in Florida. Go through Bermuda," Mike said tracing his finger along the page, "and the Azores. End up in Gibraltar. Spend some time in the Mediterranean. What would that be like?"

The Atlantic Ocean is the world's second largest ocean with a total area of about 41.1 million square miles and covering 22% of the earth's surface. In order to accomplish the crossing Mike had described, we would have to travel roughly 4300 miles. There would be a fair amount to consider in such an undertaking, not the least of which was the risk involved. Five hundred miles from land was a lonely place. In the event of an emergency in the form of weather or injury, it would do little good to call 911.

Looking across the wide expanse of blue, I wasn't so sure I would be up for an ocean crossing of that caliber. In my mind, it was life as out of control as it got. I couldn't decide if I was terrified or intrigued.

13

A farmer's field is a strange place to find a power catamaran. Mike and I drove about an hour through the lush New Zealand countryside in a rented car looking for a side street with a name like Kookaburra. Although late fall in Canada, the spring was just beginning in New Zealand, and as we drove out of Auckland, I had been relishing the sight of fresh growth.

In recent months, we had decided several things. We liked the idea of a catamaran and had looked at several options both in power and sail. We were hoping to find something between 50 and 55 feet. Anything smaller, we thought, would be less than conducive to the four of us living aboard. We had opted to look for a power vessel and since there weren't many power catamarans available in North America, we had broadened our search to Australia and New Zealand where they were more common. About a month before, I had found an ad for an unfinished power catamaran hull in New Zealand. At sixty five feet, it was larger than anything we had looked at, but because of its unfinished condition, it was still within our budget. With Lauren and Stefan at their grandparents, Mike and I had flown over to investigate.

Several miles outside of Auckland, we found the street, pulled off onto a gravel road, glanced up, and gawked. Sure enough, just like the picture in the advertisement, a white behemoth sat on stilts with trees and bushes growing around it, like it was part of the natural habitat. We got out of the car slowly, as if we had come upon an elephant in the wild and didn't want to spook it. As in the ad, she was new construction. Sixty-five feet of completed cored fiberglass husk with an empty interior, its current owner having run out of funds to complete her.

We climbed a ladder and stepped into the cockpit. There was white powdery dust everywhere. It immediately clung to our clothes and skin and made us itch. We went through a rectangular doorway into the empty galley. When I told Mike "she's big," my voice echoed, and for some reason we talked quietly after that, as if not wanting to awaken something. We went our separate ways for a time. Mike climbed down into the empty engine rooms while I made my way into the bedrooms. Staterooms, I reminded myself silently.

Without woodworking the inside seemed stark and uninviting. My imagination, so often a bane, kicked into boon mode and I imagined warm cherry wood cupboards and a settee in the pilothouse. I briefly pictured Mike at the place where the helm would be. I walked tentatively out onto the bow and leaned over the edge, imagining turquoise water below me. I could almost feel the boat rising and falling with the waves. There was a little seat in between the hulls where I sat and looked out onto a green, bushy field and attempted to picture a horizon full of water. Into my mind came a vision of a storm.

"I am not afraid," I whispered out loud.

Without skipping a beat, I heard Yoda's shaky voice in my head, saw his little cane pointing in my direction. "Oh you will be…You WILL BE."

A little disturbed, I went to join Mike in the empty galley.

"Well, it's a huge project," he said running his hand along the fiberglass doorway then flicking his fingers to get rid of the dust. "We would have to completely build the inside ourselves."

"What about putting in the engines? The electrical and plumbing? You think we could handle all that plus the woodwork?" I asked.

Mike and I had been down the construction road before. When the kids were very small we had decided that building homes on spec would be a great way to make a living. Mike had worked a couple of summers on a housing construction team while in university, and with a working knowledge of the basics, we thought, "How hard could it be?" He went to the library and checked out books like *Framing a Home for Dummies* and *Basic Plumbing*. Went to the hardware store and bought a few tools. We bought three lots, built three homes, and sold them. It turned out to be a lucrative, but physically and emotionally demanding endeavor. When a desk job opened up at a money management firm, he had taken it, initially welcoming the conventional lifestyle.

Remembering our past building experience, Mike said with a grin, "Nothing that a few trips to the library wouldn't solve. If we decided to go ahead, we should probably move her to somewhere in the States or Canada, maybe, Florida. We could move down in the spring and begin construction."

Then he sighed heavily, turned, and looked at me.

"Are you up for this? Are we up for this? Giving up a good job? Moving the kids? The building alone would be hard work, but there is the matter of living on a boat of this size with no boating experience. It's a heck of a learning curve. I would have to be sure we were in this together."

It felt like the moment of truth, but it wasn't. I had already pushed all my poker chips into the center of the table. Life sat to my right, bluffing as usual. Death sat stoically to my left, patiently waiting my next move.

"I'm all in," I said to Mike.

14

Several weeks later, it occurred to the four of us that we would need to name the power catamaran shell we had purchased that was now sitting in a boatyard in Florida. Its stern, where the name was to be inscribed, was still blank.

We were excited about the prospect of naming our boat. Stefan, a Lord of the Rings junkie at the time, hung onto "Frodo" and then "Gandalf" for as long as he could. Lauren was studying birds of prey in school and liked "Falcon" or "Peregrine." Mike liked a play on words and suggested, since it was a catamaran, "Peregrine" would be apt especially if underneath we wrote "Pair-O-Grins." Or how about "Paradise" and under that "Pair-O-Dice"? Life was a gamble, after all.

We laughed over this and I said if we wanted to be tacky, then how about adding a pair of fuzzy dice to the dashboard? Maybe glue on some Mike, Kim, Lauren, and Stefan bobbleheads? We could attach two plastic waving hands to the stern and put a bumper sticker just below that saying, "If this boats a- rockin, don't come a-knockin."

Aside from the bumper sticker (that's gross), the kids loved these ideas. Mike mentioned "Training Wheels." I tended to favor voyageur names like, "Scout" and "Pilgrim."

"What about Epiphany?" I said after a time. Mike liked it. I thought we were on to something.

"No, it's too high falootin," Lauren said.

"What does that mean?" I asked.

"Too snooty. Too fancy." Eventually the three of them sided with her and I was overruled.

Then came a list of names beginning or having to do with "Cat:"

Catatonic

Catastrophe (Quickly shelved. No need to tempt fate.)

Cat Call

Cat Nip

Catapult

Nine Lives

Cat Scan

Cathartic

They were fun words but with no deep resonance for us. Dinner was over and, with nothing solved, we decided to let our imaginations simmer for the next few days.

Growing up, I found murdering certain members of the insect world to be socially acceptable. There was a free-standing open season on flies, mosquitoes, and for very brave heroic types, wasps. Stalking them in cold blood was encouraged even if the end result was their guts violently spattered in equal measure on the kitchen counter and the back of my fly swatter. During the long, hot, restless days of summer, the malcontent gang of kids that roamed my neighborhood would rustle up a squirming earthworm (not an insect, I later learned in high school biology). Someone would be sent home to scrounge up a magnifying glass. We would form a circle and watch as the concentrated rays from the magnifying glass would begin to burn a hole in wriggling worm flesh. Sometimes there would be a small plume of smoke. The girls would turn away and say "Eeewww," the boys, "cool." Eventually, we would hear the ice cream truck in the distance and scramble off to scrounge for quarters, leaving the writhing worm to figure things out for himself.

You didn't mess with butterflies, though. There was something holy about them. You could catch them in a net, gently...gently (being careful not to touch their wings) and set them up in a posh Mason jar apartment, remembering to poke holes in the cap for air. This was the nearest you would come to playing God. I placed a stick in the jar for my new resident to cling to, some grass for her to play in, and a slice of apple for food. My Eden complete, I would sit mesmerized for about a half hour consumed with my Monarch's well being. Every once in awhile, she would go stir crazy and flutter wildly around her world, conking her head on the top of the jar a bunch of times before finally accepting her lot in life and settling back onto the stick, to slowly open and close her wings again. I had better things to do all day then just sit and watch her, but I was a responsible supreme being and checked up on her from time to time. Eventually, as is apt to happen to supreme beings, empathetic thoughts of freedom would get the better of me, and I would release her.

In an attempt to pass along my reverence of butterflies, Mike and I loaded the kids up into the minivan one Saturday morning and we went to a Butterfly Conservatory. It was early spring and the morning was cold, but we walked through the double sliding doors into a tranquil, tropical jungle. Butterflies and fuzzy moths flitted through the air or gathered at bird baths piled with fruit. One vibrant Blue Morpho landed on top of Stefan's head and decided he liked it there. It took a fair bit of combatant persuading on Stefan's part to convince the settler to seek digs elsewhere.

The air was equal parts humidity and electricity. We continued along a narrow sidewalk, deeper into a garden and found a small stream and further, a rock waterfall. Along the way, we passed a large wooden box containing several crawling caterpillars of differing color variety and a short distance away, we investigated a small display of cocoons. They were hanging, looking lifeless and drab, at different stages of development, on vertical screens framed with wood. On the last frame there were several cocoons that were intermittently shaking, reminding me of the trembling Mexican Jelly beans I used to collect when I was a kid.

Moving along, we came to a wood-shingled hut with a large picture window above which hung a sign inscribed: "Nursery." There was a woman in a khaki uniform inside and she beckoned to us saying through the glass, "You're lucky! Looks like there is a butterfly ready to emerge! Soon, she'll no longer be a chrysalis. You can hang around here as long as you want and watch."

"What's a *Chrysalis*?" Stefan asked.

"It's the name of the stage of life when a caterpillar is changing inside the cocoon. Oh look! See, she has started to come out now!"

After several minutes, the butterfly, a monarch, hobbled, fragile looking, onto the offered branch and flexed her wet trembling wings. The four of us stood with our noses pressed up against the glass.

"This is the first time this little one has experienced life with wings," she told us smiling.

After awhile, we continued down the path, and arrived at an enclave with bench seats facing a large screen. On the wall was a large red disc and underneath it the directions read: "To play, push this button."

"Just like Alice in Wonderland," Lauren said bemusedly.

Mike pushed the large, red, button and the lights dimmed. We sat down as the screen came to life.

A James Earl Jones type voice began to corresponding pictures and video: A butterfly must pass through 3 stages: embryo, larvae, and pupa or *Chrysalis*, before it emerges from its cocoon as imago-a fully developed adult. A larva, or caterpillar, lives an earthbound life. She may climb grass, bushes, or even trees, but her scope is limited. Instinctively, she senses something big is about to happen. She has no idea how long it will take or what the outcome will be, but something is expected of her. Finding a comfortable, secure piece of real estate, she creates a tough outer covering of silk, sometimes incorporating small twigs or dried grass and cloaks herself with it. Then, she settles in. She enters the *Chrysalis* or pupa stage. If she happens to be a Monarch caterpillar, it will take about two weeks to undergo metamorphosis-complete change. For other butterflies and moths this change can take months, sometimes a whole season. In solitude and silence, a butterfly waits for change.

There were several pictures of different types of cocoons which passed in silence. Then the voice continued, "Outwardly there may seem to be nothing going on inside a cocoon. To an untrained eye it appears dead. But scientists know that while the pupa waits quietly, a huge change is occurring. A pupa must be still for this change to take place otherwise it will never become what it is meant to be. It must give itself over to this change inside the *Chrysalis* and eventually it will emerge as the same entity, yet completely different. Once she has emerged, she can fly. She can view the world from a completely different perspective."

Stefan pulled on my sleeve, leaned over to my bended ear and said without taking his eyes off the screen, "Do you think it hurts when the caterpillar is changing inside the cocoon?"

"I don't know," I said. "I don't think anyone knows."

"Maybe it does hurt," he whispered back.

"Maybe," I said, nodding.

On our way out to the car, someone (I'm pretty sure it was me) mentioned "*Chrysalis*" would be a great boat name. We all froze in the middle of the parking lot.

"That's it," one of us said.

"It's perfect," said someone else.

There was no more debate. We shook hands in agreement.

Weeks later, I was explaining to a friend who had come over for lunch how we came up with the name and took the credit myself.

Mike called from the kitchen, "What are you talking about? I was the one who came up with *Chrysalis*!"

Overhearing from the sunroom, Lauren shouted, "No you weren't, I was the one!"

"You guys are all wrong, I'M the one who thought of it!" Stefan said.

At least, I thought, there was some agreement over the fact that it was a name whose conception was worthy to be claimed by each of us.

15

About a month later, I woke up early and the first thing I did was go to the bedroom window, pry open the wooden slats of the blinds and peer up into the sky. With some relief, I could see a milky blue atmosphere with a smattering of wispy, white, clouds. I was grateful for the good weather. Weeks ago I told a friend I was having a garage sale and she told me to make sure I put "Estate Sale" in the newspaper ad and not "garage sale."

"How come?" I asked.

"It sounds more appealing," she said. "Also you should mention you have antiques. You have antiques right? That always brings in the dealers. If you have a friend who needs to sell some stuff you could put, 'Multi-family Estate Sale.' That would really bring them in. Come to think of it, I have a bunch of stuff to sell, would you be up for company?"

I certainly was and not only that, but both Mike and I were up for hours the night before the sale putting small white price tags on the remaining items I had foolishly thought were much smaller in number. It seemed as soon as I moved one box aside there was another reminding me of the plate of green beans I was told to eat by my parents when I was a kid. In the wee hours of the morning, we flopped into bed, and before falling asleep, Mike peeled a tag off my arm that read "$5.75."

"Would you be willing to take $5.50?" he muttered, smiling sleepily.

By 8 a.m. the following morning, cars full of bargain hunters began to line up down the street. From my garage, I could see them through their car windows, cups of coffee steaming up the glass. They watched us drag furniture and boxes out onto the driveway and front lawn. Even from a distance their cutthroat anticipation was palpable. My sister-in-law showed up with coffee and donuts and about the same time, my friend showed up with her van load of items to sell. I stood in the middle of the garage eating a sour cream glazed and wondered if I would regret selling off what had taken the last 15 years to accumulate. I withstood a sudden urge to herd a few boxes back into the house. Laid out all around me were the vestiges of our private lives now on display. China, armoires, chesterfields, the kids' bedroom sets, books, everything out in the open.

At 8:30 some internal bell went off, folks emerged from their cars, and the race began. It was all very festive, this selling off a chapter in my life. Family and friends came in hoards. Some bought a tablecloth or a set of dishes, then set up lawn chairs, sat down, and spent the rest of the day as if watching a sporting event.

In the middle of the frenzy of doing the mental math to make change, hardly my forte, I glanced up and noticed an older woman, frail and slightly stooped, wandering around. She was smartly dressed in a grey skirt, pink blouse, and black pumps. A little overdressed for a Saturday morning garage sale, I thought, but she looked rather regal with her grey hair pulled up in a bun. She was eyeing the pine chest that had sat in my sunroom. I concluded the current transaction and went over to ask if I could help her. She wanted the chest and didn't bother to bargain.

After handing me cash, she looked around and asked, more to herself than to me, "I wonder, did someone pass away?"

"No," I said. "We have decided to sell everything and live on a boat."

She turned, then, and for the first time, briefly made eye contact with me.

"Really?" she said with what seemed to be feigned curiosity. She looked away again, her gaze scanning the rest of the furniture in the driveway. Shaking her head she whispered, "What a shame."

I flashed back to several years prior, just after my great Aunt had passed away. My grandma, mother, aunt, and I were sorting through the basement of her house and came upon a large, metal cupboard full of hundreds of empty margarine and yogurt containers complete with lids. Upon my muttering inquiry as to why on earth she would bother to keep so many, my grandma, rising in sisterly defense, said that had I grown up in the Great Depression and lived through a war I would understand the craving to save things. "This generation hasn't had to work hard enough for their possessions. Things are far too disposable these days. There is no sense of value anymore."

There was a ring of truth to her words, but what I wanted to tell my grandma and the woman who now owned my pine chest, was that as each box and piece of furniture left the property I began to feel lighter. As the day progressed, it became a sort of game for me. With each sale, I would tell myself, "That's one less dresser to dust or refinish." And minutes later: "One less box of dishes I never used that took up space in my cupboard." "There goes that area rug. I'll never have to vacuum it again or worry about the spaghetti sauce stain in the corner." By the time the hedge trimmers and lawn mower left the premises I was practically giddy. Around four o'clock in the afternoon, everything but a few boxes had been sold. Mike pronounced his first garage sale a cleansing "household enema." I couldn't have agreed more. Nothing like getting rid of the crap. My soul felt light and clean as if it had just been scrubbed with a scouring pad.

Over pizza, sitting with our lawn chair friends, we raised our glasses and said in unison, "To household enemas!"

16

We arrived in Florida at the end of May and our frigid Canadian bodies initially relished the higher temperatures. We found a small townhouse to rent until we could move onto *Chrysalis*. The place seemed cramped, but I told myself and the kids it was nothing compared to what it would be like living aboard. We went over to the boatyard the day we arrived and toured *Chrysalis* for the first time as a family. Lauren and Stefan claimed a stateroom each in different hulls. We discussed plans to build a small desk area in their rooms where they could do their school work. *Chrysalis* seemed even bigger than I remembered. I thought with some chagrin that this was likely due to the creeping realization of how much work we had ahead of us.

Chrysalis measured just under 65 feet long, including the added six foot swim platforms at the stern, and 25 feet wide. While the kids crawled happily through the empty engine rooms, Mike and I determined there was roughly 900 square feet of living space, and that didn't include the cockpit (back porch) or the flybridge (steerage upstairs and outside). Preliminary plans were discussed: where to put a galley table, appliances, settees. As we walked through, I made notes and rough sketches of our ideas.

The four of us climbed around and through *Chrysalis*, exploring as if she were a jungle gym. As we did, we had to keep reminding each other to speak in nauticalese. The "wing decks" were the side pathways you used to walk the length of the boat. If you were walking toward the bow, you'd holler: "I'm walking forward!" If you were going to the stern you'd say, "I'm heading aft!" The oblong metal thingy you attached a line to, not a rope, by the way, was called a "cleat," and from it you shoved the line through the "hawsepipe," an oblong hole in the hull well above the waterline. Onboard and facing the bow, the right side of the boat was known as the "starboard" and the left as the "port."

I would ask a kid, "What do you think of your bedroom?"

"It's not a bedroom, it's a stateroom," Lauren said.

"Yes, yes, a stateroom," I would say nodding, committing the new word to memory yet again.

Later on, someone else would say, "So this is where the toilet will be?"

"It's not a toilet, it's a head," I would remind them.

"Oh yeah right. A 'head.'"

By the end of the afternoon I told Stefan, "Check it out, your starboard shoe is untied."

At the time, *Chrysalis* had four empty staterooms, one of which we would turn into an office. There were four heads, three with showers. The main living area, or pilothouse, was on the top level. Here we planned to set up a television and a wrap-around settee. The helm station with watch berth was directly opposite that. A few steps below that, toward the stern, we would craft a galley with enough room for a full size fridge, oven, and microwave. Outside, on the top level, or flybridge, there was another helm station so we could steer al fresco. There were numerous holes cut out of the fiberglass where navigational instruments had yet to be installed. The cockpit was large enough for a small table and chairs and had a large, 36 cubic foot freezer and a barbeque already roughed in.

"What do you think of *Chrysalis* now?" I asked Lauren, when we tried to pass each other on narrow staircase leading from the galley to the pilothouse.

"Amazing. I love it!" she said happily. The prospect of life on a boat overshadowing, at least for the time being, the gut-wrenching goodbye to friends back in Canada.

"You, too?" I asked Stefan who was following her.

"Oh yeah. It's the bomb," he said. "When can we move in?"

Work commenced the following day, just when the South Florida heat was starting to rev its engines. Mike and I set up a large work area underneath *Chrysalis*, in between her two hulls. While organizing space for tools and hauling lumber into organized piles, I looked up at the curving arches and was grateful for the shade she supplied. It seemed a maternal gesture.

After purchasing *Chrysalis* in New Zealand, we had met with her designer, Malcolm Tennant, who had been a wealth of information. "In order for a catamaran to perform well, she needs to be lightweight. When you build her, keep her as light as you can," he told us. "This will be tricky, as catamarans seem spacious and you will be tempted to fill her up. Check yourselves."

Armed with this information, we used a corrugated wood product made by Tri-Cell, which was light and easy to work with. In 99 degree heat with about as much in humidity, Mike and I reverted back to our kindergarten days. We cut up 4 X 8 pieces of cored board and glued them into all sorts of pre-measured shapes and sizes. After the glue dried, I would pick up a section of galley settee or cupboards, and looking like Atlas, carry it up the wobbly metal staircase, into the cockpit, and through the galley door. Like fitting a piece into a giant 3D puzzle, Mike and I would place it into its designated spot. All of the cupboards, helm, settees, office desk, and bedroom furniture were made with the same wood. Rather than tackle the building of all the cupboard doors, we built the boxes ourselves and ordered all of the doors from a kitchen cabinet company. The same company sold us the cherry wood veneer we used to cover the corrugated wood, and also the stain they used for the doors so that we could match everything. Although it took time and effort on our part to do the work ourselves, we saved a considerable amount of money.

At every turn, the cost of materials used for boat construction and the hiring of anyone in the boating industry confounded us. I would find identical parts, one in a home store and the other in a boating store, and always the price was double, sometimes triple in the boating store. You had only to mention to any salesperson anywhere that you were building a boat and in place of their eyes two big dollar signs would appear and suddenly they had all sorts of parts you needed because your life depended on it. Once, Mike hired a guy over the phone to help us with some general lightweight construction, nothing out of the ordinary, and when he arrived and saw it was a boat he told us in no uncertain terms that the hourly rate he quoted us would have to double. "But this work is normal construction, just like a house," Mike argued. "Doesn't matter, a boat costs more," he said with confidence.

Our knowledge of home construction proved beneficial, but boat construction differed greatly in the amount of work that needed to be custom designed. There were quirky corners and rounded edges. Sloped ceilings. The weight on the inside needed to be evenly distributed so that *Chrysalis* would sit level on the water. Consideration needed to be made for the rough salt water environment and the fact that things might shift underway. Every system, including plumbing, electrical, and fuel, had to be painstakingly designed by us.

Many mornings would find the four of us up early. I packed a cooler with cold water and electrolyte injected drinks, sandwiches, and snacks. We would arrive at the boatyard while temperatures were yet bearable. Mike would give Lauren and Stefan a task: staining wood or gluing wood pieces together under the shade of *Chrysalis'* hull. Sometimes he would have them cut out marked pieces of wood with the table saw. When the engines arrived and were in place, one in each hull, they helped Mike align them using string and a level. They both helped Mike set up the generator and while doing so, got a lesson in how it worked.

When the kids were busy off on their own, Mike and I would run electrical wire, plumbing tubes, or hang cupboard boxes. While handing Mike a hammer one afternoon, I thought that it had been a long time since we had worked together toward a common goal. Certain relational embers, long dormant, were being stoked and it felt good. I had a renewed appreciation for Mike's work ethic and knowledge. The easy going way he taught the kids how to use epoxy, reminding them to use a mask. At lunchtime, the four of us sat together, sweaty and dirty, under the hull of *Chrysalis*, eating our sandwiches. Mike would say, "See that big bucket over there? A dollar to the first person who can throw a pebble into it." The game was on and suddenly we all felt a lot less tired.

17

When we weren't working, we spent a fair bit of time at the beach which, having grown up in landlocked Colorado, was a novelty to me. Every morning I climbed over a pillowy dune to access the nearby stretch of Florida shoreline and wondered what would pop up. One day the tide would be low and I would walk easily across hard-packed wet sand. Sometimes the tide was high and I was forced to make my way through small soft dunes into which I sank. Not more than a hundred feet of walking in such conditions and I would began to huff. If there had been a large surf the night before, the sand would be carpeted with shells and I would walk across them in bare feet like an amateur walking over fiery coals saying, "Ow, ow, ow."

One afternoon, I sat on a beach chair, grimacing, while watching Stefan learn to skim board. He had just come to sit beside me on a towel to rest, and I was checking out several foot-long red sand scrapes that were forming on his back when a lifeguard, a young guy in red shorts, white t-shirt, and a whistle around his neck, came over and said to Stefan, "Hey, you're getting pretty good there, dude. Just wanted to let you know the sand is really great about a hundred yards that way. Surf tends to be a bit better down there, too."

Stefan thanked him, picked up his board, and went over to give it a try.

On impulse, I asked our new lifeguard friend, "Hey, I'm just curious. How often do you actually have to swim out and rescue someone?"

As if answering a routine question, he replied, "Three, maybe four times a week. More in peak season."

Who knew there were so many of us near to drowning all the time? Since reading Marvel Comics back in grade school, I had wondered if superheroes existed, and here was one now. I told him this in all sincerity, but like a true hero, he shrugged and said, "That's my job."

Occasionally, he told me, he was required to swim to an area where he had recently, sometime minutes, sometimes hours earlier, seen sharks. He mentioned casually that there were hundreds of sharks in these waters, and he saw them all the time.

"Once," he said, shaking his head and smiling, "my buddy was keeping an eye on a heavyset guy lying on a raft a long way off the beach. He handed the binoculars to me and said 'take a look at this.' I held up the binoculars and could see a large shark fin heading straight for the guy. The fin disappeared underneath him only to resurface on the other side and continue on its way."

"You didn't try to warn him?" I asked, surprised and unnerved at the thought.

"At the time we made the split second decision not to," he said. "When we do warn people in a situation like that, they tend to panic. They get off the raft, thrash around and try to swim for shore. It makes them more of a target."

The phrase "ignorance is bliss" came to mind.

Our lifeguard friend told me he should get back to work, but it had been great chatting. The funny thing was, he didn't really leave, he just stood up, moved a few yards away and started watching the water. His eyes scanned the area for a fin or a head going under. Children playing oblivious. He wore the look of a man on serious business. I got the feeling he barely tolerated my chit chat. His brows pursed together. He blew his whistle and yelled to some young boys playing too far out, near a rip current. He told them to come in closer to shore. They grudgingly obliged. This, I thought, is what he does for a living: watch.

Later that evening I wrote in my journal, a recently revived habit: "Imagine an occupation where your sole responsibility is to be aware of what is going on around you? Like a CIA agent or a Navy Seal. Is such a thing possible in normal, domestic life? If I paid close attention for the next few years, recording my findings, could I become adept at being alert? Then maybe, down the road, if I happened to find myself in a seedy café, sitting across the table from Robert Ludlum's spy character Jason Bourne, and he asked me to describe the details around me without looking, I could give him a ten minute rendition of things even he had missed. He would be forced to throw up his hands and say, 'Well, damn! You've got me beat!'

In such training, it would be fairly easy for me to pick up on dangers and escape routes. I have a natural propensity to notice those things anyway. But could I learn to use such powers of observation for good? Instead of noticing all the perils, could I look beyond and pick up on the possibilities for growth? For joy?

I hadn't spent so much concentrated time with the kids since they were infants. It was easy with Stefan. He was ten years old. He asked little of the world, and it asked little of him. While he seemed to thrive in our new southeastern surroundings by taking up skim boarding, fishing, and body surfing, a cloudy sullenness gradually descended on Lauren. I waited in dread for the moment.

What happens relationally between Lauren and me is similar to what happens when Mike and I go on a date after an extended period of disconnectedness. There is the initial joking around and laughter, which starts with appetizers and flows into the main course. By dessert, talk has turned to politics and then dangerously close to stuff we're reading or philosophical and theological issues, which can quickly lead to all of the deeper annoyances and grievances we have been harboring against

ourselves, each other, and the world and it isn't long before
we're headed home and the date is ending in grudging silence.

Lauren was cloaked in being a teenager. She wore it like the
"Coat of Many Colors." She was unmindful of its presence, but it
was shockingly obvious to me. There were unalienable rights, she
subconsciously believed, to being fourteen. The right to choose how
she lived her life and with whom she chose to live it especially
when she was out of our presence. Our love complicated these
rights. One day about a year before, she said in frustration, "Why
do you guys have to love me so much anyway?" Assumed was that
if we didn't love her she could do what she wanted. Maybe smoke
pot with her pals back home. Return home however late at night
she pleased. Wear a bikini to school.

"Did you ever think," I asked her once, "that your love for
us complicates things too?"

"Yes!" she said with enlightenment. "Totally! How come
love has to complicate everything?"

About three months after moving to Florida, Lauren and I
spread our towels on the sand at the beach one afternoon. I had
spent that time attempting to bridge the gap between us. It helped
that I was the only female friend she had in close physical
proximity. Strides had been made, but the bridge was still a
rickety connection, and tended to sway in small relational breezes.

The day had been pleasant so far. I had been wondering
aloud how sand could manage to get into the very center of my
ham on rye. I had just said, "Maybe that's why they call it a *sand*-
wich," and we had laughed. Right after that, I asked her, "Hey,
how come you hardly ever go out into the water with your
brother?" The atmosphere grew frail between us. Her eyes
glazed and she stared out into the waves.

"I don't know," she said flatly.

We watched a guy in a black speedo pack up his chair and
head up over the dune toward the parking lot. I felt hot lava
bubbling to the surface.

"Mom?" she said, "it's just that....this isn't working for me anymore. I mean…what kind of loser am I? I have no friends. I hang out all day with my PARENTS who have this dumb idea of building a boat and for WHAT? Honestly, for what mom? To poke around some islands? Okay maybe cross the ocean, but that's like, how many thousands of days from now and in the meantime, I'm missing out on life! All my friends are going to parties and shopping and I'm stuck here on this stupid beach!"

Up until now her words had been angry, but here she switched tactics and attempted to appeal to my sympathetic instincts. Her tone became soft, conciliatory. She even touched my arm and looked directly into my eyes.

"Look, I've been thinking about this. It's not too late to change our minds. Dad can finish the boat and we can just sell it. Then we can pack up and move back. It's not such a big deal. We could easily do it, and I could start school back up in January."

I was quiet for a long time. I looked out into the waves for a magic message in a bottle. Finally, I told her softly, "Laur, there is no way we can go back."

She pulled away and scowled.

"BUT…" I paused for a few moments before continuing, "I do understand what you are saying. It has been a hard spring and summer with moving and saying goodbye to your friends, which I know was difficult, and then all this working on the boat in the heat hasn't exactly been the adventure Dad and I advertised."

She frowned again.

"Here's the thing. Dad and I really believe that this is going to be a great experience. You did, too, when you agreed to go. So we are going to push through it, at least until we have a year of living on the boat under our belts. That was the agreement. Then we can discuss the idea of moving back on land again. You may feel like you are missing out on life, but what you are doing here is not an absence of life, just a different kind of life. Maybe more real, maybe not. In life, whether on land or sea, you are going to be faced with all sorts of crap and doors slamming and lemons…And I know it sounds cheap and cliché but we've got to find ways, here and now, in the middle of the crap, of opening windows and making lemonade.

"Dad and I were talking the other day and we wondered two things: first, we found a theater day camp for a couple of weeks at the end of the summer and thought you might like to go. It's here in town, and we could sign you up if you wanted. We also wondered if you might want to take some of the money you've been saving up and go halfsies with us in buying a ticket for Emma to fly down for a week."

It was comical how her face instantly changed from grief to joy. She began to chat animatedly about all the things she could do with Emma, her best friend. And the theater camp was a great idea, she said. I could tell she was relieved. There was something to look forward to. I felt like I had temporarily dodged a bullet.

While packing up our towels to walk back, she said, "You know why I never go in the water, Mom?"

"Why?"

"Because ever since I watched the movie *Jaws* I have been so afraid of sharks. I hear the music in my head and everything."

"Does it bug you, being scared of going in the water?"

She looked at me in surprise. "Yeah…it sort of does. You too?"

"Oh yeah. I have BIG issues with fear, and it really bugs me," I said.

"I never knew that," she replied thoughtfully.

Attempting to juggle my beach chair and the umbrella, I realized that there were many other fears inherent in what we had been talking about. For Lauren, there was the fear of being alone, of being different, or missing out. For me, just now, there was the fear that I hoped we were doing the right thing.

"Then why are we going to live on a boat?" she asked.

With my free arm, I reached over to hug her and said, "To confront these fears. To change."

We walked amicably over a dune and stopped for an ice cream. She told me to smell the butter pecan mound on top of my cone, and when I did, she pushed the cone into my face and laughed. I feigned shock and flicked a clump of ice cream in her direction.

Apparently, ice cream went a long way toward building bridges.

18

Fall ebbed away and we set a move-in date for mid January. It had been eight months and we were antsy to get on with it already. We got kind of crabby and thought that we'd had enough of this journey, even though it hadn't begun. Or maybe it had, who was to say?

On launch day, a large travel lift showed up and they placed huge blue straps under Chrys' (as we had nicknamed her) bow, midship, and stern. Gradually they winched the straps tight and she rose off her jacks and swung slightly back and forth making a formidable "swoosh...swoosh" sound. The lift slowly wheeled her through the boatyard toward the ramp and the water. The four of us followed along, as did a few of the work crew who had helped with the painting, electrical, engines. Some of the boatyard personnel we had gotten to know through the months tagged along. Stefan had made friends with a boy who lived at our townhouse complex, and he and his family had come, so the whole event felt celebratory. *Chrysalis* was lowered into the water and, to my surprise, actually floated. In fact, she was above the waterline for weight, which greatly pleased both Mike and me.

We all gathered at the bow and Mike attempted to break a bottle of champagne across her, but it kept bouncing off the hull without breaking. One of the guys who helped install the engines, an old captain with a weather worn craggly face, came up to inspect the bottle.

He broke into a wide grin, looked at Mike, and said, "You guys bought a real bottle of champagne?"

"Yeah...?" Mike said.

"There are bottles that you can get specifically for breaking over hulls that will actually break. Real bottles won't."

Add it to the list of things we didn't know.

"It's okay," Mike said and he gave the bottle a shake, popped the cork, and baptized *Chrysalis* by spraying the foaming liquid over the hull. Everyone cheered and we climbed into the cockpit for our own champagne and snacks.

Baptism is an outward sign of an inward reality. After the well-wishers had left, I sat down on the galley settee to survey the inward reality of *Chrysalis*. In our impatience to "get on with it already," we had moved aboard with things less complete than I anticipated. The cupboards were in place, but there were no cupboard doors. No galley table. No cushions or upholstery on any sitting area. No wall covering which meant that in many places along interior walls, wires and plumbing were exposed. The pilothouse helm was roughed in, but unfinished. About a third of the woodworking had yet to be completed. Tools were strewn about and boxes piled in whatever free space remained. Just walking across the room required the agility of a ballerina.

The carpeting and hardwood cherry flooring had been installed, though, and the plumbing and electrical fixtures were in and working, as were the appliances. We had mounted a television in the pilothouse with a DVD player in the cupboard next to it. With no satellite or cable television, our only options regarding the TV and DVD player would be the numerous videos we had been collecting. The day before, Mike and I had shoved our mattresses aboard and I made up the beds with freshly laundered sheets because I figured after moving day we would be exhausted and there is nothing quite like crawling into bed after a day of hauling boxes around in the Florida heat.

Sitting there in the galley, I wondered how I got to such a place, so far from my normal environment. Not only did we need to unpack all our boxes, we had construction to finish and a new lifestyle to figure out, one whose ropes were not even vaguely familiar. Right then and there, I considered mounting a plank on the bow and voluntarily walking off it. The cold water would have done me a world of good, but I was saved for the moment by duty in the form of a kid yelling from the head, "Someone PLEASE find the toilet paper and bring me a roll! SOMEONE?   HELLO?" I smiled, stood up, and began rummaging through boxes. As a parent, when you are presented with such dependency, you take advantage of it. I intended to eek out a few bucks, maybe even a chore or two, from this bailout.

While I was unpacking silverware in the galley, Lauren came in with some towels and said, "Check out the backyard, Mom." I looked out over the sink, beyond the gangway, into an expanse of bluish grey, rippling, water. In the busyness of moving aboard I hadn't even noticed I was walking on water. The rest of the afternoon, every time I looked out a porthole or walked out onto the decks, I looked into its murky depths.

Up until that point in my life, sea water and I had been loosely acquainted. I took the occasional dip, stuck my toes in while sitting at a dock, or dropped a fishing line into its wetness. Wiped its stinging drops from of my eyes. Living on water elevated my status from tryst to cohabitation. If we were to be inexorably linked, I figured I better have more than a cursory hunch as to what I would be dealing with. I consulted my *Ocean Almanac*, a seagoing bible of sorts, and thus began a more intimate relationship.

Water covers seventy percent of the earth's surface. Three hundred and fifty million cubic miles give or take. In a universe where water has yet to be found, it is a hearty portion. Of that, a measly 2.5 percent is drinkable. Fourteen million cubic miles of all water on earth is ice. If you melted that ice the oceans would rise 1.7 percent or about 180 feet, enough to immerse 20 stories of the Empire State Building. No wonder folks are concerned about global warming.

The average depth of the oceans is an astounding 12,200 feet, well over two miles. I can imagine what might inhabit the bottom of such an environment. I read once that the oldest creatures on earth live there, which makes sense as they have learned to withstand the enormous pressure and darkness living on our planet so often demands. Thinking of the vast breadth and depth, it doesn't come as a surprise to learn that less than ten percent of the earth's waters have been explored by humans.

Further on, I read that a mathematician, one who obviously has a lot of time on his hands, figured out that if Christopher Columbus spilled a glass of drinking water into the ocean in 1492, by today all 1,700,000,000,000,000,000 molecules would now be thoroughly mixed into the oceans and rivers so that every glass of water drawn from every faucet in the world would contain as many as 250 molecules from the original water Columbus spilled from his glass. The next time I poured Mike and me a glass of good ole H_2O, I held mine up and said, "To Christopher Columbus and exploration." Mike, unaware of my recent discovery, smiled and clinked my glass anyway.

If you are interested in striking it rich, you might consider inventing a cost efficient apparatus that could extract the nine million tons of gold that has dissolved in the world's oceans, roughly 180 tons more than have ever been mined on the earth. While you are at it, you might as well extract the salt. There is enough salt in all the oceans to cover the continents in a layer 500 feet thick.

Next time you happen to inadvertently swallow a gulpful of seawater while swimming, consider this: not only have you just ingested salt, trace elements of gold, and about forty-six other elements, but millions of bacterial cells, hundreds of thousands of phytoplankton and tens of thousands of zooplankton. Yummy. I had done this just the other day, so I figured there had been a consummation of sorts, and water and I were officially introduced.

As I climbed into my berth on the eve of my first night to ever sleep on water's bulk, I thought about how water was holding up thirty-five tons of power catamaran, my son, daughter, husband, my whole world. It was my life support. Briefly, I also thought that if we sprung a leak sometime in the night and our bilge pumps failed, water would pour into the holds, the cabins, and the very same water that was sustaining our lives could snuff it out in a matter of minutes.

I laid back on clean smelling sheets and thought, 'Here I am. This is the day I have dreaded and looked forward to for such a long time. I am on the water and I am still alive.' I took a long, drawn out, cleansing breath. I was a little nervous, but strangely unafraid. I admit this was partly due to the fact that I was exhausted. That and the gentle rocking of the boat seemed to placate my imagination. Just before nodding off, I looked directly above me through a hatch, roughly two feet square, and was surprised to see a dark sky full of stars.

19

For the next week, every morning I would wake up and think, "Well wonder of wonders, I made it through another day and another night. The boat is still floating. I haven't drowned, yet. Mike and the kids aren't dead. It's going to be a good day."

Thus would begin a bombardment of sensory perceptions unlike any I had experienced. While having coffee I would look out the window and both sense and see that I was in motion. The horizon, forever stable and stationary in my previous life, now continuously moved up and down. Sometimes a boat would go by and the wash would bounce around my universe. This, I imagined, was what it felt like to be a bobblehead.

The sheer amount of auditory signals being chucked in my direction made me, on more than one occasion, want to sit in a dark stateroom, put my hands over my ears, squeeze my eyes shut, and say, "Na, na, na, na." At any given moment, several machines could be counted on to whirr, thump, or growl when you least expected it: generator, watermaker, bilge pumps, freezer compressor, twin 330 Cummins engines. The first few times I ran the water at the galley sink, I would simultaneously hear a strange noise, sort of a combination between a hum and a distant reoccurring thumping. I froze and asked, "What was that?" Had we been holed? Was it time to abandon ship? A scavenger hunt ensued until one of us yelled up, "Oh, it's just the watermaker!"

Around 2 a.m. on the second night aboard, I awakened to an eerie intermittent moaning. I opened the pilothouse door and looked around half expecting to see the ghostly crew of the Black Pearl marauding through the marina. I was all set to tell some grubby pirate, "Parlay," when I determined it was the air flowing past the large mast of the sailboat next to us, the resulting sound similar to someone blowing into a plastic two-liter pop jug. Back in bed, I listened to our lines groan and the fenders creak as we moved on and off the dock. I hoped the lines would hold us.

As I scrubbed the galley floor the next morning, I heard an odd "rubbing" noise coming from underneath the hull. I got the rest of the crew to come into the room and we all stood together, with our eyeballs rolled up and off to the side, our brows furrowed as if trying to guess the final question on *Jeopardy*. The four of us trooped en masse to the pilothouse to listen some more. The sound was faint. It seemed to be coming from the cockpit. Back we went, through the galley, outside, where we looked down over the starboard swim platform to see a manatee rubbing its belly on the bottom of our starboard hull. What next, I thought.

When tasting wine, oenophiles credit the nose with as much importance as the tongue. This is why, when I want to impress the sommelier at my favorite gourmet restaurant, I nod at the bottle he's presented, the label of which means about as much to me as reading a menu in Klingon. I then bring the minnow portion of wine swirling in the glass up to my nose and take a deep breath in. Of course, whether it does or not, I always say "It smells delicious." On impulse I might add, "Like after a fresh rain in California wine country." This will impress the sommelier, even more so if the bottle is actually from California. Then the sommelier might enthusiastically ask me, "Have you been to California wine country?"

"No," I would be forced to say.

This was where it got tricky.

The nose is a finely tuned instrument and plays a large part in our interpretation of life. I have a particularly acute sense of smell and routinely use this fact as an excuse as to why I love to eat. My nose gets going with my tongue making eating chicken curry like riding the careening teacups at an amusement park. This gift became a betrayal when, during the first forty-eight hours of living aboard, the starboard head malfunctioned twice, resulting in stench more putrid than anything I had smelled before in an outhouse. I mopped up, then disinfected, with a clothespin uncomfortably pinching my nostrils shut. Afterwards, I went outside to cleanse the palate of my nose. I breathed in the fresh smell of salt air for several minutes, only to come back into the galley to be confronted by the smell of diesel. Mike was testing the engines.

For days I walked around like a bloodhound, my nose in the air, sniffing for potentially harmful fumes or smoke. Learning to decipher the difference between smoke resulting from my botched attempt at Moroccan Chicken on the BBQ and the electrical smoke I smelled later that night became a survival lesson in discernment. Faulty wiring in the davit solenoid, the crane used to haul the dinghy up and down, had released a smell around 4 a.m. strong enough to wake only me up. After sniffing around I found the exposed wiring in the galley and noticed with some apprehension that the area around it had been scorched. Even then, a wisp of smoke was wafting toward me. Since we had yet to install our fire alarms, had I not caught it, the whole boat might have gone up in flames before sinking while we were snug in our beds. As if the perils of water weren't enough, now there was a new adversary to worry about: fire. I installed the fire alarms the next day.

The davit incident aside, I lived for the day when I would be able to sort through all the sounds, smells, and other sensory perceptions into a mental manila file folder, their repetition causing them to be automatically filed under "Just a Normal Day."

~~~

Back on land, I had a large walk-in closet. I have heard it said that "perceived needs rise to meet an income," and I can tell you the same is true of closets. As soon as we moved into that house and I realized my wardrobe only filled half of it, I instantly had the desire to fill it. After five years, I had succeeded and then some. When we decided to live on *Chrysalis*, I knew I had to simplify this area of my life, as there would not be room for all the stuff I had accumulated. I gave a lot away. I was feeling pretty charitable and pious about all the giving and simplifying I was doing right up until the day I sat on the bed in our stateroom on *Chrysalis*, surrounded by boxes of my clothes and shoes, and realized it was going to be impossible to cram it all into my assigned 4 ft. by 2 ft. "locker," one small cupboard, and four six inch by three foot drawers.

And another thing, I had been so proud of myself for paring down my shoe collection to only twenty pairs, including flip flops and sneakers, but it was clear there was no way they were all going to fit in that locker. I tried stacking them with an ingenuity that would have impressed the ancient Egyptians, but every time I opened the locker doors, five or six pairs would come tumbling out. With some dismay, I realized I was going to have to increase my ruthlessness which, months ago when initially packing, I thought would be impossible. While stuffing a garbage bag with items I had previously considered as "necessary" including a favorite red sweater, I hesitated. I opened Mike's locker and tried to sneak the sweater and a few shoes in, but he later found them and said "forget it." By the end of the second day aboard I had a box and a bag to give away, most of which I never missed. Except that red sweater. When I am supremely frustrated with having nothing to wear, I am certain that red sweater would magically cure all my fashion woes.

20

The boatyard had agreed to let us stay at their dock only for the weekend, as they had other boats to haul out of the water Monday morning. Like it or not, we were going to be flushed out into the open. Since we were amateurs, we hired a captain to take us north on the Intracoastal Waterway to the small marina at which we had reservations. Captain Preston showed up around 9 a.m. in Bermuda shorts and a red and white Hawaiian shirt. After we gave him the tour he commented, "Not too shabby," which under the circumstances was very kind.

We shoved off the dock, with Captain Preston barking orders from the flybridge. Mike stood next to him at the helm. Lauren, Stefan, and I, looking much like the amateurs we were, attempted fender and line duty for the first time. Although unfamiliar with the jobs required and who should do them as they emerged, we managed to push off unscathed. After rolling up the lines, I joined Mike and Captain Preston on the flybridge.

It was a typically sunny day in South Florida. It was January so it was cool. Cooler, once underway, and thankfully calm. Lauren and Stefan sat at the bow, their chatter rose up in wafts to where I sat on the flybridge. They were cheerful. Lauren had told me earlier that it had all been "worth it." Novelty had its rewards.

We cruised slowly along the Intracoastal Waterway. Past miles of mansions and through stretches of vacant sandy shoreline populated only with palm trees. For a mile or two, there was nothing but clumps of twisted mangroves. While motoring north, I kept track of our progress on a large paper chart. With the binoculars, I checked the numbered green and red buoys, anticipating our course. I noted out loud the shallow areas, but Captain Preston had traveled this stretch of waterway "too many times to count" and was well familiar with the obstacles. Many medium sized boats, mainly fishing craft, flew by us generating large wakes that caused *Chrysalis* to bob around. One time, my silverware drawer opened and its contents spilled out onto the floor. Captain Preston was not impressed with the fly-by culprit. He told us in disgust, shaking his head back and forth, "Jerks! This is a no wake zone! Most people going up and down the Waterway have absolutely no idea how to operate a boat or follow the rules." I told him that sounded a lot like us, but he smiled and said, "That is why you have me. And anyway, you guys will learn in time."

Two hours later we pulled into a small posh marina, the only one that could take us on short notice. As we floated by all of the immaculate, gleaming, white yachts, I thought how much we must look like the hillbilly Clampets when they pulled into Beverly Hills. Sheets of lumber and Mike's table saw sat behind us on the flybridge. A workhorse was set up close to that. The pilothouse door had yet to be painted. I was certain we were trailing a cloud of sawdust behind us similar to Pig Pen's cloud in the *Peanuts* cartoon.

As we pulled deeper into the marina, I spotted a dockhand waving us into what seemed an impossibly tight berth. I was nervous. I was at the bow with a line, Lauren was midship, and Stefan at the stern. I threw the line but missed the dockhand by about ten feet, and the line slipped into the water. I hauled it up as quickly as I could, gathering the line in large loops like I had practiced. I re-threw the bundle, this time with more accuracy. When the dockhand had secured the line, we began to pivot off the bow, and when we were close enough, Lauren threw the springline (the line midship), then Stefan threw the stern line. We scrambled to replace a few fenders and although we misjudged a couple, resulting in a few tense moments and a small scratch, we were finally secure and had successfully completed our first docking maneuver.

Lovely as it was, those first two weeks at the marina, our stay was brief. The marina needed the space for a previous reservation. Captain Preston came again for the last time and helped us move to a large, nearby bay, where we anchored and remained for over a month.

While at anchor, we began to get used to substitutes. Instead of a car we had a twelve foot inflatable RIB (Rigid Inflatable Boat) or dinghy, which had the unfortunate name of *Crabcakes*. In the morning I might say, "I'm heading in to get some groceries," and instead of hopping in the car I would hop in *Crabcakes*. I had never started an outboard motor in my life and found the yanking annoying. After several pulls, I would get it humming and then I would bounce along over the waves feeling very nautical, to the small beach where several dinghies were pulled ashore and tied to low lying scrub brush. After purchasing my groceries, I would haul the bags out into the parking lot and down the street a few blocks. Inevitably, the tide would have shifted one way or the other during my absence. I would find the dingy either further up on the beach imbedded in the sand, requiring me to push with all my strength to get it back into the water, or I would have to wade in water up to my shins to load the groceries.

Hot and sweaty, the slightest bit of live-aboard romance having leaked away, I would climb aboard *Crabcakes*, yank the motor to life, and bob back over the waves. As I approached *Chrysalis*, someone aboard would hear me. A smiling face would greet me on the swim platform and help me secure *Crabcakes*, then assist me in carefully hauling the provisions on board while the breeze shifted the whole scene gently around our anchor.

For the first couple of weeks on board, we had a cell phone. It had followed us from Canada and held at least a hundred of our most important, can't do without, phone numbers. One day while attempting to leap from the dinghy to the swim platform, Mike misjudged the distance and fell into the water. When we were through laughing our heads off, we realized that along with his wallet, the cell phone had been in his pocket. The wallet was salvaged, but despite our best life saving efforts, the cell phone never regained consciousness. We purchased a new one and only gave the number out to family, close friends, and the nearest Chinese restaurant whose delivery guy, Lee, would actually come to the small dingy beach to deliver our take-out. I was surprised at how much I enjoyed life without a telephone. When the cell phone occasionally rang, I would stop what I was doing, look up, and ask, "What was that noise?"

We did have a VHF, or Very High Frequency radio. Attached to the receiver was a telephone cord that ended in a speaker or microphone. This is the main mode of communication between boaters. It is your telephone. With it you can hail the power Sportfish coming directly for you down the Intracoastal and inquire sweetly if his intent is to ram you. Or, if you happened to be sinking, you could use it to calmly relay a "Mayday" in hopes that someone close by would come to your aid. Under more pleasant circumstances, you could use it to hail friends anchored nearby and ask if they wanted to come over for drinks. If you are nosy, as I am, you can listen in on everyone else's conversations.

We had never used a VHF before and practiced communicating on working channels back and forth between the helm and our portable handheld unit. At first we were very official, but then it all seemed so cloak and dagger, so 007, that we began creating elaborate messages in code. The kids made up nicknames for us. For reasons we'll not discuss in detail, they gave Mike the name "Bald Eagle." For myself, "Mother Bird." After picking a friend up at the airport and loading her luggage into the dinghy, I hailed Mike on a working channel from *Crabcakes* and our transmission went something like:

"Bald Eagle, Bald Eagle, this is Mother Bird do you copy?"

"Mother Bird, this is Bald Eagle on *Chrysalis*, go ahead."

"Bald Eagle, the tuna is in the bag. I repeat, the tuna is in the bag. Over."

"Good news, Mother Bird. Return *Crabcakes* to base for the ceremonial roasting of the tuna. Over."

"Roger that. Mother Bird heading to base with the tuna and *Crabcakes*. Over and out."

Aside from the fact that my friend didn't necessarily like being the tuna or the sound of eminent roasting, I thought our communiqué was fairly clandestine and it went a long way toward amusing the crew.

21

Being at anchor, I discovered, was vastly different from being tied up at a marina. For one thing, you were far more exposed to the elements. Wind in particular could be a problem, especially if you were anchored, like we were, with many other boats in tight quarters. A strong breeze could force an anchor from its holding and cause you to be rudely awakened to the sound of crunching fiberglass as you dashed into the sailboat off your stern, or into one of the many docks belonging to the multimillion dollar waterfront homes nearby. While sound asleep, your anchor could pop up and you might simply float, wraithlike, across the bay and get stuck on the rocks along the shoreline. Unable to remove yourself, the waves would bash your boat against a jagged rock creating a hole in the side of your hull. The little red bilge pump lights would come to life and you would wonder why-oh-why you had ever decided to live on a boat.

With the wind howling around 3 a.m., I sat alone in the cockpit with a blanket wrapped around me and tried to gage our position from lights on a dark shore. With each gust, *Chrysalis* would swing wildly around her anchor, the rode straining and groaning. I cringed. I thought the stress on the line would be too much and it would snap. As I studied the shore, it appeared that we were dragging, and I would experience bouts of gripping panic.

After a week of particularly windy weather resulting in several sleepless nights on my part, Mike was poking around our GPS computer program and exclaimed, "Hey! I think we have an anchor alarm here!" On the screen, I could see where the computer had recorded our path to the anchorage in the form of a red line. I could tell where we had dropped the anchor because the red line suddenly shifted directions and went in a straight line back to where *Chrysalis* was resting at anchor in the form of a flashing red ball. Circling us was a dotted line, the perimeter Mike had set up. With the aid of GPS, an alarm was set to go off if we moved outside a set perimeter.

That night I slept in the pilothouse, where I could see our GPS location on the computer screen. Not long after that, the windy conditions subsided, and I was able to move back to my berth. Knowing the alarm would go off, I slept a bit better.

Being at anchor required that we consider our power usage. While most yachts opt for an AC generator, we had installed a DC generator designed by a former NASA engineer. It was smaller, quieter, and more fuel efficient than a typical AC generator. We also liked the idea that we only had to run it a few hours a day. It charged our batteries, and we then ran our power directly off of our battery bank. We programmed it to run an hour and a half in the morning and the same at night before we went to bed. As long as we remembered to conserve our usage, it supplied our batteries with more than enough power to run our freezer and air conditioners. We reminded each other to turn off lights and computers.

We installed a watermaker that took sea water and, through reverse osmosis, created up to 400 gallons a day of clean drinking water. When you consider that there were four of us wanting to shower, do laundry, and dishes, it went rather quickly. We spread out our showers and made them quick. Lauren and I turned off the water while shaving our legs. We made a conscious effort to use smaller amounts of water for dish duty.

In the mornings, I would sit in the cockpit and watch the sunrise over the water between the masts of two sailboats. While sipping hot coffee, I considered the difference between living on land and living on the water. When I was a kid, I was a swinger.

My mother would take me to the park down the street and I would head for the nearest swing-set.

I remembered it. The rush as I sped down toward the ground, then the weightless feeling when the horizon disappeared and all I could see was sky and the tops of trees. A few times I couldn't help myself. Just when my progress was at its highest point, I let go of the chains and flew gloriously through the air for a few seconds, before experiencing land's selfish desire to keep me to herself in the form of gravity. I could never decide if the harsh and often painful landing was worth the few seconds of soaring.

From the roof of the flybridge, Lauren and Stefan paused to look down at the water some fifteen feet below. There were dares and "C'mons!" and finally one of them would hurtle themselves off the edge, tuck their knees to their chest, and fall through air howling "whoo hooo!" Unlike land, water was merciful. From that height, it received them, cushioned the blow, swallowing them in a single gulp, only to spew them up again, laughing. Unlike the hard-packed grassy earth, water was forgiving. Here in the harbor there was room for mistakes. Belly flops, similar to the painful one I performed off a swing when I was eight, were accommodated. I appreciated this.

As on land, there were chores, work, and school to accomplish during the day. I had initially thought that living in smaller quarters would mean less "house" work, but there seemed just as much to do on a boat. The white hull of *Chrysalis* was a magnet for whatever dust or grime might be floating in the air. When I finished scrubbing down her huge carcass, I would notice that there were small circles of rust forming on our stainless rails. Just about the time I was done shining the stainless, the hull would need washing again. While attempting routine upkeep on our systems, watermaker, engines, generator, Mike juggled the installation of doors on all cupboards and fabric wall covering.

In the afternoon we swam or fished off the stern. Stefan took up crabbing. He laid several traps with raw chicken and set them in our vicinity. Every morning he would go off in the dinghy to see what might have crawled in overnight. Almost always he brought in a couple of stone and blue crabs. By law, you could take one claw from a stone crab that had two as one would eventually grow back. If you took both claws the poor crab would have no way of defending or feeding itself. Over the course of a week, we collected several claws and had ourselves a small, but tasty, feast.

There were days when Stefan caught several small blue crabs, too small to eat, so we set up a small raceway using our teak deck chairs and a few unused school binders. Each of us would look over the crabs inspecting the length of their legs, their apparent liveliness, and choose one. We would line them up in the cockpit and someone would say "GO!" Of course the crabs didn't get it at first and we had to shove them along. But eventually one would get going in the right direction and a couple others would follow and then things got very exciting. As the winning crab crossed the finish line there would be shouts and groans, and Monopoly money would exchange hands.

22

The ancient Phoenicians would have loved GPS. If they had it, they would have ruled the seas for much longer than they did. They were master sailors and making charts for ocean navigation as early as 1200 BC. Included in these often sophisticated maps were the locations of rocks, shallows, and suitable channels through narrow straits. These handmade charts were highly valued, and information on them was passed down to fellow Phoenician sailors but never to strangers. In times of war, charts with misinformation were circulated among the enemy in hopes that they would run aground or get lost.

Much later on, in the Great Age of Discovery, Spain kept her maps under lock and key in the royal vaults. In those days, the breadth of a country's cartography often indicated its success and wealth as a nation and their secrets were tightly guarded. Charts and maps were given only to captains making official journeys on a ruler's behalf. In addition to geography and aids to navigation, these charts could hold specific information on hard-to-find treasures, like spices. During the course of a journey, if a ship was threatened by an enemy, the captain would order the charts to be gathered and bound with a lead weight and thrown overboard rather than risk them falling into enemy hands. Many ancient charts were lost in this way.

Today, if you live on a boat, you use charts, not maps. Maps describe certain topographical and geographical information pertaining to land, including roads and elevations. Charts display information applicable on water, like depth, buoys, currents, where to anchor and what holding you might expect there, right of way, and aiding landmarks. All this is laid out in minutes and seconds according to longitude and latitude.

I discovered during the first month of living on a boat that I had an affinity for GPS, and I loved charts. Especially paper ones, with their crisp, tactile edges. In my chaotic world, their organized lines laid out before me on the chart table gave me a feeling of security. For a woman who likes being in control, or at least the illusion of it, there is nothing so reassuring as finding your exact coordinates, down to the second, on a chart.

"Look," I would say while pointing to a coordinate, "there I am and all is well."

~Part Three~

Splice: the joining of lines by tucking strands or otherwise interweaving parts of each rope inside the other.

23

When I was in university, I read *Thoughts in Solitude*, by Thomas Merton, and mistakenly interpreted silence, solitude, and simplicity as life lived on my terms in peace and quiet with little or no interruptions. Not long after I got married, I discovered that all three were interrupted by a significant other who had the quaint idea that our lives were meant to be shared.

We shared a bed, which he hogged, leaving me with about six inches of sleeping room. Not only that, he stole the covers. I would wake up, late for work, and make my way to the one bathroom we shared and find he was already in there and that it would be quite some time before the bathroom would be in usable condition. He depleted the last of the milk for his Cheerios leaving me a stale loaf of bread for breakfast. His wet towel lay on the floor. Instead of bringing home supreme pizza like I asked, he would "forget" and bring home meat lovers. After a long day at work, I would go to bed and there he was, asleep on my side again. "For the next fifty years, this is how it will be," I thought.

Just about the time I had made some wriggle room in my soul for marriage, I got pregnant, and life has been one continual adventure in how many ways I can be interrupted in a single day. In a single hour. Early on, it was crying in the middle of the night and exploding diapers in the nice restaurant where we were having brunch. Just when I was doing something important like reading the evening paper, some tiny version of humanity would go and topple down the stairs and require a run to the emergency room. I would happen upon my potted fern, overturned, the soil all over the newly vacuumed carpet.

The small culprit, covered in potting soil, would deny all responsibility. Later, it was incessant "whys?" or "can I have's?" interspersed by calls from the school nurse who told me that my kid had thrown up all over another and could I come and pick them up?

After being interrupted all day, I snapped an irritated, "What now?" to the kid's inquiry of "Mom?"

Smiling up at me, they said meekly, "We've brought you some flowers."

I don't like interruption because I have things all worked out in my mind. Even while my kids were still in utero, I had their lives mapped out, and mine by association. I imagined for them a fulfilled childhood brought about by wise and witty parents, followed by loving teen years, and their subsequent marriage to a polite, clean cut, hardworking person, with defined goals. Down the road, there would be a few cute, well-behaved, grandkids living nearby so I could see them whenever I wanted. In my script, everyone was healthy, stayed happily married, and lived well into their 90s, or at least long enough to care for me in my old age.

Interruptions to my script were a reminder of my lack of control. For a long time, I assumed these interruptions to be an affront, an oddity, to an otherwise "normal" existence. It won't come as a big surprise to find that I had a positive, albeit unrealistic, dream of what living on a boat might be like. It was full of space brought about by having much less housework to do and much less running around, space in which I could think all sorts of lofty thoughts, the result of hours of communing with God, nature and with family members who always did their chores and cleaned up after themselves. Profound insights would pour forth, and I would be able to write them all out while lounging on an inflatable raft drinking a mojito.

The financial reality of our situation dictated that living on a boat could not be a holiday or early retirement. Occupations would change but remain important. I determined early on to write. I got up each morning with the intent of churning out megabytes of pithy wisdom. Just before descending into our small "office," currently used as storage for lumber, I would hit the galley and grab some breakfast. I mentioned to whatever family happened to be in the vicinity that I was going down to write and unless someone was being tortured by Jack Bauer or had an eye hanging out of a socket, no one was to bother me. Even then, best to think twice before knocking on my door. While I carried cereal down the stairs, Stefan called out, "What makes you think we'd call YOU if we were being tortured by Jack Bauer?"

Once situated at my desk, I would handcuff myself to the blank page and then try desperately to get away. I drummed my fingers on the desk. Watched the thin arm on my desk clock measure the seconds. I got briefly inspired and wrote a few bumpy lines, then found that even though it was only an hour after breakfast, I was starving. I went back to the galley for peanuts. I ate them one by one at my desk, but their texture and saltiness made me thirsty. Off I went to find something to drink. I was too hot. Too cold. I looked around at the disaster in the form of lumber and wall fabric laying around, and told myself no one could be expected to work under such messy and unorganized conditions. I putzed around at shuffling the clutter from one end of the room to the other. Several hours would end in a disgruntled sigh on my part. Writing was hard work, I told myself.

About the time I was hot on the tail of a quick moving Pulitzer winning tidbit scurrying around like a white rabbit in my brain, a husband, a daughter, or a son, take your pick, would knock on the door and inquire as to where the dish soap was or if I had taken their geography book. My attention diverted, the white rabbit escaped down a hole never to be seen or heard from again.

I told them calmly, sternly, "Creation doesn't just happen. You have to work hard for it. Now that I have been interrupted, I will have to start over. Please, LEAVE ME ALONE!"

Not a minute later, I looked at the clock and thought happily, "oh good it's time for lunch."

It began to dawn on me that the dream of living on a boat was not going to involve a naval-gazing interruption-free existence. Living in tight quarters with three significant others and their stubbed toes, spilled milk, broken bones, and lost keys, was par for the course on sea as well as on land. This in itself was an interruption to my idea that by living on a boat I had discovered a magical loophole towards serenity. It was unfortunate that my script did not dictate to the Universe. The Universe would have its say. I came to the conclusion that interruptions weren't the exception to the rule. They were the rule. And living on a boat was no exception, either. In fact, living on a boat was the biggest interruption to my life so far.

For many years, Mike and I tried to teach our kids to think for themselves, and not just "full of knowledge" thinkers, but wise. You had only to take a cursory glance through the pages of history to know the dangers of not thinking for yourself. So we taught our kids to be suspicious of face value. Dig deeper, we told them. Don't be afraid to speak up. Ask questions. Even in matters of faith, politics, science, and history. Just because someone with big hair on television, in a pulpit, a lab coat, or a textbook tells you how it is, doesn't necessarily make it so. You think about it. Search for it. Conduct interviews. Compile various sources. Find the Pearl. Work hard for an ongoing friendship with Truth.

This meant that learning the ropes of life onboard was continually interrupted by four strong personalities, all with a lifetime of practice in questioning the status quo and thinking for ourselves, and all willing to share their opinion while attempting to dock a 65-foot power catamaran in a 20-knot cross wind. On approaching a fuel dock for the first time on our own, Lauren, Stefan, and I had a heated debate through clenched teeth and barely controlled voices, over which line should be thrown first. This diverted our attention from the stern, which proceeded to bang into a concrete piling resulting in a foot-long scratch in the fiberglass. Captain Mike was not pleased. He left the helm and stomped down the stairs looking as miffed as I had ever seen him, and proceeded to toss a line to the heavyset, bearded dockhand who asked us jovially, "And how is everyone today?"

We grumbled our salutations.

Docking, we discovered, could be a tricky endeavor. For the kids and me, it involved making use of two skills, line handling and fender placement. In subsequent approaches, we placed large fenders forward, midship, and aft with several small fenders close at hand because inevitably the large fenders were not quite in the right place and at any given time a barnacle-encrusted piling could be counted on to threaten our shiny, smooth fiberglass. We attached several lines to cleats, then through the hawsepipes, on the *outside* of the rail. Once this was accomplished, we threw a line to the dockhand, who might know what to do with it. Many dockhands would catch our line fine enough, but then hold onto it as Mike attempted to pivot thirty-five tons of power catamaran with twin 330 Cummins engines off the same line. I can tell you that in a game of tug of war, *Chrysalis* won every time. The sheepish dockhand would be forced to let go of the line and one of us would have to quickly draw it in, and Mike would have to reposition *Chrysalis* for a second attempt. We learned to instruct the dockhands to secure our line as quickly as possible.

Just when you thought you had everything under control, a gust of wind or a current could be counted on to push you right toward the lovely multimillion-dollar yacht about two feet off your stern. So far, I have not found much in life that instantly gets my heart rate into high-efficiency fat-burning mode as watching our stern float silently within inches of another boat. While sipping drinks along a boardwalk at a marina one night, Mike and I witnessed the docking misfortunes of a seventy-foot Sportfish who misjudged the amount of space at his stern and rammed into a gleaming 100 foot Broward. The resulting sound of crunching fiberglass and yelling was something we hoped to avoid.

We held a family meeting to assess the docking situation. It was widely agreed that in the future, stopping to hold an irate meeting in the middle of such a task was going to be impossible. We decided it would be in the best interest of all concerned, including *Chrysalis*, to hold our planning meetings prior to our arrival or departure. We assigned jobs: two on line duty and one in charge of fenders. This, we thought, would go a long way toward curbing impromptu pandemonium and facilitating a more team-like attitude.

We had decided earlier on that because Mike knew the most about our systems, he would assume the title of captain. I am all for equal rights in a marriage and everywhere else for that matter, but there is a longstanding nautical tradition that someone on board needs to have the responsibility of the final word. That person is the captain. In tense, sometimes dangerous situations, this is important. During maneuvers, if we could not come to a unanimous decision, we would defer to his judgment.

That we were bound to have differing opinions was a given. These opinions, however sacred they might be to us individually, had to take a backseat to the value of the person(s) we were attempting to persuade or debate. We might be mad, but yelling, rude gestures, and snarky comments pretty much flew in the face of this nugget and were squelched as a viable communication option. As incomprehensible as it might seem at the time, there was a slim chance our personal idea was not the best one. Keeping an open mind was essential.

"This includes you guys," Lauren said looking back and forth between Mike and me. "If we are going to work as a team, you have to treat both Stefan and I as equals. We have good ideas and they should count."

Mike and I looked at each other, bewildered, then nodded. She had a point.

We practiced docking at the fuel station a few more times that month. Even though we discussed approach and departure beforehand, we were still learning, and there were numerous times when we all screwed up. Afterwards, doors closed a little harder than usual. Things were said that were later regretted. I learned something those first few months aboard. Cruising makes a poor escape from a landlocked life. You can be sure that whatever problems you had on land will follow you right down the dock, over the gangway, and into the cockpit. The stress of living in such small square footage will fan the smoldering embers into a roaring blaze, and after that there is no point in attempting a cover-up.

It was at this very juncture, when there was nothing and nowhere to hide, that we discovered the value in being able to admit we were schmucks and that our love for our neighbor was more important than our own schmuckyness. After a humble apology, sometimes right away, sometimes later on in the day, there would be claps on the back. Hugs. Letting go. A hearty, "not to worry." I could never have anticipated the important roles that respect, kindness, and forgiveness would play in the living-aboard learning curve. In the safety of the four of us, the borders of who we were began to expand. It was okay to mess up, be sorry, ask forgiveness, and move on. After that, life on board had mostly to do with being able to laugh at yourself and your neighbor and especially yourself while your neighbor was good-naturedly laughing at you.

Headway was made. The next time we docked in a particularly tight situation in large winds it went something like this:

"Laur, how many feet to the dock?" Mike said calmly but audibly from the flybridge.

"About ten feet. Five feet now, I'm throwing the bow line to the dockhand. Bow secure, I'm walking aft."

From midship Stef's voice would call out, "Springline secure! Mom, we need a fender midship."

"I'm on it, Stef. How's the stern fender, Laur?"

"Good, but I need another line."

"I'm on it," I said while scurrying to deliver both.

After the successful completion of our sixth docking in between two sparkly 100-foot yachts with about two feet to spare on either end, there were grins and high fives. It was a satisfying feeling, this delicate art of teamwork. The journey was shared. Confidence and trust in ourselves, in each other, began to grow. With incredulity, I thought, "we can do this."

24

I am not a member of the Mothers Against Video Games Association. I am not even sure there is such a thing, although I wouldn't be surprised if there was. On the contrary, I appreciate the good folks at Nintendo, who go to great lengths to create new and engaging games. You just have to have all things in moderation. I once asked my Swedish grandmother how her large family spent their evenings on a farm in rural Iowa when she was growing up.

"Well," she said, smiling as if some fond memory presented itself, "we spent a lot of time playing Yahtzee."

In my grandmother's day, there was likely a group of protesters against Yahtzee. After all, it was played with dice, which could be associated with all manner of ne'er do well's and busty wenches.

An interesting thing happened to the social structure on *Chrysalis*. There was a meeting of minds in the middle among the four of us. It occurred to me one day, that with the responsibility of docking and learning to occupy themselves and be content in their own company, our kids were maturing beautifully. Mike and I, on the other hand, seemed to be regressing. We spent a lot of time thinking up pranks to pull on the kids. We teepeed their staterooms and covered their doorways in plastic wrap. We snuck outside with cups full of water and then urgently called one of the kids outside, only to douse them when they appeared. In the afternoons, we played a version of tag combined with hide and go seek. We ran, which you aren't supposed to do on the decks of a boat, up the steps to the flybridge or along the wing decks. A vague feeling was resurrected in my brain. A feeling I hadn't felt since the long hot days of childhood summers.

"Lauren? Stefan? What are you guys doing?" Mike would shout down into a stateroom.

"Go away. I'm busy doing chemistry," Lauren would say in a monotone voice without looking up from her textbook.

"And I'm doing math. I can't play with you now," Stefan would call up from the desk in his stateroom.

"Oh c'mon!! You guys are always doing work! Mom and I want to play MarioKart! C'mon, just a couple of games! You guys have been working all day!" I noticed Mike's voice bordered on whining.

"Oh all right. You guys are like a couple of kids!" Lauren said in exasperation.

In MarioKart, there was something artistically and relationally beautiful about sending a red turtle shell to halt a loved one's progress right before the finish line so you could pass them and end up in first place. In the realm of simple pleasures it ranks up there. A whole boatload of stress could be relieved under such circumstances. Living on *Chrysalis* had taught me this.

When playing video games, things can quickly deteriorate. Even the well chaperoned and instructed kid can take perverse pleasure in verbally wounding a grade school colleague. Early on in my experience as a mother, I witnessed children's cruelty on more than one occasion. One of my sweet and intentionally parented kids, incensed over some colossal injustice like their sibling's use of the Big Wheel, would yell, "You big stupid-head, it's my Big Wheel!" This was yelled while bashing their rival over the head with a plastic shovel and subsequently pushing them headlong off the Big Wheel resulting in a goose egg bump, tears, and further name calling and finger pointing.

I had little patience, then and now, for name calling in anger and forbade it. "And I don't want to hear you say 'shut up' in anger either," I said.

"Why not 'shut up'? Everyone says shut up!" they responded.

I told them: "What I want you to understand is that your brother or your sister is more valuable than, say, a Big Wheel or anything else for that matter. The words you use are important. They mean something. We treat each other with respect in this family, and there will be no saying "shut up" in anger, or any kind of name calling in anger, ever.

"You mean we can't ever get angry?"

"Yes, you can get angry. I just want you to remember that you are in control, not your anger. And also, that the person you are angry with is more important than the issue you are angry about. That is why we don't call names. Do you understand?"

They nodded obligatorily in unison.

A few minutes later I would hear the beginnings of a skirmish and yell up the stairs at them, "Are you being loving and kind to each other?"

"Oh yes," one would respond, their tone dripping with honey through clenched teeth. "It's just that this sweet little dork, this darling idiot, won't give me the remote control. See Mom, I didn't say it in anger!"

When they became teenagers they developed an interest in verbally "slamming"each other. At first I was adverse to what seemed to be insulting behavior, but then one of them sat me down and took my hand in theirs and talked to me like I was about five. They explained that their insults were about being creative, not inflicting wounds. They brought up my own love of good stand-up comedy, and how it takes a great deal of attention to the small details of life to find the humor in it. One of them said, "You know how you're always talking about the heart behind the actions? Well, when we slam each other, we are really just joking around, and everyone knows it."

"Doesn't it ever hurt your feelings?" I asked.

"Sometimes. But then we just stop and say sorry."

"Yeah, Mom, it doesn't mean anything. It's just funny. You should try it," said the other.

So I did. We started to keep a running tally of our best work in a small notebook we affectionately called "The Burn Book." Anytime one of us said something creative or jovially insulted someone else, one of the kids would run to record it. With some dismay, I thought, we had no tangible photo albums, but we had a book of insults. What kind of a mother was I, anyway?

One night over tacos, Lauren decided to read what we had to date. She said, "Okay, I'm going to read you some of our best insults and creative comments." In between bites of taco, she read: "There was that time Dad was flexing his muscles in the galley and said: "Don't you think I'm a bit like Samson in his strength?"

Stefan: "Like if you grow any hair you'll get some?"

Lauren (commenting on her love of bread): "I'd do really well in jail…All I need is fresh bread and water."

Mom: "Good to know you're thinking ahead, babe."

Laur: "I don't have a mirror or an alarm clock in my stateroom."

Dad: "That explains a lot."

Dad to the rest of us in exasperation: "I don't know what's worse, you guys breaking something, or you guys trying to fix it."

Dad said to Mom on a bad day: "Well, it's better than living in a housing project!"

Mom muttering: "This IS a housing project!"

Dad to the rest: "You people drive me crazy!"

Laur: "That's a short trip."

Mom: "I laugh in the face of fashion."

Laur: "It laughs in your face, too!"

Stefan: "Guys, you're supposed to spare the rod AND spoil the child. You've got to do both. I'm pretty sure an Xbox would be considered spoiling, so can I get one?"

I could tell that a relational climate was beginning to develop on board *Chrysalis*. Seeing the same three faces day after day was ceasing to freak us out. We had started to mesh our lives together and work as a team. A simple rhythm developed to our days. We glued the whole thing together with trite sayings and practical jokes.

And then, we began to look outward.

25

While at anchor, I would hear the intermittent clackety-clack of one of our sailboat neighbors hauling up their anchor. The sound would draw me to the cockpit or a porthole, where I would watch them slowly exit the bay to the south and continue down the short stretch of Intracoastal Waterway. There, I would lose sight of them. I knew that just beyond was the Lake Worth Inlet and open water.

I had conflicting emotions. I was comfortable where we were, but there was something compelling about watching those sailboats leave the harbor. An instinctual urgency developed. We all sensed it. We began to study the weather online. At night, Mike and I sat together at the galley table with our heads bent over our charts and Waterway Guide. The plan was to head south to Miami for a few weeks. The trip down there was about four hours in open water. This, we figured, would provide a decent initial testing of our systems outside the sheltered waters of the Intracoastal Waterway. From Miami, we would wait for weather to cross the Gulf Stream to the Bahamas and a more extensive offshore maiden voyage.

One afternoon, our own anchor came up out of the water. We made the short trek down the narrow Intracoastal towards the Inlet. As we wound our way toward the cut, I kept an eye on our depth sounder and watched it descend: 5ft...4ft...3ft...2.5ft...2ft. I was sure that at any moment we would run into a rock and it would rip a hole in the hull.

"Well, that was it then..." I would be forced to say. "Our journey lasted all of an hour and we sank in the middle of Lake Worth."

In my head, I was already charting a swimming course through the water to the nearest marina, whose restaurant we had eaten at a number of times. I remembered they had good Irish coffee and thought how nice it would be to warm up with a cup after nearly drowning. Instead, the depth hovered at about 1.5 feet and then began to climb. We approached the inlet and my attention was distracted from the depth by the open water stretching out in front of us.

The winds were from the east that day and the tide was going out, which made the waves stand up in steep four-to-five foot chop as we exited Lake Worth Inlet. *Chrysalis* heaved and rocked. I held on, grim, with wide eyes. The further we got into deeper water, the more things calmed down both in terms of wave height and my own heartbeat. We pushed away from land for the first time.

With the wind whipping my hair and the rise and fall of *Chrysalis*, I temporarily forgot my fear. Even though I was sitting on the flybridge of a catamaran with every modern convenience, I began to feel myself part of a wild, untamed, world. There was the incredible feeling of being released. Set free. Behind me lay the land-locked life with all the things I was so familiar with; traffic, high-rise buildings, media, hurry. But out in front of me existed an expanse of unobstructed space. Who knew what lay ahead? Distant lands. Creatures unknown. Something shifted inside of me and instead of being freaked out, I found the feeling expanding. I began to imagine myself in the same league as Juan Ponce de Leon, who sailed these waters back in 1513 in search of the Fountain of Youth. I wondered what it had been like for him to push away from shore and head to foreign waters. Were thoughts of drinking from this fountain enough to motivate him to travel around the world, or was it this feeling of liberation he craved?

Liberated as he might have been, Ponce de Leon never did find the Fountain of Youth. Instead, he landed in what is today known as St. Augustine. He named it Florida, Land of Flowers. From there, he continued south, making his way through the Florida Keys and turning around near what is now known as Charlotte Harbor. While sailing through these very seas, I knew that he had been without GPS, local knowledge, depth sounder, VHF, radar, and satellite phone. There were no buoys or charts marking shallow water. I considered what it must have been like for him and his crew to sail here all alone, so far from what was known to them, wondering, as they floated in uncharted territory, what to expect of the land and its occupants with the long journey home across the Atlantic yet to be accomplished. I changed my mind. In the bravery department, I decided Leon and his crew were a little out of my league after all.

For four hours, as we made our way south, my body and mind attuned themselves to the cadence of the open sea. I became accustomed to the upward and downward rhythm. The slightly sideways tilting movement. The sound of the waves pulsing by our hulls. The cool air that came in gusts to drum on my face. By the time we approached Miami, I felt the smallest stab of regret to be leaving the ample, uncluttered, domain of Poseidon. We entered Governments Cut, past the numbered red and green buoys, reminding each other, "red right returning," and kept an eye open for shallow areas. Once inside the Cut, we went to starboard and dropped anchor off Belle Island on the other side of Miami Beach. The anchorage was a busy one. We spent the first few days rocking and rolling, the result of wash created by numerous small boats and jet skiers who zoomed by within a few feet of our swim platforms.

Miami was the first big city I had spent significant time in. The first few days we were there, I kept looking for the metropolis portrayed in the television show of my high school years, *Miami Vice*. I expected to see Don Johnson, as Sonny

Crocket, dressed in his white suit and black t-shirt come barreling around a decrepit building, his gun out of pocket, chasing some seedy "cocaine cowboy" in between retirees in plaid shorts. But this was not the Miami Beach of the '80s.

I discovered this when I needed groceries. Every few days, I took *Crabcakes* up a small canal, right into the throbbing heart of South Beach, and walked about three blocks to the nearest market. Beautiful people, well pecked or amply bosomed, wearing designer athletic wear, jogged by me and the numerous society castoffs sitting against the fronts of banks with their caps in hand. Everyone was tan, and from a Canadian perspective, wore very few clothes. Cars honked. I heard footsteps coming up behind me. Music blared from outdoor cafés and pimped up ancient Cadillac's. There were trendy restaurants, haute shops, and boutique hotels housed in retro art deco buildings in pastel colors. The whole place reminded me of a giant Easter egg. At night, this egg turned Faberge, with the glitz and glamour of painted people making their way to Ocean Drive and the many nightclubs that seemed to appear after dark out of nowhere.

After a week at our original rolly anchorage, we moved *Chrysalis* to a more serene location. With architecturally attractive office buildings and posh apartment buildings lining the shore about one hundred yards off to port and several mega mansions across the water off to starboard, *Chrysalis* swung at anchor in a small, shallow bay that our charts noted had "poor holding." Anticipating the convenience of the location, we ignored the notation on our chart and anchored there anyway. It was a pristine spot and out of the path of most jet skiers. Although we had anchored several times back in Lake Worth, we had yet to be in a large blow, and had no idea how many rpms (revolutions per minute used to measure torque or power) from the engines it would take to set the anchor well enough to hold us in a weather system that generated a significant amount of wind. We had taken a guess, backing down in reverse, at about 600 rpms.

Except for large ships, not many new pleasure yachts utilize the traditional kedge anchor with its cross and hook shape. In researching what kind of anchor to use for *Chrysalis*, we had come across several lightweight versions of different shaped anchors: the plow, claw, and fluke being the most common. We chose to go with twin Delta plow anchors mainly for their versatility in holding on different sea bottoms. When sitting on the bottom under the water, the plow, looking very much like a piece of farmyard equipment, lies on its side, but when pulled by a yacht going in reverse, it rights itself and the point is driven into the bottom until it becomes completely buried. Then, the captain or crew member will place his engines in reverse, measuring the force used in rpms and "back down" on the anchor in an effort to further bury it. In poor holdings, or if you back down too hard or fast with the engines, the anchor can pop up, requiring it to be hauled up again and re-set.

Before moving aboard, we read several accounts of how to set an anchor and the amount of rode, or line, to let out in proportion with the depth, approximately 5-7 feet of rode to every foot of depth measured from the anchor roller. This was easy enough to remember. It was setting the anchor that proved to be an art perfected by experience and knowledge of our own vessel.

One late afternoon in Miami, I watched with interest the approach of dark storm clouds from the north. From a distance I could see flashes of lightning. The air was warm and still, as if it was holding its breath in anticipation. When the clouds were nearly on top of us, the air stirred slightly before accelerating to over forty knots in what seemed the space of a few seconds. A prolonged gust of wind hit *Chrysalis* with great force and whipped her around the anchor. At the same time, sheets of rain materialized, decreasing our visibility.

Concerned, Mike and I had been making our way from the cockpit to the pilothouse to keep an eye on our anchor alarm, when it went off. Hurrying to the helm, we could see a red line exceeding our anchor perimeter. For a split second, Mike and I looked at each other with wide eyes and a knowing look. All around us were shallows and submerged pilings and numerous docks. Running into one or more was now a possibility. While shouting to each other, the kids and I ran to put on rain coats and within seconds, Mike had the engines started, and I had made my way through the wind and rain to the flybridge. Mike showed up at the bow with Lauren and Stefan. Squinting through the blowing rain, I could tell they were attempting to bring in the anchor.

Our roles in anchoring had only recently been decided upon. Mike and the kids had opted to take control of the anchor and windlass at the bow, and I agreed to set the anchor at the helm outside on the flybridge using the engines. I was still a little uncertain in my skills at controlling *Chrysalis*. I had yet to establish the intimacy that Mike had in using the throttles, but I was learning. After taking control of the engines on the flybridge, I looked down at Mike, who was yelling something up at me I couldn't distinguish due to the howling wind.

My main objective was to keep us in the center of the bay, as near to our original anchorage as possible. This proved to be difficult as the rain was so thick I couldn't see the shoreline. I got the sense, though, that we were still dragging our way across the bay. With my heart pounding in my chest, I noted the direction of the anchor line and moved us forward in an effort to make up for the distance we had dragged. I did this while keeping a nervous eye on the depth beneath the keel which hovered around 2 feet. I also moved us several feet to starboard, remembering the red line on the anchor alarm had been veering to port.

Lauren, looking back toward the stern from the starboard bow, suddenly turned toward me and began to point excitedly toward the stern. Turning around, I realized two things: one, I was running over the dinghy, *Crabcakes*, whose bow was now wedged under the swim platform and whose stern was rising off the water. This immediately made me wonder if I had run over the line holding *Crabcakes* and, if so, had it wrapped around my propeller? Losing the starboard prop at this stage could not only prove disastrous, it could wreck the engine as well. The second thing I noticed was that through the rain, I could clearly make out the white slats of a glamorous dock, complete with gazebo, and we were about twenty feet from ramming into it.

While Lauren and Stefan ran to the stern to see about *Crabcakes*, I revved the engines and tried to move us forward in the opposite direction of the dock, but our depth reading suddenly went from two feet to zero. I felt *Chrysalis* give a slight shudder as she touched bottom. I backed up slightly to dislodge us, but didn't want to complicate matters with *Crabcakes* and was worried about not being able to see exactly what Lauren and Stefan were up to in its regard. I then became completely disoriented and uncertain what to do next. I was cold, and my whole body was quivering. From the bow, Mike turned to look at me. He must have sensed my panic, because he left the anchor, still somewhere in front of us, and came up to help steer *Chrysalis*. He bounded up the steps, two at a time, and I moved aside without a word, relieved to let him take over, but disappointed that I couldn't finish the job.

I went down to check on the kids and *Crabcakes*. With some effort, the kids had managed to get it unstuck and the line was clear of the propeller. I went inside the pilothouse and switched on the radar, which unfortunately had yet to be installed on the flybridge, and called up sketchy directions to Mike so he could move us to the center of the bay. By that time, *Crabcakes* was secure, and Lauren and Stefan were back at the bow bringing in the anchor. About fifteen minutes later, the wind began to decrease and the rain stopped altogether. *Chrysalis* was once again in the center of the bay, and the rest of us were on the flybridge, breathing heavily, and trying to decide what to do next.

I was a bit shaky. That is not altogether the truth. I was actually as near to a nervous breakdown as I had ever been. In that moment, all the tension from moving and adjusting to life on a boat that I had been doing so well at repressing, suddenly erupted in a spew of verbiage. I told Mike that two and a half months of change and adventure was enough for me. I was tired of living in a nautical world where I knew next to nothing. I certainly hadn't anticipated the strain of existing in the perpetual mess of living quarters yet to be completed. And it wasn't that I didn't adore my crewmates, but it was so hard to get any privacy and no one ever put away their dirty dishes.

After over sixty days at anchor, I was worn out from wondering if we were seconds away from a shipwreck. The romance of life on the water was highly overrated. I was done with stupid dreams. I wanted to return to land and my LazyBoy. I told Mike that if I didn't get some stability in my life, like right this instant, well…I couldn't predict the outcome because I had never been in this emotional space before. Whatever happened, it wouldn't be good. I looked up from my little tirade to find Mike and the kids staring at me.

I remembered, then, something Mike had said years earlier while he was playing university hockey. Toward the end of a game, we had watched one of Mike's teammates, a friend of ours normally cool and collected, beat a member of the opposite team, eventually getting kicked out the game. Meeting Mike outside the locker room after the game, I had asked him about it. He told me that the stress and excitement of playing hockey often brought out the issues of the athlete that were less than exemplary.

I was not exactly thrilled with the issues that the stress and excitement of living on a boat was bringing out of me: I felt scared, emotionally weak, disappointed with my ability to act under pressure, and ready to quit. There it was. It was me exposed, and it wasn't pretty. I told myself to remember this the next time I decided to play "scientist" and experiment with my own journey by placing myself in crazy situations just to see what would happen. My original hypothesis of: "If I immerse myself in an environment of change, I will rise to the challenges presented with wisdom, strength, and grace" was now refutable. Upon observation, my assumed conclusion would need to be altered.

This is the thing about dreams, about change, I thought. The exertion stirs up all sorts of things lurking beneath a usually cool and calm exterior. Books and movies on following your dream, plentiful as they are, should, like a pack of cigarettes, come with a warning label: "CAUTION: Following a dream can be hazardous to your emotional health and may result in the loss of cherished illusions and ultimately coming face-to-face with the Truth. Proceed at your own risk." Why hadn't anyone told me this? Consider yourself warned.

After a few minutes, I calmed down. I knew enough not to make the decision to quit the boating life while in the heat of a stressed-out moment. I told Mike that before I decided to pack it in, maybe we could take a breather at a marina for a few days. Everyone thought this was a great idea. We hailed a couple of marinas in the area and found one that could take us. That night, another big storm came through, but I crawled into my berth with the comforting knowledge that we were tied up, secure, to a dock. I didn't have to keep an ear out for any anchor alarm to go off or be ready to spring into action if it did. I slept the sleep of the dead.

Of course, in the following days my sanity gradually returned. I relented and told the crew I was committed to living aboard. The consideration to quit *Chrysalis* had made me realize all the things I appreciated about the lifestyle. The large amount of quality time we were spending together as a family and the proximity to nature. Most days, I did relish the learning curve. I wrote in my journal:

"If I am going to be honest about the dirt, my weaknesses and limitations that this dream is bringing to the surface of my life, then I need to be honest about the good things in me it is bringing to the surface as well. Mainly, and perhaps most surprising, that despite my fear, weaknesses, and limitations, I am willing to keep pushing forward. Who knew I had such reserve power inside of me? And would I have ever recognized this if I hadn't placed myself under these circumstances?"

26

From Miami it is 42 nautical miles, through the Gulf Steam, to the island of Bimini in the Bahamas. The Gulf Stream is a warm flowing ocean current which is birthed in the Gulf of Mexico, exits through the Strait of Florida and then continues northward up the eastern seaboard of America and Newfoundland, Canada, before heading east across the Atlantic where it becomes known as the North Atlantic Drift. It is between 50 and 100 miles wide and between 2,600 and 4,000 feet deep. The current can flow fast at its hump, or midpoint, up to just shy of five knots, but it tapers off to zero at its outskirts.

In good weather, the Gulf Stream poses little problem for boaters. You must factor the current into the crossing, but a good GPS and charting program will keep you right on course. Winds from the north can pose a problem, as they can stack the waves of the northerly flowing Gulf Stream and significantly increase wave height. From the marina in Miami, we kept a close eye on the wind forecast for several days before deciding to raise the hook and attempt our first maiden offshore voyage.

In midday sunshine, we cast off from the marina and emerged from Government Cut into calm waters. About an hour later, we began to skirt the Stream. The water changed from green-blue to a vibrant purple-blue. This being the maiden offshore voyage, there was a lot to do. We checked the fuel lines, filters, temperature of the engines, steering, GPS, and compass. All systems were working well, and *Chrysalis* was handling better than expected. Since it was calm, Mike decided to bump up our speed from 10 knots to 18 knots in order to test the engines. The engines roared and the bows rose up out of the water before falling slightly, as if she had planing hulls. This was curious to us because *Chrysalis* has twin, full displacement hulls, and should not rise out of the water. We traveled this way for awhile going at 18 knots, about 22 miles an hour. Just about the time I was thinking, "What's the big deal traveling offshore?" our starboard engine sputtered several times, then failed. With a concerned look, Mike left to check on it. Before he could make an assessment, the port engine quit as well.

I sat at the helm and nervously considered the possibilities should both engines fail to restart. We might drift in the Gulf Stream all the way up to Cape Fear, named, I suspected, for a reason. A more probable scenario would find us calling Tow Boat US. They could come and tow us back to Miami. It was fortunate for us that the coordinates between Miami and Bimini were well traveled. Help might not be minutes away, but likely a few hours at most. Not so if we were in the middle of the Atlantic, say, between Bermuda and the Azores. Even with a satellite phone, assistance of any kind would be several days away, possibly more. Self reliance on any kind of ocean passage was imperative.

Mike returned to the pilothouse and proceeded to explain what he thought was the problem. While we were an anchored, he had transferred most of our fuel and water to our forward tanks. This caused the boat to sit bow heavy. It also caused our fuel gauges on our day tanks to misread the level of fuel. Once we picked up speed, the bow rose so that the fuel now moved to the rear of the day tank. Since the fuel pickup was at the forward end of the tank, we would be "out of fuel" while the gauges had us at a quarter of a tank.

"So, we just need to remember to keep our day tanks more than a quarter full if we are going fast, right?" I said.

"Right. Every boat has its quirks and this is the first that we know of. We won't be going 20 knots regularly anyway, we would burn too much fuel. Our cruising speed is around 10 knots which won't cause a problem no matter how our fuel is situated on board."

Since air had gotten into the fuel lines, Mike had to suck it out and get diesel back through the lines in order to feed each of the engines. At the time, he could do this only by sucking it out with his mouth, receiving a mouth full of diesel once the air had passed. Diesel breath, I discovered later on when he tried to kiss me, was an even bigger turnoff than garlic.

It took about an hour to rid the engines of air pockets before they resumed their rumbling. The afternoon had worn on. It was late. We weren't thrilled about navigating the shallow waters of the Bahamas in the dark, so we decided to return to Miami and try again another day. We anchored, this time in a different bay, making sure to set the anchor at 1000 rpms.

Unfortunately, a low passed through the area and for the next few days a northerly kicked up winds over 30 knots. Although I was nervous, the anchor held. We waited impatiently for the low to pass. When things had calmed down slightly, we decided to make a second attempt. The forecast was for six-to-seven foot waves outside the Gulf Stream. Although we were wary, we were curious as to how *Chrysalis* would handle seas of that kind. We decided to venture out.

Skies were clear and the sun shined brilliantly, but as soon as we exited Government Cut for the second time, we were met with significantly heavier seas. True to the weather forecast, we plodded through six-to-seven foot waves. The further east we went, the taller the waves became. Foam capped large, breaking, confused seas. We were bombarded from every direction. Mike attempted to navigate from the flybridge. The kids and I sat flanking him. From this vantage point, twelve feet above the waterline, I looked out with an even gaze to the top of the waves approaching us. Spray erupted over the sides up at us. The rocking was substantial and uncomfortable. We hung on.

I decided I wanted to see what the waves looked like from the cockpit. I inched my way down the stairs on my posterior, standing only briefly to open the pilothouse door. Once inside, I radioed up to Mike to tell him I had made it indoors. I groped my way into the galley and out the back door. From the hollow or valley between waves, I looked up on the crest of waves that were higher than the flybridge, making them about 12 to 14 feet high. I considered: these waves approached the size of waves I had seen in my dreams.

Since all of our systems were working and *Chrysalis* seemed to be handling the situation, there was no immediate danger. I studied the power of the waves with a surprising neutrality. Just a few steps over the stern existed a world with little mercy. The waves cared nothing for my past, present, or future. They cared little for my life as a woman or that I was a wife and a mother. If I was to stand along the wingdeck, a misstep, a sudden awkward jerking motion, and I could slip overboard and even with my lifejacket on, the water, with impartiality, would likely steal me away indefinitely.

I crawled back up to the pilothouse. I could only crawl as walking had become impossible. At the helm, I radioed Mike to tell him that I was coming back up. I crawled to the flybridge, getting doused along the way by a large wave that hit us broadside. The four of us sat on the settee in silence for a few minutes before I said, "There doesn't seem to be much sense in continuing on in these conditions for another four or five more hours. Should we head back?"

"I was just thinking the same thing," Mike replied.

We turned slowly, in a wide arc, and once again pointed the bows toward Miami. Nearing the shoreline, Lauren said in a hoarse whisper, "I never imagined the sea could be this wild."

I had imagined it. Unlike my visions of horror, everything had turned out just fine.

Back at our anchorage, we discussed how well *Chrysalis* had maneuvered in such conditions. Although tossed, no green water hit the pilothouse windows. Nothing leaked or ceased working. What a great boat, we both said, pleased.

Mike asked me how I had felt seeing those large waves.

"It is becoming obvious to me that my imagination is far worse than the reality," I said. "How did you feel about it?"

Smiling, shaking his head, he said, "Those were some pretty significant seas out there. I think a few of those waves that hit us were over fourteen feet. Once I saw how well *Chrysalis* was managing, I wasn't nervous. But that rocking was uncomfortable! I am glad for the experience, though. Knowing how *Chrysalis* handles seas that large will go a long way in building our confidence should we ever encounter those kind of seas again, don't you think?" he asked.

I told him I thought it would.

Stefan, who had been sitting in the cockpit listening to our discussion, said with dismay, "I don't think we are ever going to get to the Bahamas."

The northerlies gradually abated that night, but it wasn't until two days later that things calmed down sufficiently for us to try again. Experiencing the seas of our last attempt, while going a long way toward building our confidence, was not something we wanted to repeat. We exited Government Cut for the third time. The waters were tame and although the skies were overcast, the wind was almost non-existent. The land disappeared and for three hours we saw nothing on the horizon but water and sky. During that time, it occurred to me that I was in the middle of nowhere. Timbuktu. There were no buildings, no cars, no people, and no land. Time could fast forward or rewind. How would I know? It was an ageless ocean. Spin the wheel and set the date. With binoculars, I scanned the horizon for a galleon with a Spanish flag. Maybe, I thought, I could wave to Ponce de Leon.

The middle of nowhere was actually somewhere, for there I was in it. The motors hummed. The sun was shining, the breeze, cool. I sat alone on the flybridge under the shade of a Bimini canopy. I had volunteered for the first official watch. On lengthier ocean passages, taking a turn on watch is important. Each crew member is assigned a block of time, while the rest of the crew takes a break. The person on watch keeps a lookout for other boats, rocks, and debris in the water. They record longitude and latitude, mark any mechanical notes down in a ledger. I took my job seriously. My head scanned from left to right like a metronome searching for any possible danger. For the moment, there was little to be concerned about. The waves were on the nose, roughly one foot swells. I barely felt them. They were just enough to combine hypnotically with the motors to put me in a trance-like state.

So, I was lulled. I sat for an hour, a day, a month. My mind was completely void of thoughts. As was *Chrysalis*, I was on auto pilot. There was nowhere to go. Nothing to buy. No plans to make. No news from the outside world. Nothing to be concerned about for miles and miles. Nothing between there and the moon.

As I floated brainlessly along the space-time continuum, I was jolted out of my stupor by rush hour. A cigarette boat materialized from the southeast and passed in a blur. It took me a few moments to comprehend it. It smacked of some other world I once knew. The craft turned suddenly northwest toward land. I was sorry to see him go. This was a newsworthy event in la la land. A head poked up through the hatch from down below.

"Did you see him whiz by?" Mike asked.

"I certainly did," I replied. After all, I was on watch and it was my job to notice such things. As soon as I said this, I saw the arced bodies of dolphins approaching.

"Dolphins ahoy!" I yelled down a hatch, which, gauging from the response, was similar to saying, "Here comes the ice cream truck!" The crew emerged from below and we made a beeline for the bows. A pod of spotted dolphins raced towards us as if they had an urgent message. They were after our bows, which was their playground. Upon arrival, they began to jump exuberantly back and forth directly in our path, darting under one bow, perilously close to the hull, only to reappear on the other side. Two or three of them discovered the space between our two hulls and were content to leap there. The more we cheered them on, the more they seemed to enjoy their own antics. We whooped and leapt ourselves as if sharing some inside joke. For a full ten minutes we relished their company, and then they disappeared just as quickly as they came. We stood leaning over the rails, heaving and smiling, before wandering off in contented silence.

Since it was rush hour, the traffic continued. As soon as I was back at the flybridge, a small bird appeared. I noticed it was not a water bird, but some kind of sparrow. I wondered how he had come to be almost forty nautical miles offshore. I considered that he might be taking the scenic route on his way north after a warm winter in Florida. He did a complete 360 around our boat, chirping at me for the duration. I assumed he was wondering what we were doing this far out into no man's land. After receiving little response from me, he turned and, interestingly enough, headed north.

"Land Ho!" I shouted. Through the binoculars, I saw the grey loping outline of land between water and sky. The water gradually began to change from greenish blue to milky turquoise. Lauren and Stefan emerged and made their way to the bows in order to keep a look out for reefs and rocks. As we pulled in through the narrow entrance of Bimini Sands Marina, they began jumping up and down, hollering "hooray! We made it!" Stefan turned to me and yelled, "Mom this is the happiest day of my life!" They both proceeded to do the chicken dance.

The dockhand helping us asked where we had come from and what the seas were like. He nodded his head at our report.

"Nice day for a crossing," he said smiling at me as I handed him our stern line.

"Sir," I said, "you have no idea."

Not long before, I had read Nathaniel Philbrick's *The Mayflower*, in which he described the journey of the Pilgrims and their attempt to make a life in a new world. As they became friends with the natives, they began to realize that the land that was new to them was already ages old and had a history all its own. While on scouting exhibitions with the locals, the Pilgrims noticed many circular, foot-deep pits, several feet wide, placed along trails through the forest. Upon inquiry, the pilgrims learned that these were "story" holes. When the course of their travels took them by a pit, the natives would stop and everyone traveling with them would get into the pit. Someone would then recount the story of what had happened there, thus keeping history alive for their community.

I consider the Gulf Stream a story pit. In the future, every time I cross over it, whether by sea or by air, I will gather everyone together and tell the tale of our first offshore voyage and the struggle to get to the small island of Bimini. All the hard work of building the boat. Learning to tie a bowline knot. The color of the water. The smiling faces. Large waves. The relief. It is possible that I will begin to take a little license on the story pit idea and just start telling the tale in any old place. I'll even recount it to grandchildren who will roll their eyes and say, "Not again, Grandma! We've heard this story a hundred times already!"

27

The next day, after the kids completed some neglected school work, we left to explore the area. The Bimini Islands consist of two, low lying, main islands with a few tiny ones lying to the south. Although there has been talk in the past, North and South Bimini are not yet connected by a bridge. Since the marina where we were docked was in South Bimini, we took a taxi about a mile or so to the small ferry service. This took us to North Bimini, and the main hub of Alice Town. We disembarked the rickety, wooden ferry, and proceeded to walk by several whitewashed, ramshackle shops selling trinkets and shells. For a dollar, you could buy a conch shell, smooth, pink, and polished. A few restaurants, one advertising Bimini Macaroni and Cheese, were scattered along the main thoroughfare. Since macaroni and cheese was a favorite, I made a mental note. When we went by later for lunch, I found the mac and cheese, cut into squares and sparsely populated with peas and carrots, to be a delicious rendition of the dish I was familiar with.

While in town we discovered a shop that rented golf carts, the general means of island transportation, and set about securing one. Upon signing the back of a scrap piece of paper legalizing the transaction, I inquired about a map. The guy we were renting from threw his head back and laughed. He said we certainly wouldn't need one as there were only two roads, "Dis one, and dat one" he said pointing first one way, then the other. "You ride up three or four miles and then catch da linking road and ride back, mon."

The rest of the family found this amusing, me asking for a map, and throughout the remainder of the day, kept inquiring if

I needed a map to: find the toilet in the restroom, the cheese in the small grocery store, and once back onboard, the way to my stateroom.

Since traffic was sparse, we let each of the kids take a turn driving up and down The Kings Highway. Stefan, new to the automotive world, hit almost every pothole and narrowly missed a goat within the first hundred and fifty feet. While traveling down the left hand side of the road, dodging carts, pedestrians and the occasional chicken, he said with exuberance, "This is better than playing Frogger!"

All the way up and then back down again, friendly locals waved, nodded, or called out "Hello there!" We were smitten. What Bimini lacked in Internet and convenience, it certainly made up for in hospitality.

Ernest Hemingway lived and wrote on the North Island from 1935 to 1937. From his yacht, Pilar, he trolled the surrounding waters for tuna and mackerel. When he was on land, he lived and wrote at a local pub, The Compleat Angler, which used to be a hotel. Mike, Lauren, and I went to the pub where he used to write. It was just as I had pictured it, an antiquated version of an "old boys club" with carved dark wood paneling, tables, chairs, and pictures of Hemingway's glory days covering every inch of spare wall. Here he was standing on a dock next to a hoisted sailfish. Over here it was a grouper and next to that a shark. Other memorabilia, glasses, a pen were kept in enclosed viewing tables. Interspersed were written snippets about his life and sound bite quotes from him, some of which I tucked away for future reference.

I sat in what the bartender told me could very well have been his chair. He told me this with a smile and wink, so I wouldn't bet my life on it. Even so, my writing self was all alert hoping some of his residual talent was still hanging about the place and if I inhaled it, perhaps it would attach itself to my brain. I looked out the window on to a dusty street, and wondered what it would have been like for him to sit in that chair, or somewhere close by, writing *To Have and Have Not*. I wondered what drew him to Bimini. Was it just the fishing? Or did the lonely solitude and beauty of the turquoise waters become the muse he was looking for?

Today, fishing still draws people to Bimini. For the duration of our stay, a steady stream of sportfish yachts pulled into the marina just long enough to check in to customs, ready their gear, and buy baitfish. We would hear the rumble of their motors early in the morning as they pulled out. Sometimes they would return later in the day and clean several tunas at stations set up along the dock. We gathered to watch with envious eyes. Inspired, Mike and Stefan spent several afternoons reorganizing our fishing gear and discussing lures. They read local fishing books, talked over strategy, and asked everyone they met where the best fishing was.

Anxious to try ourselves, we left Bimini on a sunny morning, in calm seas, and went east toward the Berry Islands. The only ship we saw that day was a cruise ship, anchored off the northern end of the Berries, to give its passengers a taste of Caribbean life on their "private island."

"Not so private when the 2,000 passengers disembark," I mentioned casually to Mike.

From the flybridge, I had just watched the cruise ship disappear behind the island, when I heard a noise. I concentrated. It was a whirring noise. Instinctively, I tilted my head and sniffed the air as irregular sounds can often be accompanied by burning smells, electrical or chemical, neither good. But there was only a whirring. I looked around, following the sound, and noticed the last bit of fishing line running out of a recently placed fishing rod. The only thing now holding the line to the rod was the knot at the end. The rod was at a ninety degree angle.

"FISH," I yelled, "FISH!"

I ran to the throttles and stopped the engines.

Mike came up, "What? What's the matter?"

I pointed urgently at the rod. "FISH!"

One by one the crew materialized, confused at first. Then, we scrambled to find nets, the gaff hook, and a bucket. Mike ended up in the cockpit struggling to reel in what turned out to be a whole lot of line and attached to the end, a fifteen pound tuna. It flopped around in the cockpit, getting a fishy scented slime all over the deck. The stripe along its back was neon blue and its rigid, silvery body flashed in the sunlight. Delighted, we stored it aboard and put out three more fishing lines.

All afternoon we heard whirring. Twice that day, we had fish on four separate lines at once which resulted in the four of us fox-trotting around each other in order to keep the lines from getting crossed. After reeling in several more fifteen pounders, we stopped for a brief rest, our chests heaving, and consulted our *Fish of the Atlantic Guide*. Clearly, we had hauled in two kinds of tuna. Several had black spines with distinctive yellow sides and silver bellies. Looking through the pictures in our guide, we determined that these were Blackfin Tuna, also known as the Bermuda Tuna Football due to their characteristic form. They are found in the Western Atlantic from Cape Cod to Brazil. Weighing in from two to 45 pounds, they are among the best fighters relative to their size. Food quality: excellent. Someone mentioned sashimi for dinner.

Earlier, upon reeling in the tuna with the bright blue stripe, I had yelled out, "Hooray, a Bluefin!" But on closer inspection we discovered that, instead, we had several Bigeye Tuna. Their spines are royal blue, with silver bellies, and their first dorsal fin a bright yellow, the finlets yellow with black edges. They run about the same size as a Yellowfin, from a few pounds to upwards of 400 pounds. I didn't know that the Bigeye is among the species of tuna most endangered due to commercial fishing. In light of this we let the smaller ones go and kept only what we knew we could eat. Like the Blackfin, Bigeyes are hearty fighters. Food quality: excellent.

We let the four lines out again and it wasn't long until we recognized the now-familiar whirring and the bent rod. Mike wrestled with a mystery for quite some time. Abruptly, the line went slack. We all groaned figuring the fish had come off. When the end of the line finally presented itself we were surprised to find the head and remains of a larger tuna. His body had been cleanly sliced in two. It lay on the floor of the cockpit, its large eye wide as if in terror. The four of us stood around it in silence as if attending its funeral.

"Sharks," I whispered the benediction ominously.

I looked over the edge of *Chrysalis* into the dark swirling water and imagined the tuna's violent end.

Stefan broke the lull by yelling out, "Fish! We've got another one on the line!" and I quickly forgot about our unfortunate friend.

In between reeling in tunas, we spent about 15 minutes taking turns reeling in a forty pound Amberjack and just after that a sleek Spanish Mackerel. We kept the Mackerel and five tunas, intending to store the fillets we didn't eat in our freezer. Tired, but excited at the prospect of dinner, we reluctantly pulled in the lines. The sun was low on the horizon and we had arrived at our anchorage. Pulling into Devils Cay, we found it deserted. No boats, no homes, just a ring of small islands, scrubby with brush, rock, and several vacant, smooth beaches. As much as I believe that peace can be found in the city, this topography, stark and quiet, spoke the native language of my soul. I felt something shift inside me, and expelled a long breath. I was settling. We anchored in the center of the wide, shallow bay, and began the task of cleaning fish.

~~~

When the kids were toddlers, Mike and I discussed the best way to educate them. Private versus public school was a source of lengthy debate. At the time, there was a family in our church who homeschooled. They all wore matching clothes. The eight of them lived several miles outside of town on an acreage property and raised cattle. The parents never let the kids go to their classmates' birthday parties. I had a couple of the children in an after school club. They were serious types and found it difficult to relate to the antics of their immature counterparts, but they were well versed in farmyard animal anatomy. From my perspective at the time, it did not go a long way toward promoting a viable educational option.

My own school experience was one of drudgery and regurgitation. I was a wriggly kid who liked the outdoors. Being strapped six hours a day to a school desk for 13 years nearly squelched whatever instinctual wonder I originally possessed. I was not quick on my feet, a trait that exists to this day, and when called on to answer a question in the classroom, I stumbled in my performance. Being a sensitive whelp, I was hurt by a teacher's disregard or animated frustration at my lack of knowledge and communication skills. I slunk to the back row and tried my best to blend in. I cruised through without much effort on B's and C's. In high school the rote memorization all but sucked the joy of learning right out of me and it has taken years to recover. As an adult, I was shocked to discover I loved learning, just hated school.

With this in mind, I thought homeschooling required a second glance. I liked the freedom to explore the world under less structured circumstances. Even more, that the pace of learning could be carried out to accommodate the needs of an individual child as opposed to the progression of theory being dictated by a class of thirty students as well as the pressure on teachers to accomplish a prescribed amount within a certain time frame, often leaving slower or more deliberate learners in the dust. I began to have visions of nature walks through the woods, tracking rabbits through the snow, building and launching rocketships, and lazy afternoons spent reading aloud together. I hoped a shot of holy curiosity could be injected into my kids' brains. Erase the line between education and life.

Early on in my research, I was overwhelmed at the large number of companies putting out quality curriculums. If you wanted, some of these companies would keep a record of achievement in the form of grades and transcripts. There was a fair amount of hand- holding and this went a long way to reassuring me that quality education at home was possible. Although Mike and I felt unqualified to create a curriculum, if one was prepared for us, we were confident we had the capacity to be educational mentors for our kids.

We decided to give it a try for Lauren's kindergarten year and see how it went. We subsequently homeschooled off and on for the duration of their educational experience.

I was a keener in the early years of homeschooling, a passionate believer in hands-on education. To demonstrate the human digestive system I lined up pillows in my bedroom and told the kids the pillows were teeth. The bedroom was the mouth. I told them we were pieces of food in the mouth and we rolled against the pillows. This they loved. From there, we then crawled through a long, plastic play tunnel down the hall.

Midway through the tunnel, I said, "Pretend this is the esophagus. The food, us, must pass through here on its way to the stomach." We emerged into the dining room, the stomach, where I had us all bounce into each other to animate the stomach's role in breaking down food, churning with gastric juices. Stefan, small as he was, bounced into a wall and there were tears. Just a little indigestion, I told them. It happens to the best of us. When antacid in the form of a few hugs was administered, we moved on. Descending the stairs, we talked about the purpose of the small and large intestine, and then we went out the front door, the anus where, I said, waste was released.

"Let's do it again!" they said, running back inside.

All afternoon we played "digestive track," alternately being swallowed and eliminated, until finally I lay on the grass in the front yard and told the kids, "I'm wasted."

Because we had experience in homeschooling, this was the one element of moving aboard that required little adjustment. Both Lauren and Stefan were registered at a correspondence school, which sent them accredited curriculum and kept all of their grades and records. Many of the courses they did were online with discussion groups. Lauren joined the photography club and worked on the school newspaper, submitting photos and articles over the Internet. We continued our schedule of schooling in the morning with the remainder of the day for exploration. During this part of the day, learning happened spontaneously, and experiences prompted them, out of curiosity, to further explore their environment.

Lauren had her fifteenth birthday in the Bahamas. She had recently taken an interest in medicine and decided to clean a tuna by herself. She got out the long thin filet knife with the leather handle and read the chapter on "Filleting Fish" in a book on Bahamian fishing. Without a grimace, she sliced into it, beginning at the anal opening and running a slit along the length of the belly up to the jaw. Watching her, Stefan grabbed a tuna out of the bucket and proceeded to do the same.

They were in their bathing suits, wet and disheveled from their recent swim, sitting on the cockpit floor with newspaper spread out around them, and an open fifteen pound tuna each in front of them. There was fish slime, blood, and guts everywhere, spattered in globs on their own legs and up their arms to their elbows. The whole place reeked like a fish market. They didn't care.

While preparing sashimi and sushi in the galley, I listened to their conversation. I could hear them talking back and forth as they dissected.

Lauren said with breathy excitement, "Oh! Check it out Stef, here is his stomach."

"Really? Let me see. Cut it open and see if you can tell what he had for breakfast!"

There was a pause. I went to the galley doorway to watch them. Lauren had sliced open the stomach and had pried it open between two fingers. Their blonde heads were bent together and they were peering inside.

"Hmmm," Lauren said poking around, "I can't really tell what he had for breakfast, but look… here is his intestinal tract and you can follow that all the way to his anus, right here, where poo or pee comes out his body."

"That's hilarious," Stefan said.

I smiled and wondered why pee and poo were standard humorous fare for pre-adolescent boys.

Awhile later, Stefan called out, "Hey! I can see my guy's brain. Look how tiny it is!"

"Sort of like someone else's brain." Lauren said, looking up at him and smiling.

"Ha ha, very funny."

After Mike cleaned the remaining fish, reserving some meat for bait, he threw the carcasses into the water off our stern. It wasn't long before two six-foot nurse sharks arrived on the scene. The water below us was eight feet deep and clear. We had a perfect view of the sandy bottom. The four of us hung our heads over the side and watched them circle the area before gulping down chunks of flesh.

Stefan said, "Hey, this is just like the Discovery Channel."

A large ray floated gracefully by, looking very much like a bird in flight. He kept his distance until the sharks left the area before cruising around for remnants. 'Hello neighbors,' I thought to myself.

I told the kids to wash up for supper which took awhile. After their showers, we sat at the galley table dipping barely seared, sesame-crusted cubes of tuna into soy sauce, and I asked Lauren and Stefan, "So, how was your day at school?"

28

Breakfast the next morning consisted of freshly caught barbequed mackerel and the last of the mango I had brought from Florida. We ate it with our fingers in the cockpit while wearing our bathing suits. As I removed a small bone from between two of my teeth, I wondered out loud what it would be like to be stranded on a deserted island.

"You mean like Tom Hanks character in *Castaway*?" Lauren asked.

"Yeah. On an island just like this one," I said.

After a pause, Mike said, "I've always thought it would be fun to go on the TV show *Survivor*. Try to exist with the bare essentials. Make a shelter. Fire." He looked at Lauren and Stefan, "You guys wanna try it?"

Duh.

Alexander Selkirk was born in 1676 to a Scottish shoemaker. He evidently had better things to do than take over the family business because in 1695 he ran off to join a crew of buccaneers and by 1703 was sailing master on the privateering ship, Cinque Ports, sailing the Pacific. A man of some passion, in 1704 he had a huge quarrel with his captain, Thomas Stradling, and asked to be put out ashore on the uninhabited island of Mas a Tierra in the archipelago Juan Fernandez, 400 miles west of Valparaiso, Chile. There was little doubt in his mind that he would be picked up shortly by the next passing ship and that the inconvenience of a brief wait on a secluded island would be better than spending one more day with an incompetent captain on a leaky boat. He gathered together some necessities: musket, gunpowder, carpenter's tools, a knife, flint and steel, few pounds of tobacco, and a kettle. Fuming, he was dropped off on the island and as the ship sailed away, immediately regretted his decision. He called after the ship to no response.

For 52 months he lived there alone, making resourceful uses of what little he had, including the goats living on the island, until 1709 when he was picked up by an English ship and finally returned home in 1711. Although his circumstances as a castaway were unfortunate at the time, he met a better fate than the crew of Cinque Ports, which sunk off the coast of Peru, drowning all but the captain and seven men, who were captured and sent to rot in a Peruvian jail.

Upon his return to England, journalist Richard Steele interviewed Selkirk and ran a piece on him in *The Englishman*. Selkirk may have been the model Daniel Defoe used for his character in his book, *Robinson Crusoe*. For his own part, Selkirk seems to have missed the solitary life, saying to Steele, "I am now worth 800 Pounds, but shall never be so happy as when I was not worth a Farthing."

Armed with a small hatchet, two blankets, fishing line, a bottle of water, and at my request, a handheld VHF, Lauren and Stefan were ready for their own experience as castaways. They balked at the VHF.

"Why do we have to carry a VHF? Robinson Crusoe didn't have a VHF!" Lauren asked.

"No, but the real Robinson Crusoe, Alexander Selkirk, was almost twice your age and a seasoned sailor. Plus, half of surviving in the wild is learning to make use of your resources. In case of an emergency, you will be happy to make use of this one."

Mike dropped the kids and their meager gear off at the beach and then returned to *Chrysalis* in the dinghy. In between cleaning the heads and shining stainless, I watched Lauren and Stefan through binoculars. They spent their morning hacking away at the dry dead scrub brush that littered the island. There was a small rocky outcropping about 30 feet up from the waterline, which they used as the rear of their shelter. They stacked up the sides, using rocks to brace the twigs and branches, and by mid-afternoon had begun to gingerly place palm fronds and lighter brush on top as their roof. They spread out their blankets and sat down on them in the shade of their lean-to for a break.

After finishing my own work for the day, I set up my own camp in the cockpit with the essentials of survival: mojito, book, chips, and binoculars. Every so often I raised the binoculars, continuing to check on the survivors' progress. Late in the afternoon they had made a clearing for a firepit, being mindful of the wind direction and not placing it too close to their shelter. I was impressed. They hauled rocks over and placed them in a large circle, mounding kindling in the center. Then they hailed us on the VHF to come for a visit.

"Oh and by the way, we've been trying to start a fire for like two hours using a piece of glass we found, but we couldn't do it, so bring matches okay? And maybe some supper, like hot dogs," Stefan said.

"Pretty sure Alexander Selkirk didn't have hot dogs when he was marooned," I said.

"Too bad for him," Lauren's voice came on over the VHF. "When you are surviving, you have to make use of your resources, and lucky for us we have you. Oh yeah, and bring stuff for s'mores too. And our pillows and my guitar would be great. Thank you, Mom!"

Just before loading our provisions, a sailboat entered our bay and anchored nearby, reminding us we were not in the year 1455. Mike and I hopped in the dinghy and went over to invite them to our bonfire. We knocked on their hull and a young couple emerged. They introduced themselves as Nick and Alice, both from Alaska. They had just come from West End through some substantial seas and wanted to have a rest and some supper, but they promised to join us for dessert after dark.

Our Survivor Hosts were gracious. They gave us an extended tour of camp and their lean-to as well as taking us a short distance to where their "outhouse" was conveniently located down wind and on the other side of a hill from their camp. With Stefan's jackknife they had pared some long sticks to use for roasting the hot dogs and marshmallows. With the matches, for which they were now grateful, we made short work of starting a fire and getting supper prepared.

By nightfall the fire was roaring. Mike and Stefan were attempting to juggle hot coals, Lauren was strumming her guitar, and I was leaning against our picnic backpack close to the fire, listening. In the distance I heard the hum of a dinghy motor and it wasn't long before Nick and Alice showed up with popcorn and wine. The four of us went down the beach to help them pull their dinghy ashore, shaking hands, and saying hello. We made our way to the fire, where we settled down to swap stories.

Nick was a retired professional skateboarder. *Who knew that skateboarding had been around long enough to have retirees?* I wondered to myself silently. Heavily tattooed, in baggy shorts, with shaggy hair sticking out from under his offset baseball cap, he looked the part. He was lanky, thin, and tan, and sort of swaggered when he walked. I could tell right away that Stefan thought he was the coolest. His wife, Alice, was blonde, trim, a massage therapist with an easygoing, lighthearted way about her. Over s'mores and popcorn they told us that in the summer they farmed their land in Alaska and sold their organic fruits and vegetables to local markets. Nick hunted moose and deer; the meat they mainly lived on, although they kept chickens as well. Sometimes, Alice said, there were so many salmon running upstream not far from their property, that she would simply hike down in the morning with a net and scoop up a four pounder for dinner.

While holidaying in Florida several years ago, they found their 32-foot sailboat, in a dilapidated state, and purchased it on the spot for just under $5,000. Before the cold Alaskan winter set in, they shut down their farm and drove their jeep ever southeast, all the way to Daytona Beach, where they began to refit their boat. This was their second winter and spring in the Bahamas. They had anchored in this very spot a year ago. Alice asked me how our provisions were holding out. I told her we were just beginning our journey, so were well stocked. She said kindly, "Well, if you need any meat I've got a bunch of canned moose. You would be welcome to have some."

When the stories of building the inside of boats, malfunctioning water makers, and large seas had dwindled along with our fire and the wine, we said good night and left Lauren and Stefan to sleep on the beach in their lean-to. As Mike and I pulled away in the dinghy, I could see the beams from their flashlights bobbing along the shoreline, traveling the short distance to their lean-to which I could barely make out in the moonlight. By the time I reached *Chrysalis* and turned back toward the beach, their lights had gone out.

The next morning, Mike and I made our way to the beach to see how the Survivors had fared. It had been a good night, they said, but a few things had happened. The wind had kicked up and blown a few of the palm fronds off their roof, causing a bit of a ruckus. The mosquitoes had been fierce. Stefan had to use "the facilities" during the night and made this comment, "Boy, is it dark in the middle of the night on an uninhabited island!"

Adding to the description, Lauren said, "After you guys left last night, Stef and I looked at the stars for awhile, and then I said good night and tried to get to sleep, but the island was so noisy!"

"What kind of noises?" I asked, curious.

"Insects whizzing by. Leaves and branches rustling or falling down in the wind. It was kind of creepy at first, but then I realized it was just the island settling down to sleep. After that I slept just fine. When I woke up, everything was quiet."

Packing up her water bottle, flashlight, and guitar she continued, smiling, "I don't see what the big deal is. I definitely could go on the TV show *Survivor* with no problems at all."

Soon after we had boarded *Chrysalis*, Nick and Alice came by and offered to show us a profitable spear fishing hole. Mike and the kids were thrilled. Although we had brought equipment, a couple of "Hawaiian Slings," we had yet to try them out. I do enjoy snorkeling, but I had no desire to spear fish, so I told the crew to go ahead without me. Plus, the thought of a little alone time was more than a little appealing. From the cockpit, I watched the five of them head across the bay and tie up to some rocks. Several hours later they returned. Nick had caught a lobster, but my crew was empty-handed. Evidently, it took some practice.

Sitting around the fire the night before, Nick had mentioned that at the gate to their farm in Alaska, they had a mailbox with the words inscribed, "Time stops here." Whenever they had guests over, they warned them that upon their arrival they would be expected to leave their watches in the mailbox. "Our culture's addiction to knowing the time is unfortunate," Nick had said in between mouthfuls of popcorn. "If you believe in an afterlife at all, then we are timeless beings and should act as such. Western Civ needs to take a few breaths and slow down," he continued.

At this, Mike had glanced in my direction with a knowing look.

Several weeks before coming to the Bahamas, Mike misplaced his watch. It was an expensive one, the last reminder, along with a few neckties, of his previous life working in an office. Since beginning the live-aboard lifestyle, I often thought its black and gold shiny face and band looked a little funny worn with shorts and a t-shirt. Although I was distraught by its loss, Mike released it with little fanfare. Both kids were sporadic watch wearers to begin with, and it wasn't long before their drugstore watches disappeared into a nook or a cranny never to be heard from again. It was a good thing, I thought, that I still had my watch.

Then one day my three crewmates sat me down in the pilothouse.

"This is an intervention," Lauren said gravely.

"What are you talking about?" I asked, wide-eyed. Innocent.

Mike said gently, concerned, "We have come to the conclusion that you have an addiction."

I thought they had finally realized that my love of chocolate might be a problem bordering on addiction, but if they thought I was going off chocolate cold turkey, they had another think coming. Besides, I could stop eating it anytime I wanted to.

Instead, Mike continued, "We think you are addicted to knowing what time it is so you can schedule your day, and ours by extension. Your watch is enabling you to make to-do lists and we think this is criminal here in the Bahamas. One of the reasons we are living on a boat is to experience a little more freedom from conventional restraints. We want you to hand over the wristwatch."

"You can't be serious?" I was sure this was some kind of joke. I backed away and covered my watch with my opposite hand. This was ridiculous.

"Hand it over, Mom, then step slowly away, and no one gets hurt," Stefan held out his hand.

"Fine." I said while unclasping my watch and plopping it into Stefan's hand as if I didn't care. "You guys will see. Giving up this watch will be no problem." Then I reminded Stefan that the watch was expensive and to please put it in a safe place.

I started out just fine, but a couple hours later I caught myself in the act of raising my left arm to check the hour and was greeted instead by a naked wrist. I immediately felt disoriented. Lost. How was I supposed to know when it was lunchtime? How could I be expected to schedule school and work with no watch? I wandered aimlessly among the hours unable to "place" myself in the day. I grew fidgety, cranky, and sweaty. I paced the rail like a tiger. I shielded my eyes with my hand and looked up at the sun's place in the sky hoping for discernment. Out of habit, I kept asking Mike and the kids what time it was, until they got frustrated with me.

"For the last time, Mom, we don't know and we don't care! We're on island time, mon!" they said.

At the dinner table one night, I stood and confessed, "Hello, my name is Kim Petersen, and I'm addicted to knowing the time." They all patted me on the back and told me they accepted and loved me even though I had lots of quirks and imperfections. Oh, the joys of community.

As I thought about it later on, I realized there were deeper issues surrounding my task oriented compulsions, and that I placed a great deal of my self-worth in what I accomplished during the course of a day. Letting go of my watch, painful as it was initially, reminded me of my value simply as a human being, not solely for accomplishing a to-do list.

It took a couple of weeks to get used to the feeling of being adrift in my day, but gradually, I started to feel myself a part of the day as a whole instead of carved out pieces of 60-minute intervals. The hours seeped into each other. When I woke up I had breakfast and worked. I played and read in the afternoon. When the sun went down, we ate dinner. Returning from an afternoon of snorkeling, I would glance at the battery-operated clock in the galley that had recently been restored to me as a gift for good behavior. It made no difference if it was 4 o'clock or 7 o'clock

About a month later, Stefan found Mike's wristwatch buried under papers in an office drawer. Mike seemed genuinely glad to have it returned and thanked Stefan profusely, but I noticed the timepiece ended up in his night table drawer. Eventually, my watch was returned to me, but it joined Mike's in the same drawer.

29

The geography of the Bahamas, the shallow waters and numerous protected harbors scattered throughout nearly 700 islands, made it attractive to past pirates who could loot passing merchant ships and disappear into its complicated waters. Even in the early days of Discovery, its location in a burgeoning shipping lane led to the downfall of many Spanish and English boats on their way to and from the New World. These ships were plundered by famous marauders such as Henry Morgan, Blackbeard, and Anne Bonney. Henry Morgan, whose treasure was never found, hid out in the dangerous reefs off Andros. Captain Kidd preferred Kidd Cove in Elizabeth Harbour, Exuma. By 1700, pirates essentially ruled Nassau and had driven out most of its law-abiding citizens, who moved on to Great Exuma. Edward Teach, otherwise known as Blackbeard, took up residence in Fort Nassau until the British Navy had enough in 1718 and kicked him out.

Rapacious behavior was not limited to privateers and pirates. In the Abacos, pirates settled and joined forces with a growing population of British settlers. Like the Siren daughters of the Greek sea god Phorcys who lured sailors to death with their lovely song, from the shore at night these islanders would see the lights of a passing ship and set up lanterns in the shallows as if to direct the ship to safety. The ship would follow the lights, run aground or bash into the rocks, and the looting would commence with often murderous results.

Back on land I used to watch with interest a television show called *Treasure Seekers*. Each episode started with a story of intrigue. A pirate treasure that had been buried on a long-forgotten island. A recounting of Egyptian thieves losing stolen burial goods. Ancient civilizations booby-trapping their wealth in some hard-to-reach canyon. Sometimes fortunes were unexpectedly lost in storms at sea or thrown out of car windows with the cops hot on their tails.

One episode featured a middle-aged man who had it on good authority that bank robbers had buried their loot somewhere on an acre of land running along a stretch of highway near his home. He stood, sweaty, dirty and rumpled, leaning on a shovel in front of a field full of craters he had dug. He said shaking his head, "Dag nab it, it's got to be around here somewhere. I won't quit until I find it." Later on in the episode, the same guy looked intently into the camera and made this remark, "You know what will happen? If I don't find this treasure, one day, long after I'm gone, some young kid will kick over a rock and find it with no work, time, or money. That's just the way life works."

The modern-day treasure hunter comes equipped with a water bottle, cell phone, and the latest map printed off the Internet. If you do not have access to a 15 million dollar yacht equipped with sonar or drilling equipment, you might at least be able to purchase a metal detector. With it you can explore some open-ended plotline in hopes of providing a financially lucrative denouement. Every now and again, one of your treasure-hunting colleagues will happen to find what they were looking for and end up on the front page of the newspaper. Their picture, in the midst of crumbling pottery and crusty coins, will inspire you to invest your last bit of savings on a treasure map you buy off some shady character in an old tavern. He will no doubt assure you of its authenticity.

Sensing my interest, Mike got me a metal detector the Christmas before we moved aboard. I tried it out on a stretch of Florida coastline. I waved it slowly back and forth a few inches over the small dunes of sand, stopping to dig at the appropriate sound in my earphones. Hearing those beeps and pushing the sand around was invigorating, but I only dug up loose change and several bottle caps. With dreams of discovering a more substantial buried treasure, I had high hopes for the deserted islands of the Bahamas.

Pirates were known to frequent the protected harbor of Royal Island, our next destination, originally named Real Island for the Spanish silver coin. This, I thought, might serve me well as a place to use my metal detector. After a little over a week at Devils Cay, we hauled up the anchor, waved to Nick and Alice, and made our way to Royal Island Harbour. Here, we joined a few other anchored sailboats in the wide bay.

Spurred on by thoughts of buried treasure, the four of us combed the beaches, taking turns with the metal detector. We became adept at recognizing the distinctive "beeping" noise indicating a mystery. We would stop and dig around excitedly, but except for a few odd shaped pieces of metal we found no coins and no priceless jewelry. When I was busy with chores or work, the kids took the metal detector to the island and tried to work systematically inland, but the ground proved to be rocky and in the end we abandoned the hope of striking it rich. Eventually, the metal detector ended up in storage. As so often happens, we moved on to activities whose rewards were more immediate, like the ruins of a 1930s hotel on top of the hill.

My cruising guide said little about the hotel, except that it had thrived in the 30's and then, perhaps due to the economic depression, it had been abandoned. There were rumors that a few famous people, entertainers and politicians, had stayed in the hotel, but I could find nothing to confirm this. One morning the four of us landed on Royal Island, tied up *Crabcakes*, and pushed our way through an overgrown stone footpath. Along with our own animated voices the air was full of the sound of chirping birds. After a while, we emerged into a clearing and found the crumbling remains of several coral and wood buildings whose roofs were missing or only relatively intact.

Carefully walking through them, we identified several bedrooms, one with a rusty metal bed frame, and a bathroom with patches of blue and white tile still on the floor.

Continuing down a roofless corridor, we entered what appeared to be a spacious dining hall complete with coral fireplace and attached to that, a kitchen whose cupboards had long since been emptied. Breaking the silence, I said, "I wonder what kind of food they served here?" my voice echoing strangely across the open expanse. Climbing a short, stone, stairway, testing the stairs as we went, we emerged onto a broad coral-hewn deck overlooking the north part of the island from which we could view a picturesque teal sea. At the end of the deck, the curved remains of a bar could be seen. I tried to imagine folks with martinis sitting on deck chairs listening to a Benny Goodman record. I wondered where they were now.

Up ahead of me I heard Stefan say to Lauren, "I wonder who laid the tile in that bathroom back there. Just think, it was all fresh and new one day."

"Yeah, and who made the meals in this kitchen, and who served them to the guests in the dining room? And who WERE the guests anyway, and where did they come from? How did they get here? And where are they now?" Lauren was running her fingertips along the top edge of the bar.

"I wonder if there were any kids that came whether they liked the lizards here on the island like I do," Stefan said, eyeing a small lizard climbing up the wall and slowly approaching in an attempt to capture it. He lunged, but the lizard was much faster and escaped into a crevice.

"Don't you wonder what the story is behind this place? Mom said she couldn't find out much on the Internet. Maybe we'll never know…"

"Maybe some people, way into the future, will walk through our boat or our old house and wonder the same thing about us," Stefan mused.

As we walked back to the dinghy, Lauren and Stefan forged the trail ahead of me. The moment of contemplation had passed and they were hip checking each other, trying to make their sibling crash into the bushes. When they tired of this, they attempted to kick each other's butts while walking side by side, or step on each other's heels. They pulled ahead of me and I lost sight of them through the dense, island growth. Every once in awhile, I would hear their laughter ring out from somewhere up ahead, and I would smile to myself.

I had come to Royal Island hoping to find buried treasure, cashing in on some long forgotten hoard with my metal detector. And although I had been disappointed not to unearth anything of cash value, that little voice of wisdom in my head was reminding me that feelings of monetary success would pale in comparison to the richness I felt walking down this deserted path, listening to the ruminations and giggles of two teenagers who had moved aboard *Chrysalis* as strangers but had, out of necessity and convenience, become the best of friends.

The day after exploring the hotel, we moved on from Royal Island. We anchored briefly in the small town of Spanish Wells and the lovely New England village of Dunmore Town on Harbour Island before journeying north to anchor in the Abacos. From our Alaskan friend, Nick, we had learned this was a prime fishing, diving, and snorkeling area.

When school was finished for the day, Stefan spent hours swimming around the boat hunting schools of small fish with his Hawaiian sling, until one day his shouts of excitement brought us all to the stern. There on the end of his spear wriggled a tiny fish no bigger than 4 inches long. We all cheered. With the youngest crewmember's success, the bar was set. Mike, Lauren, and Stefan began taking the dinghy to offshore reefs. They practiced their accuracy. Sometimes I went with them to snorkel, but more often than not, I stayed on *Chrysalis* to write. Late in the afternoon, I would hear the hum of the dinghy, and I would meet them on the swim platform to help them tie up. They would be eager to show me the day's catch. Regularly there were five or six different varieties of fish, often more. We would look up the ones that were unfamiliar in our *Florida and Bahama's Fishing Guide*. We began to recognize favorites. The hogfish, reddish in color with the long sloping snout, was a prize. The homely looking grouper and the elusive, quick-moving snappers were plentiful, a challenge to spear, and always delicious.

During all that time, the kids never asked what was for supper. If I had told them "pizza tonight," they would have put up a ruckus.

"How about a big banana split for dinner tonight?" I might say enthusiastically.

"But Mommm! We want grouper."

"Oh all right, fine then," I would acquiesce.

Early in their spear fishing careers, they came home one evening subdued but strangely electric. I asked them what they were hiding. They glanced at each other knowingly.

"Maybe you should sit down for this story," Mike said.

After shooting several small fish a shark had showed up. He swam below them and kept his distance. Seeking to reassure me, Mike offered, "As soon as we saw him, we got out of there."

I was more interested in how Lauren had managed the event. Recently she had told me, "I'm spending so much time in the ocean it's becoming a second home!" Still, a shark was the presentation of her worst fears. I asked her how seeing it had made her feel.

"The three of us were in the water. I had just speared a snapper and gone up to put it in the bucket on *Crabcakes*, then I dove back down to keep fishing. I didn't see the shark at first because I was hot on the trail of another snapper that had disappeared into a crevice on the reef. All of a sudden, I saw

Dad motioning me to follow him. He pointed down and I could see the shark about fifteen feet directly underneath me, swimming in the same direction I was. He was… about six feet long?" she looked over at Mike who nodded in agreement, "Not too big, but big enough."

"Were you afraid?" I asked.

"Right away, my heart started beating so hard and fast. But then I thought, here I am with this shark and I'm okay. If he had wanted to, he could have come up and bit me, like in my dreams, but he didn't. So, I didn't freak out, I just calmly followed Dad and Stefan back to the dinghy and climbed in. It wasn't as bad as I thought it would be. I'm not missing a limb or anything. I think I'm going to be okay with it."

We all congratulated her and told her how proud we were of her. She told me later, "You know, Mom, I think you're right. The imagination is often far worse than the reality."

Sharks became routine, a normal part of their day. Like driving 75 mph down a highway, carrying laundry down the stairs, or eating a plate of Fettuccine Alfredo. Always, once a shark was sighted, they would climb into the dinghy and move on to other fishing grounds. Routine yes, but still respected. Mike took an underwater camera down with him and photographed one. After studying it, we determined most of the sharks they saw were Caribbean Reef Sharks. Generally between four and six feet long, they rarely grow larger than eight or nine feet. In one book we read, "The Caribbean reef shark is not an aggressive species and is not considered dangerous to humans unless provoked. However, it is excitable and may make close passes at divers and may bite in the presence of speared fish."

I instructed the kids, "Whatever you do, don't provoke him!"

"Really, Mom? Wow! Because that's exactly what I was going to next time I saw a shark. Wave a fish in front of his snout and then pull it away saying, 'Sike!' Stefan said.

30

While at anchor, we met a nice couple from PEI, Canada, Will and Pat, who invited us over to what we thought was their 75-foot sailboat. Later, we found out that they captained the yacht for part of each year, keeping the boat in top shape for whenever the owners might decide to spontaneously arrive. In the meantime, the owners gave Will and Pat the freedom to cruise the Caribbean Islands. After touring the yacht, we sat down in the cockpit with drinks and discussed all the things we loved about Canada: Tim Horton's coffee, Saturday night hockey games, great political television satire like *This Hour Has 22 Minutes*, the Rocky Mountains, and Alexander Keiths beer. Then, Captain Will called us over to the galley settee and spread out some charts. He had circled two or three spots in blue pen and had written "blue hole" next to them.

"What's a blue hole?" I asked, taking a sip of rum punch.

"A blue hole is a cave or a cavity at least partially filled with water. Usually they exist below the waterline, but sometimes the surface may be visible on land. They can reach depths of more than 3,000 feet. I dove several on my last trip to the Abacos. The one I was in had stalactites, which meant that at one point the hole would have been above the water line."

"So a blue hole is basically a deep, dark, underwater hole in the earth with God knows what lurking inside it," I said with a mocking smirk.

"That, my dear, is part of the excitement," Captain Will said.

~~~

On January 23, 1960, Donald Walsh and Jacques Piccard climbed into a bathyscape named Trieste and proceeded to sink to the bottom of the world. The Mariana Trench, near the Philippines, was their blue hole. A converse Mt. Everest. At almost seven miles, it is the deepest location on the surface of the earth. God only knew what lurked there as no other humans had ever explored the area. After sinking for five hours, Piccard and Walsh were 35,000 feet down the deepest blue hole on earth.

Not many people have an interest in diving the deepest deep, as indicated by the fact that as of 2008, Mr. Walsh and Mr. Piccard still hold the record. This is partly because it is extremely inconvenient to get there. Whatever craft you are in must be able to sustain 16,000 pounds of pressure per square inch. And it is dark down there. Very dark. At a depth of about 500 feet, light ceases to exist in that world, and you might as well get used to it because, if you are Donald and Jacques, you have got another 34,500 feet to go. This makes it anything but a popular travel destination. People might be lining up to reserve a spot on the next space mission, but I haven't heard of anyone standing in a queue for the Mariana Trench.

Evidently, there is life in the dark places. Teeming, abundant, and lived out fully in what we would assume to be blindness. On their dive, Piccard and Walsh discovered, not five, not 100, but 5,000 new species of sea creatures. Most of these seldom migrate, live their entire lives in the dark and have an incredible longevity, some living for over 100 years. Scientists believe that many of these species have changed little in millions of years.

I am very interested in being an armchair Trieste diver, but have little desire to go to the Mariana Trench myself. I wouldn't mind peering into a blue hole in the Bahamas while sitting safely in the dinghy with my lunch close by. One afternoon, Mike, Lauren, and I spent about three hours trying to locate the one circled on our charts, with no luck. Part of the problem was that the tide had gone out and we kept running aground on the sand. The whole area was shallow. In addition, we had yet to learn how to read the water accurately. One of us would say, "Check out that dark patch over there," and off we would go, only to come upon a shallow area of grass, rocks or reefs. This happened numerous times, always beginning with excitement and ending in disappointment. We returned to *Chrysalis* to recheck our charts and see if we couldn't pull up any more information. On a little used chart we had buried in our chart drawer, we found a more precise location. We decided to give it another go, this time at high tide.

Early the next morning, we loaded our snorkel gear, Hawaiian Slings, bottled water, handheld GPS and VHF, charts, and lunch into *Crabcakes* and set off. The air was chilly as we bounced across the water to resume our search. With an extra three feet of tide water under us, we maneuvered easily between tiny, rocky islands filled with low lying bush. It took about half an hour before we noticed a black patch about a hundred feet off our bow. It was darker looking than the usual coral or grass, and we moved forward to investigate.

Sure enough, cruising in about eight feet of water, the four of us looked over the starboard side to view the gaping, jagged, mouth of a deep cavern roughly forty feet in diameter. We anchored the dinghy close by and began to suit up. Now that I could see the hole, and feeling a little peer pressure, I decided to hop in the water for a closer look. I gingerly let myself into cooler-than-anticipated water. I sucked in a deep breath and my head went under. I adjusted my mask until it was comfortable and I could take in the sea world without it pinching my face or pulling my hair. Mike was out in front, Lauren and Stefan were trailing, and I followed closely behind.

Circling the outside of the hole, we made nasal, hollow-sounding comments to each other through our snorkels.

"It's huge!" Stefan called out through his snorkel.

"Totally spooky," Lauren called back.

Earlier we had read that this particular hole might be as deep as 3,000 feet. It was inky even at the top. I was reminded of the scene in *Star Wars* when the Millennium Falcon makes an emergency getaway down a hole in an asteroid, only to find it inhabited by a large monster who, as expected, attempts to eat them. As I cautiously made my way around the perimeter of the blue hole, the only monster I came across was a plump grouper, close to three feet long, swimming in and out of the entrance, apparently at home and undaunted by our presence. In fact, the grouper was curious, approaching Stefan closely, and turning around only after Stefan, a little anxious, pulled back, making a "shoo-away" hand gesture.

There were other fish swimming placidly in and out of the hole and Mike tried to spear one, but missed. The spear shot horizontally through the water, then the four of us watched it fall to the edge of the hole where it continued to drop about 10 feet down inside of it. Through the murky water, I could just make out the tip of it. Up until that point, the four of us had been observing the hole from our vantage point at the surface. Without consciously thinking it, I had believed that we were safe surveying the deep from a distance. Now one of us, Mike, would have to enter the hole.

With the three of us shouting encouragement at the waterline, Mike took a deep breath, and dove down to retrieve the spear. We watched his progress through our masks. His head and torso entered the shadows and as he reached out to pick up the spear, out crawled the anticipated monster, the largest lobster we had ever seen. He scuttled straight at Mike as if challenging him. Mike snatched the spear and swam swiftly back to the surface and sputtered, "whoo hooo, did ya see that?"

We had seen it and were already dreaming of supper.

"Get him! Get him!" the three of us cheered, pounding the water with our fists.

Mike inhaled and dove down. As if acting as guardian of the hole, the lobster hadn't moved. Afraid of losing the spear again, Mike jabbed at leviathan repeatedly to no avail, his tough shell was impervious. Mike resurfaced to a backseat warrior wife yelling, "Just pick it up!"

Bahamian lobster, or crawfish, are without claws, which makes it seem like they would be easier to nab. But they can be spiny. This one, with its many spindly legs, reminded me of a giant spider. Its antennae alone must have been 2 ½ feet long, and were waving back and forth like radar checking for enemies. The beast was quick and agile.

Mike said, laughing, "You pick it up!"

I conceded.

After repeated attempts at grabbing and stabbing him, we eventually watched dinner slip into the safety of darkness where the crawfish, no doubt, is still grinning and shaking his head. After some further exploration, the crew haphazardly began to make their way back to the dinghy, but I hung back. There was the feeling that I had missed something. An inner prompting that made me turn in the opposite direction from the dinghy and swim several strokes.

Snorkeling had yet to become familiar to me. I was always a little nervous swimming in the ocean, feeling myself a visitor, and uncertain of protocol. I was well aware of the food chain and had a good idea of where I might fit into it and that didn't go a long way toward curbing my uneasiness. Glancing around for predators with sharp teeth that were bigger than myself, I wondered if I could ever feel completely relaxed in an underwater environment.

I longed to feel at home in the ocean. I had a close friend who was a deep water diver. She had told me that she felt more at home in the ocean than she did on land. The silence, the lack of distraction, spoke to her. She would return to land after exploring the underwater world feeling rejuvenated and reminded of the things that were important in her life. "Diving," she had told me, "has become a spiritual discipline."

Close to the blue hole, there was a trench where the water got deeper. Seeking the connection she described, I swam over to it, sucked in a breath and dove down about ten feet to hang, suspended in the water, relishing the feeling of weightlessness. Small, brightly colored fish swam around me. At the surface, the water was a bright turquoise, but at that depth and below me, the color softened. I recognized a couple of orange and white clownfish and a black triggerfish. Nearby, tall grasses waved back and forth as if in a breeze. Brain coral amassed in random heaps.

All was silent. Like the lobster's antennae, my eardrums scanned the surrounding area in an attempt to hear something. Strangely, there was no hum of the refrigerator, music from the other room, or the sound of distant traffic. Nothing. I felt the weight of silence, deep and penetrating. I looked toward the surface and both saw and felt a soundless wave pass by me. The fish and I rose slightly with the wave before being re-placed. I could swim for miles and miles, I thought, and never escape this silence. I resurfaced briefly, took another breath, and hungrily went back for more. For the hearing, total cessation of sound in our culture is a rarity.

There was nothing to say, either, and no one to say it to. The fish cared little for my garbled attempts at speech. I existed, mute and deaf, like the sea whip coral, with limbs stretched upward. The tide or the current, unseen and unheard, began to push me along, back toward the mouth of the blue hole. I let it carry me, closer and closer, until my shrinking lungs begged for mercy. Willing them to hold out a little longer, I pushed myself to swim right over the mouth of the cave, my heart beating like mad. If there is a God, a Divine Being, omnipresent as I have been taught and hope for, then that Person exists in the far reaches of the unknown, like this blue hole or the Mariana Trench, where I can never go. And if God exists, somehow, inside my being, then maybe this is why I feel curious about exploring the I fear I have over the things I cannot control. In my searching, I hope to find God there.

When my lungs finally overruled my brain, I surfaced with some regret, to find that Mike and the kids had already climbed into the dinghy and were waiting for me. I put my mask on my forehead and did the breaststroke across the expanse of separation. With considerable effort, I hauled myself aboard, panting and exhilarated. As we bounced back toward *Chrysalis*, I thought, 'Once you get familiar with the surface of the deep, it's not so bad.' I wondered if I would feel the same 1,500 feet down a blue hole.

I consider the blue hole I witnessed that continues to exist, even now. I wonder if anyone has been there since. The tide continues to push water in and out like a broken record. Fish live and die, live and die, as they have for a thousand years and will continue to for a thousand more, with only God as their witness. Our lobster dinner will grow old and perish and none will be the wiser. Why is it surprising that all this is completely outside of my jurisdiction? One night, I dreamed that I went back to the blue hole alone. Hovering over the chasm, I peered into the darkness, my eyes squinting, straining to see something. Anything.

"I know you're in there," I heard myself whisper.

The only response I got was a large, brown grouper that swam out of the darkness, eyed me for an instant, then turned and gradually disappeared. It wasn't much, but I'd take it.

~Part Four~

Steerageway: sufficient motion through the water to enable a vessel to respond to its rudder.

31

"Mom?! C'mon, you have to wake up!"

Someone was rudely shoving me on the arm. Why must they do that?

"Wha'? Why are you shaking me?" I answered, my speech slurred with sleep.

"C'mon sleepyhead, it's 2 a.m. and it's your turn on watch. Get up already." I comprehended it was Lauren's cheerful voice and Lauren who was shoving me.

"Okay…Okay, I'm on my way." I heaved myself up and sat on the edge of the bed.

I oriented myself. I'm on a boat. *Chrysalis*. Something about a crossing. Right. Our first overnight crossing from West End, Bahamas to St. Augustine, Florida. My turn on watch. Need something…Coffee. Must have coffee.

I padded groggily up to the pilothouse. I passed Lauren, sitting at the helm, without a word. As I walked by, she told me, grinning, that I looked all hunched over and shaggy, like a Neanderthal. By the time I had finished making coffee, I was a little more coherent. I tied my hair back, stood erect, and felt a little less like a cave-woman. Back in the pilothouse, Lauren briefed me on the night's happenings so far. There had been a few tankers. Engine temperature good. Oil good.

"All systems go, Mom. Good night. I'm going to bed."

Then I was alone and wide awake on my first nighttime watch. I was all excited thinking about how I was going to relish the beauty of the moon on the water, but when I looked out the windows, I was greeted by total blackness. There was no moon and no residual city glow. I took the binoculars and scanned back and forth in search of the horizon, but the water and skyline blended together. I had the disconcerting feeling that I was blind, or that I was inadvertently closing my eyes. I opened my eyelids as wide as I could and peered out the pilothouse door. All was dark. Curious, I flipped on our searchlights, which illuminated our bows, but little else. I turned them back off. I checked the radar. It revealed a little red ball, us, floating across a white expanse of nothingness. It was an odd feeling to be cruising at 10 knots through such complete darkness.

After about an hour, I began to get used to the feeling. Sitting in the helm chair drinking my coffee, I thought that our decision to head up the eastern seaboard had been a good one. In the Bahamas, Mike and I discussed the second part of number six on our old dream list, the larger dream of crossing the Atlantic. I agreed with Mike that it would be beneficial to gain some additional offshore experience before attempting the task. We could refine our weather watching abilities and develop a more concrete routine of caring for our systems. Plus, I had told Mike, heading north for a few months would allow us to get some work done on *Chrysalis*. The office and staterooms still had no wall covering. Shelves needed to be built and installed in several cupboards, and many of our storage cubbies needed to be reorganized so that things didn't fly around underway. Our swim platform hatches were leaking. We had found replacement hatches online. We would need to cut out the existing 2x3 foot hatches and epoxy in the new ones. The air conditioners and venting system had yet to be installed. I was planning to sew some blinds for the pilothouse.

Crossing the Atlantic to spend a year in the Mediterranean involved an emotional and relational commitment as well. As the kids pushed further into the teenage years, we wondered if they would be able to survive such an extended journey, just the four of us on *Chrysalis*. While it was true that we had adapted to life on board, meshing our lives together, there were some days it was still a struggle for Lauren. She held on to the idea that she was missing out on a life lived in a more conventional manner. And even though Mike had no problem hurtling himself over a cliff, it was another thing entirely to take your family across an ocean to a completely different part of the world. At the time, the only one who seemed up for anything was Stefan, who still loved fishing, video games, and skateboarding. As he was nearing thirteen, I wondered how long this easy going attitude would continue. Mike and I had decided to revisit the Atlantic crossing decision when we were in Boston.

The crew was asleep and, except for the hum of the motors, it was quiet. Every hour, I logged down our longitude, latitude, oil and temperature of the engines, and fuel left in the day tanks. I went down into the engine rooms to sniff and listen for anything unusual. I walked around the inside of the boat and looked out over the stern encountering the same inky blackness. I got myself a second cup of coffee and made some microwave popcorn.

Two hours later, the moon finally appeared on the horizon, a great red orange ball that lit up my world like a giant light bulb. With its help, I could distinguish the horizon and the bows. I could see what lay ahead. Up until that point, I hadn't given the moon much thought outside of its beauty. I was glad, then, for its utilitarian purpose.

Tied up at a berth in St. Augustine, we watched the weather along the Eastern Seaboard. We were charting a course for Norfolk, self-proclaimed city for lovers. There was a push to get north for hurricane season, officially beginning in June, as our boat insurance did not cover us south of Norfolk during this time. We considered the crossing carefully as it would be our first extended offshore journey, two nights and three days. I was getting used to the routine of preparing to go offshore. During the encounter with rough seas in the Gulf Stream, drawers opened and spilled all over the floor and a treasured bowl from Africa was hurtled through the air and smashed. I learned my lesson. I made my way through *Chrysalis* and took books, magazines, playing cards, dishes, and the paraphernalia of life that sprouts up on counters and tabletops and I stowed them or tied them down. I locked all of our drawers and cupboards. When a weather window opened up, we were ready. It wasn't a perfect window, but we decided to take it anyway. On a lovely sunny but disconcertingly breezy afternoon, we made our way through the cut and were immediately greeted by six-to-eight foot waves, coming in short succession, hitting us on the beam.

Although catamarans are a fairly new concept in the leisure yachting world, at least in the west, they are hardly a recent discovery. There is evidence of their use as early as the 5th Century AD in Tamil Nadu, India. Utilizing their speed and agility, the Tamil Chola Dynasty was able to invade Burma, Indonesia, and Malaysia, likely bringing the design further to Polynesia. British sailor and buccaneer William Dampier was the first Westerner to mention them in his English journals back in the 1690's as he traveled through India. On the coast of Coromandel he wrote in 1697, "They call them Catamarans. These are but one Log, or two, sometimes of a sort of light wood … so small, that they carry but one Man, whose legs and breech are always in the Water." Some historians now believe that the Polynesians made use of the catamaran's stable design, traveling all the way to South America almost 100 years before the Europeans.

Chrysalis has a curved, shaped underplatform. The double curves are designed to alleviate some of the pounding catamarans can experience in larger seas. So far, we had experienced very little pounding and assumed our curved underplatform to be part of the reason. The living space aboard is low on the water as opposed to monohulls of similar size whose decks are stacked vertically making for uncomfortable conditions in relatively small beam seas, or so we have been told. Ships of this nature, although they can be larger than ours, are typically called coastal cruisers. They may have the fuel capacity, but they are not meant for longer offshore passagemaking.

We may not experience the sideways rolling motion many monohulls experience, but we were not immune to the elements. Six to eight foot seas on the beam results in a sort of jerky up-and-down motion. Side to side. Not long into the crossing to Norfolk, we found secure places to sit and held on in stoic silence. After a couple hours, I saw both Lauren and Stefan hanging over the rails. It was not long before I followed.

When I think of the famous naturalist Charles Darwin, I automatically place him in the Galapagos cataloguing species, and forget that there was a great journey involved in simply getting to the islands 600 miles west off the coast of Ecuador. From 1831 to 1836, Darwin lived aboard HMS *Beagle,* a ten gun brig-sloop, whose crew was to chart the coast of South America and explore the Galapagos Islands. Darwin did not find living aboard much to his liking. He suffered a great deal from seasickness during his voyage, and upon returning to land wrote, "If a person suffers much from sea sickness, let him weigh it heavily in the balance, I speak from experience; it is no trifling evil…"

The second night into the crossing, I discovered that I agreed with Darwin. There not much in life worse than seasickness. It is no trifling evil. It is similar in violence to the 24 hour stomach flu, but at least with the flu you are likely to be in a comfortable land-based bed that is not eternally moving up and down. Your husband or partner can take the kids to a movie and you can call your mom or your best friend who will drop off homemade chicken soup and place a cool washcloth on your forehead. With both kids down and Mike driving solo, it was everyone for themselves. I reminded the kids to drink water.

"Dehydration," I called out to them from my prone position on the pilothouse settee, "is your worst enemy!"

They grumbled something incoherent, and made no attempts to comply. Staggering, I brought them each some bottled water and gave them and myself an herbal seasickness remedy, an oil applied behind the ears, which did nothing but make us smell like a combination of lavender and Echinacea. We finally resorted to Dramamine, which promptly knocked us out.

Around 4 a.m., I was blessedly asleep in my berth when Mike gently shook me awake.   Miraculously, he had been unaffected by our seafaring malaise. To allow us time to rest, he had been on watch since 6 p.m. the night before and needed a break. Was I okay to watch for a couple hours? I was not, but I stumbled shakily up the stairs and lay down on the watch berth in the pilothouse. Mike brought me a large, stainless mixing bowl and, without another word, went to bed.

I watched the radar through weary eyes. I was keeping track of a couple of tankers in close proximity, about 2 miles away, and I dozed off a couple of times as we were approaching Cape Henry. Into my mind came the numerous voices of fellow cruisers telling me that tankers were notorious for not having someone on watch. They put the ship on autopilot and played poker. What did it matter to them if they ran over anything?

I was concerned about this. Afraid I might fall into a deep sleep and a tanker would mow us down. I set up an alarm clock to go off every fifteen minutes so I could make sure that if I drifted off it wouldn't be for very long. In between the buzzes and dozing, I threw up again and again. I decided I didn't care if a tanker ran into us. Bring it on. Blowing up or drowning would be preferable to the incessant rocking. In moments of lucidity, my lack of care startled me. I forced open my eyes with my fingers, slapped my cheeks, and attempted to sip ginger ale through a straw.

Mercifully, the wind died down around 6 a.m. Almost immediately, the waves began to settle and I felt relief. I determined that once we got to Norfolk, I would look into a more potent, non-drowsy, seasickness remedy. I eventually settled on the Transderm Scop, a patch worn behind the ear, and both myself and the kids rarely wrestled with seasickness after that.

32

While docked in downtown Norfolk, Mike and I renewed our vows for about the hundredth time. There had been too many bowls of rocky road ice cream and barbeque chips, and not enough cardiovascular effort on our parts. We both agreed that we weren't getting any younger and that if we weren't careful, our organs would end up on display during a segment of Oprah, with some charismatic physician leaning over them with a probe saying, "And this is a particularly fatty heart…"

"Okay, so we will begin tomorrow morning," I said reaching out to seal the deal with a handshake.

Mike shook my hand, saying, "Tomorrow it is…in the meantime, could you pass me that donut?"

In the early morning hours, I would feel Mike leave our bed, hear him quietly pull on shorts and a t-shirt, and a few minutes later, hear the muffled sounds of him climbing out of the cockpit and onto the dock to jog. I would stare guiltily at the red digits on my alarm clock and think, "Crap." After listening to him patter away for a few mornings, I followed him groggily out the door. A few minutes of sunshine and fresh air caused me to wonder, yet again, why it was that doing what I know is best for me is often the hardest thing.

Norfolk is a navy town, home to the world's largest naval base. During the first few days we were there, several large battleships passed by less than a few hundred feet off our stern. We stood, gawking, in the cockpit. Later we would look up the ship's name and number on the Internet to find out what kind of ship it was and where it had been. Stefan would often wave up at one of the armed military men lining the gunnels, but didn't arouse much notice. Lauren, sunbathing in her bikini on the flybridge, got a far different response with considerably less effort.

Mike and I settled on a routine jogging trek that took us along the downtown Norfolk seawall, past the numerous active naval ships docked on the opposite side of James River in Portsmouth, past Nauticus, the Maritime Museum, and all the way around the corner where the Iowa -class Battleship USS Wisconsin, now part of the Museum, impressively took up the view for almost a whole city block as I panted beside it.

We spent longer than we anticipated in Norfolk, almost two months. Part of the reason for this was that we were bombarded with more than the usual amount of bad weather. This led to a greater conviviality among the numerous live-aboards and transients in the marina who gathered in small groups on the docks to discuss the wind. There is nothing that boaters like more than talking about the weather, past, present, or future. In importance, it ranks up there with elections and taxes. This is because weather plays such a large role in a nomadic water-based lifestyle. It determines whether you stay or go and what kind of journey you have while at sea. It can mess with your plans for weeks on end or play right into them. The weather cares little for your sleep patterns. On land, I used to savor the sound of a storm at night. On the water, even tied up at a marina, a storm in the middle of the night generally means that you will be required to leave your cozy berth and go out in the rain and wind to readjust a line or a fender in order stop your boat from ramming into the dock. While doing so, you will likely see the dark form of your neighbor doing the same thing, and you can share an early morning casual salute before heading back to bed.

Live-aboards are a unique slice of the culture. They are often anti-establishment, expats living in their own country. Most are deep-thinking folks who have considered long and hard their choices in life, which is to say that over half are retired and have the wisdom and financial means to be choosy. The smaller segment consists of mid-life past professionals who have done the 9 to 5 thing and decided that it isn't for them. Most of these vacillate between jobs and living aboard depending on the state of their wallet. They proudly wear t-shirts that say things like, "A bad day at sea is better than a great day at the office," which, in my opinion, is debatable. The younger boating crowd, the ones running around in logo button-down shirts carrying groceries bags, work as crew on larger yachts, the kind that have placards that read, "Private. No boarding." Although they haven't done the 9 to 5 desk job yet, they've seen it in action and prefer the gypsy nautical life. They are all saving up for their own sailboat. Once in a great while, we ran into a live aboard family with kids younger than ours, homeschooling as we were, but these were a rarity.

At impromptu pot-lucks on the dock, meaningless chit chat among live-aboards is nominal. Because time to connect with others is brief, live-aboards are an open bunch and often deep friendships are made on the fly. They are most interested in your story. How did you come to be living an alternate lifestyle? What led you to be here, living on a boat, in the middle of the eastern seaboard? Was it an actual or metaphorical birth or a death? A divorce? Loss of a job? Did you smack your head with a 2 X 4? Did you look too long at a sunset? Where have you been and where are you going? What kind of fish did you catch, and if you weren't so lucky, then there is a great little place I know of, corner of Main and something or other, that serves the very best Cajun catfish you'll ever taste. Ask for Joe and tell him Mel sent you.

Jogging along the dock one day in Norfolk, Mike and I struck up a conversation with a salty old sailing captain from Maine who, when he heard we were thinking about crossing the Atlantic, told us in no uncertain terms that he would never attempt a crossing again.

"About ten years ago, I was delivering a lovely 70 foot sailboat from St. Pierre and Miquelon, just off the coast of Newfoundland Canada, to England, and suffered through the worst seas of my life. Mind you, I have been sailing my whole life, so this was no small storm. Seas were well over 25 feet and the wind didn't stop wailing for five days! Five days I tell you! I thought we were goners. It was the most miserable, terrifying five days of my life! I swore right then and there that I would never make another extended offshore crossing again, and I never have. Never will."

"Thanks so much for that," Mike said quietly, rather sarcastically I thought, and before I could ask any further questions, he grabbed my elbow and propelled me along the dock and away from any more tales of woe and despair. Back on board *Chrysalis*, I had just been saying, "See! There is a seasoned captain who won't ever cross an ocean again…" when we heard a knock on the hull. We emerged to find a dark-haired, very tan guy around fifty in a red polo shirt, tan shorts, and brown top-siders, who introduced himself in a slight French accent as Jean from Montreal. He had seen our Canadian flag and had been meaning to come and chat with us. He was sailing solo at the moment, heading south to Florida to deliver the forty-foot sailboat he was on to a friend there. He was embarrassed to say that he had overhead our conversation with the captain from Maine, and he wondered if we might like to come over for drinks to talk about the Mediterranean. He had sailed there for many years. He might have a few charts we would be interested in. Since it was already nearing happy hour, I grabbed a bottle of wine, and we went over directly.

Right away I like Jean. He was full of nautical knowledge and experience without being egotistical or grandiose. Like the captain from Maine, he had lived on boats his whole life. While setting out a plate of cheese, crackers, and green olives, he mentioned casually that he had crossed the Atlantic five times.

He looked directly at me as he said this, continuing, "I couldn't help but notice the concern in your eyes, Kim, when you were listening to that captain tell the story of his, shall we say, bad time crossing the Atlantic. I wanted to talk with you. To tell you that not everyone has this kind of bad experience. In crossing five times, I only experienced rough seas once, nothing life threatening, only annoying. If you are smart and plan carefully the ocean is a wonderful teacher."

He went on to ask what our plans were once we got to the Mediterranean, and since neither Mike or I had really thought that far ahead, he went on to describe with some passion his travels as the captain of a large sailing yacht there. Were we going to Spain? We must stay in Spain for the tapas, the flamenco, and the paella. Go to Barcelona and you will never want to leave, he told us. The whole city is a work of art. And France? Well, France was obviously his favorite. It oozed wine and cheese and history. If we docked in Marseilles we could take the train into Paris. Who didn't want to go to Paris? And once we got to Italy, he said, we should visit the mainland, Rome, Naples, of course, but even more than that, we should go to Sicily and Sardinia. They will blow you away with their beauty! Everyone is so friendly. They will fill you up with gnocchi and cannoli. In Sicily, you can walk Roman and Greek ruins and no other tourists will be around. Did we think we would get further than that? Maybe to Greece? We didn't know. The food isn't the greatest is Greece, Jean said, but it was a spiritual place. Rugged and full of history, of course. The wind always blows there, so set your anchor carefully. This, I told Jean with a sideways glance at Mike, we could do.

Jean said, shaking his head back and forth, "Oh! To think you are doing this with your children. It is so good! They will learn so much."

When the wine ran out, and I realized the hour was late and that back on board *Chrysalis* Lauren and Stefan would be wondering about supper, I mentioned to Mike that we should be going. We asked Jean to supper, but he said he was meeting a friend in town. We should get together again before we leave Norfolk, Mike said. Just before we climbed onto the dock, Jean kissed both my cheeks, then looked directly into my eyes and said, "There will always be someone around with a grand tale of disaster no matter what life you are living. Try not to listen to them. Cross the ocean! You can do it! If you are prepared and careful you should be fine. On the other side, there is another world just waiting for you to discover!"

I hugged and thanked him. His words meant more to me than I could say at the moment. Back on *Chrysalis*, as Mike and I began to make supper I said, "I haven't been able to get excited about cruising the Mediterranean because I have only been able to focus on the crossing and not the opportunity beyond it. For the first time, someone whose nautical knowledge and experience I respect has opened my eyes to the bigger picture. His stories were a great encouragement to me. I have a clearer idea of the potential, now. It might, just might, be enough to motivate me to push through and get to the other side. Can you believe he has crossed five times?"

"Who knows, maybe you will cross five times," Mike said, chuckling.

"I'm pretty sure I'll be lucky to make it once," I told him.

33

From Norfolk we went up the Chesapeake and entered the quiet, scenic waters of "the Nation's River," the Potomac. With the passage of each nautical mile, I had the feeling that I was, like a psychiatrist, delving deeper and deeper into the psyche of a nation. As with any exploration, mental or physical, there were issues to contend with. For the duration of our journey we encountered groups of bobbing crab pots, small colored buoys haphazardly scattered everywhere. We kept a keen lookout to avoid their lines becoming entangled in our props. Nearing Washington, D.C., the water turned murky brown and filled with trash and debris. As we were docking in the Washington Channel close to the Francis Case Memorial Bridge, a dead, bloated rat floated by.

Off and on for several months Lauren had writhed and moaned about living on a boat. In a unanimous decision, we were several months over our one-year live aboard goal. She vacillated. Some days she relished the travel, but other days I would find her sitting in the cockpit with a look I translated to be one of a small animal caught in a trap. Even though crossing the ocean and spending time in the Mediterranean was enticing to her, there were some days, she told us, when it was torture making her live on a boat. She should report us to child services. We did not tell her it would pass or make light of it. We reminded her that whether by land or by sea, crappy things were bound to happen in life. How would she survive? Listen, I told her. That's all you have to do right now. Open your eyes and ears. There were good things happening. Focus on them. Let go of the things you can't control. Mike and I kept things as normal as we could. We laughed, played, worked, prayed. We let her win a few games of MarioKart. We reminded each other to practice what we preached: stop, look, and listen. Be still. And if your soul can't be still and know, then at least be still and make peace with the not knowing. This, I told her, was something I was still learning.

In recent months, we had begun to develop an appreciation for the extensive travel living on a boat was affording. The cities and places we had spent over a month in, Miami, the Bahamas, Norfolk, and now Washington, were opening our eyes to a bigger piece of North American history, yes, but it was more than that. Because we were continually arriving somewhere we were unfamiliar with, there was this feeling of expectancy, or curiosity, that had been developing in all of us. A habitual feeling of, 'I wonder what this place will reveal during our stay?" Our environment was constantly changing. Continually fresh. Our senses were on perpetual full alert.

I believe it was this constant outward focus that caused Lauren to mellow while in Washington. Inquisitiveness overcame her desire to hold on to an alternate ideal of the land life she might be missing out on. I got the feeling she had reluctantly unzipped her self-imposed mental strait jacket and was finally taking a peek at the world outside herself. I could feel things beginning to shift in her soul. 'Pay attention,' I told myself, 'and one of these days you will watch her wake up.'

In the dim light of the National Archives Building, the Rotunda for the Charters of Freedom was not yet packed with tourists. We had arrived early in the day and were coexisting with other sojourners in hushed reverence, waiting for our turn to see the Bill of Rights, Constitution, and the Declaration of Independence.

While waiting I looked at two paintings flanking the Declaration of Independence. My guidebook told me they had been done by Barry Faulkner in 1936. One depicted the signing of the Declaration and one the Constitution. On the left, gallant, noble men, clad in stately garb, some in powdered wigs, faced a young-looking Thomas Jefferson who held the newly penned Declaration in his right hand. They wore determined, if not smug, looks on their faces. Across from it, the picture of the Constitution centered around a tall and regal George Washington in a flowing, pale cape. It featured the men the United States calls their Founding Fathers. Reading through the list of names, there were many I hadn't heard of before. In both pictures the day was bright, the trees in the background were perfectly proportioned. Not one of the men had any spots on their clothing and their wigs were all in place. An unlikely portrayal, I thought.

I looked around the room at my fellow pilgrims whose names I would never know but whose lives would intersect with my own for just these brief moments in time. In contrast to the perfectly portrayed gentlemen in the oil paintings on the wall, we seemed a motley assembly. A few older types wore pastel shorts and sandals with calf high tube socks. A young couple, looking exhausted, tried to rein in their three young, noisy, children, one of whom had just narrowly escaped knocking over a large American flag. The father had grabbed it at the last second and then looking embarrassed, glanced around the room to see if anyone had noticed. He caught my eye and I smiled at him. He shook his head. Two teenagers were kissing on the threshold and the security guard told them in animated disgust to move on. A scholarly, annoyed-looking man, who despite the heat was wearing slacks and a tweed sport coat, was shushing the couple with the kids. Right about then, Mike told me I had green stuff in between my two front teeth. We weren't a perfect bunch, I thought. But we were there. And we were interested.

When it was our turn, we stood next to the Declaration of Independence. You aren't supposed to put your hands up to the glass, but we forgot about that. We instinctively stretched them out as if hoping to connect with the moment or maybe the emotions of the people who were present at the birth and design of a nation. Make some sort of sense as to what it meant to us individually and as a community. A few moments later, a woman in a uniform loudly reminded us not to touch the glass. We pulled our hands away and leaned closer.

I turned my head to look at Lauren. It was fortunate, I thought, that she happened to be studying the American Revolution in her online American History class. She was scrutinizing the Declaration, attempting to read the faded script. Her brows were furrowed. Her lips were moving but no sound was coming out. Then she straightened upright. She looked up at the pictures by Barry Faulkner on the wall. She went into the middle of the room and turned a full three hundred and sixty degrees, before looking back at us. She was blinking hard as if recognizing where she was for the first time.

In a voice sounding louder than it should in such a place, she said, "So all this actually happened? I mean you read about it books, but it is so hard to make the connection. Here is the actual Declaration of Independence! The very one! Look," she walked back to where we were standing, "there is Benjamin Franklin's signature and John Adams, Samuel Adams, and Thomas Jefferson. They were actual people, you know! Who the heck are the rest of these men? And look, there is John Hancock's signature. Is this why when you sign an important document they ask you to 'sign your John Hancock'? I bet it is. That saying must come right from this document…and look up here," she pointed to a plaque on the wall before continuing to talk in a fast and excited voice, "here are all the grievances the colonists had against King George. There were so many of them. No wonder they revolted. And now I remember learning that there were many who disagreed with the revolution and they were called Loyalists and they made their way up to Canada, where we are from. Just think, since this time, we have all been affected by the decisions made by these people during the American Revolution. And omigosh!" she turned to look at us with wide eyes, "That means we're all connected!"

She stopped her monologue and found the three of us staring at her with dumbfounded expressions.

"What?" she said shrugging her shoulders, nonchalantly. "Don't you see? It all makes sense to me now."

As a mother, I live my days like a hunter dressed in camouflage and wait all afternoon in the bush for a white furry tail in the form of a connection. I stalk that flash of insight between my kids and the world around them, when their eyes widen, they grab my arm, and say, "So that's how it is?" The moment can present itself when you least expect it, so it is best stay alert. If I get distracted, if I become chatty or busy, I will miss it. Sometimes, you can predict the moment is coming. You hear the sound of rustling leaves and prepare yourself. But most of the time, it will take you by surprise, at the end of the day when you have all but given up and have decided to eat your chicken sandwich. Then, it will crawl out of the trees and you will gape in surprise. Cautiously, you put down your sandwich, and just as you reach for your camera, the prize will nimbly disappear back into the bush. No one back home will believe you saw it.

This was one of the reasons I had decided to live on a boat. It was, I was learning, one of the rewards of a simpler lifestyle and large chunks of time spent in each other's company. I had grown to have the mental and emotional capacity to be present at those miraculous moments of complexity in my kids, when the universe shifted into focus. I noticed the furrow of a brow, felt the metaphysical tremor of a brain's rapid computation; links being formed. I reeled when I noticed eyes that widened. Who needed flashy healings supposedly instigated by a preacher in a three thousand dollar suit or random last minute snatches from death, when you could stand witness to the evolution of life? Was this not worthy of thousands of people standing in a stadium with their arms outstretched? If I checked, would there be a star shining in the east? A heavenly host singing "Hallelujah"? Surely, the very ground I walked upon was holy. Should I remove my sandals? Avert my eyes in case the glory blinded me?

I walked out of the National Archives Building feeling inundated with miracles. "Enough, already," I told God. "There is too much glory. I am simply up to my eyeballs in miracles." Later, I would catalog those brief seconds of connection in my journal: "new species observed today."

For the next week, Lauren appeared hungry. This happens sometimes after a prolonged stay in a desert wasteland.

"C'mon you guys. I want to hit the Monument, the White House, and the Lincoln Memorial today, so let's get moving," she said while tying her shoes one hot and humid morning.

I told her to pace herself. It was a well known fact that starving people who had been rescued needed to eat carefully or they could OD on food and get sick. I said this mainly because she was wearing the rest of us out. She didn't seem to care. After a full day at the Smithsonian, she saw the Library of Congress, and had to go in RIGHT NOW. When we went to the Vietnam War Memorial, she ran her hand slowly along the engraved list of names and afterwards, was quiet for a very long time.

Nearing the end of our time in Washington, D.C. she said, "You know what, Mom? Something has happened to me here in Washington. It is like I connected a bunch of dots in one of those coloring book pages I used to do when I was a kid. It is hard for me to explain. When I think about history and how big the world is, my life seems so small in comparison. And yet, there is a place for me, here. Now. I can enter in. The strange thing is that I am not afraid to be alone anymore. I mean, I still want to hang out with my friends sometimes, but lately I find that I am pretty good company, too. It's like I am finally comfortable with my place in the universe. And I am learning to be comfortable with myself too."

I envied her this knowledge of herself at sixteen years of age.

34

By the time we got to Boston, I was in deep. American history and the Revolution percolated in my brain. I studied it during the day and dreamed about it at night. I walked it out along the Freedom Trail in the afternoon as I made my way to the small mini mart to pick up bread. The lines between now and the past blended together. I was so immersed that while Lauren and I walked through Fanueil Hall, it didn't surprise me to notice a short, stocky, balding, older guy obviously dressed for a part in some play as Benjamin Franklin. He was walking hurriedly towards us as if late to sign the Declaration of Independence. As he passed, I nodded to him as if I had done it every day of my life.

"Mr. Franklin," I said casually, "Trust you are well today?"

"I am well, Ladies, well. I wish you a pleasant morrow," he responded in character while polishing his spectacles. He kept right on walking. I thought nothing of it.

We loved Boston. We loved how they said, "how-wa-ya?" and "gidadaheah." We ate clam chowder from a vender in Quincy Hall even though it was the end of August and 90 degrees in the shade.

Mike said, "This is the best clam chowder I've ever had."

"Gidadaheah!" I said smiling and shoving his arm.

This resulted in him jovially hip checking me and my clam chowder sloshed over onto my pants.

We had spent the past month docked in Charlestown, across the Charles River from downtown Boston. There was another family that lived aboard tied up in a powerboat along the same dock. Their four children were similar in age to our own. Lauren and Stefan had been enjoying the camaraderie. One hot evening, Mike and I escaped the antics of four teenagers playing Nintendo, by heading out into the cockpit with cold drinks. The sun had just set and we were enjoying the view of the downtown Boston cityscape. Just about the time I started to unwind, Mike left and returned with the Atlas. He opened it up to the two pages showing the Atlantic Ocean and pointed.

"So what do you think about that?" he asked me.

I took the Atlas and looked at the six inch circle encompassing North and South America, Europe, and Africa with the tiny specks of Bermuda and the Azores splitting the body of water into chunks. Even after living on a boat for over a year, a small pit of fear formed in my brain and settled in my gut.

"We could do it, Kim," he continued softly. "We could cross the Atlantic. *Chrysalis* has proven herself. She is seaworthy. We have been able to gain experience traveling up the eastern seaboard. Since Washington, Lauren has been more content, and Stefan just wants to say he crossed an ocean. They could continue on in their studies, sending their work into the online high school. We could keep living life as we are, writing and working from home. As long as we can keep earning a living, we could spend a year in the Mediterranean. From here in Boston, we could make the journey back down to Florida, and from there, we could prepare *Chrysalis* and wait for a weather window to Bermuda."

He paused and looked at me to make sure I was still conscious. Noticing I was still coherent, he kept on, "Look, we made the two night, three day crossing straight through from St. Augustine, Florida to Norfolk, Virginia, so we have some extended offshore experience. We can run the same distance as we head south to Florida, giving us more experience. From Florida, if we travel at 9 knots, we can make the trip to Bermuda in four nights, five days. Weather prediction, as you know, is pretty accurate for that time window. From Bermuda, if we make 9 or 10 knots, it should take us 8 nights, nine days to make the trek from Bermuda to the Azores. After that, just another 4 night crossing to Gibraltar and we're there."

It was true that going up and down the coast had further prepared us both in experience and confidence. Even so, for a woman with control issues, I was interested in guarantees or at least the illusion of probabilities. On land, you might see a suspicious, shadowy figure cross your neighbor's lawn around midnight and become concerned. You can pick up the phone and call the police. There is a high probability that a squad car will arrive ten minutes later and two officers will emerge from the car to investigate. If your house catches fire on land, someone in a red truck with flashing lights will come to your aid. If you fall and can't get up, or if someone you love gets in an accident, there is a high probability that several uniformed and well prepared individuals will arrive on the scene in a white van with flashing lights to give you life support. They will take you or your loved one to a tall building and put you into a soft, comfortable bed. Hook you up to drugs of varying sorts that will alleviate your pain and bring you your meals in bed, which will make the whole experience similar to a very expensive vacation.

I knew that many people had successfully crossed the ocean in their own boat. Many had died trying. Being hundreds of miles offshore did entail placing yourself at risk. If your boat catches fire in such a location, you had better be prepared to deal with the situation because there is a zero percent probability that anyone is going to show up with a big hose and an oxygen mask. If you have engine trouble, it will do you little good to call a tow truck for roadside assistance. Should one of the crew develop a fever or happen to break a leg, there are no hospitals with warmed up blankets. If you happen to get caught in a serious storm, and find that your boat is sinking, you can call someone. By all means try to hail anyone. If you are exceptionally lucky, you might reach a tanker 50 miles away who is sympathetic to your plight, but in a storm, he'll be making around 10 knots or less and won't be able to reach you for another five hours. A lot of things can happen in five hours.

In the middle of the ocean you are well outside the bounds of conventionality, and this is where I began to understand some of the benefits of conventional culture. You stand together. You help each other out. There is protection, shelter, reinforcement. In between Bermuda and the Azores, you are alone, with no broader support system. Life as you know it is on the line, and you and your crew are the only ones who can deal with problems as they arise.

To complicate matters further, weather prediction nine days out is a gamble and this really stuck in my craw. The longer you expose yourself to the elements, say more than three days offshore, the more unpredictable the weather can become. The low pressure system you thought would pose little worry suddenly gains momentum and strength and approaches faster than you had anticipated. When you are cruising close to shore, you can head toward land and safety. When you are 800 miles from the nearest land there is nowhere to run. You can try to alter your course, but on such a long journey, we would carry only such reserve fuel as could be used for an emergency. If we chose to alter course and then had a fuel leak, we could find ourselves out of fuel and in a bit of a pickle.

I told Mike, "I do like living on a boat, but crossing the Atlantic in a homemade powerboat is a different sort of animal. If anything ever happened to one of the kids, I am not sure I could forgive myself. It would be as if we were intentionally placing them in harm's way." Even as I said this, I reminded myself that just by giving them birth I had placed them in harm's way.

He came and knelt by my chair and took my hands into his. "But what if the crossing was a success? Think of the story, we would be knitting into our lives; the value of pushing through our fears and accomplishing a difficult task. Think of the things it would build in our future. I feel like we are so close to accomplishing this goal. We've already done the hardest part: built the boat and learned how to live aboard. To turn back now seems unthinkable to me."

He paused here and looked away before saying softly, "If you don't think you can do it, I would understand. We certainly have had enough adventure in our lives lately. How would you feel if the kids and I took *Chrysalis* over without you? You could fly across and meet us in Gibraltar. There would be nothing wrong with this. I would think nothing less of you. I would understand completely! We all have our limits. But, Kim, this has always been our dream, yours and mine, and it won't be the same if you aren't there. I would love to be able to accomplish this together. I believe in you. I believe you have the capacity to accomplish this. How about we just move in that direction, and see what happens? We can always change our minds."

I told him I would think about it.

Evidently, the giant woman Fear was still around, she had just been sleeping. Now she woke up sputtering, "What? What did I miss? Did someone mention crossing the Atlantic? You can't be serious. Oh that's rich!" She made up for lost time. She amassed forces on the battleground and switched tactics from mental to physical.

Obviously, I still had some issues regarding crossing the ocean, because after returning to Florida, I woke up one night with pains in my chest. I had fallen asleep and dreamed that *Chrysalis* was caught in a huge whirlpool, spinning out of control, and was about to sink. It happened again a few nights later when I was just beginning to drift off to sleep. When it happened a third time, I went to a doctor.

I told him it felt like I was having a heart attack. I could feel my heart fluttering in my chest and it was hard to breathe. After taking a detailed history and considering my current lifestyle, he asked,

"Are you concerned about anything in your life? Stressed out for any reason?"

I explained the little bit about crossing an ocean.

He looked at me speculatively above his black framed glasses.

"Well there you have it," he said closing the beige manila folder with my patient history. "I believe you are having panic attacks. I can give you a sedative, but what you really need to do is talk to someone about this. Do you have a counselor or psychiatrist you could talk to?"

I told him I didn't but could probably find someone.

"Good. Find someone to talk to. If you are still having the attacks, come back to me and I can prescribe a sedative. Maybe run some further tests."

When I got home, I remembered my friend Dave who specializes in sports psychology. A couple years previous he had told me that one of the main things athletes struggle with is fear in some form. Since Dave was a member and coach of Canada's National Free-Style Ski Team and holds two Guinness World Records for duration skiing, I figured he might be able to help me out.

I called him up and told him we were thinking about crossing the ocean and I was pretty sure I was having panic attacks and was wondering if he could help me. He asked me to describe them.

"Shortly after I have fallen asleep, I wake up with a gasp, my gut is totally constricted and my heart is pounding. I feel like I am hyperventilating."

"Sounds about right," he said. "Okay. Normally I don't like working with someone over the phone, but since I'm familiar with you guys and your situation, if you have a few minutes, I'd like to work through something with you. So get yourself comfortable and alone. No one else should be in the room. You ready?

I went to my stateroom, shut the door, and sat cross legged on the bed.

"Ready."

"Okay," Dave began, speaking softly and slowly, pausing in between sentences, "I want you to close your eyes. Now, I'd like you to imagine that you are in a movie theater. It is one of those lovely old theaters with carved moldings and ornate balconies, and there are those big, heavy, velvet, red draperies with gold trim, hanging in front of the screen at the front. The chairs are padded and covered in red velvet and very comfortable. I want you to sit in one of them. It is quiet. You are the only one in the theater. Can you picture that?"

"Yes," I said, my eyes closed.

"The drapes are slowly parting now and a movie begins to play. It is a movie of you and the rest of the family in your boat. You are crossing the ocean. There is no land for miles. Can you see it?

"Yes."

I want you to describe the scene for me as you see it played out in your worst fears. Make sure you describe yourself in the scene and how you are responding."

"Okay. We are in between Bermuda and the Azores. Miles from help. I notice dark storm clouds forming on the horizon. I am worried. Eventually they catch up with us. The wind is howling and the waves get big. Maybe twenty-five feet. They come at us from all directions. We are tossed around inside. Things fall over. Mike bashes his head. He is bleeding. Water is pounding against the windows. One of the pilothouse windows breaks and water comes crashing in. The kids are crying and afraid. Mike is trying to fix things. I am….I am frozen with the fear that we are going to sink and die. I can't move. I can hardly breathe."

I paused and heard Dave's soft voice, "Are you feeling anything other than fear?"

"Mostly fear, but….also hopelessness. Helplessness. And regret that we ever did this in the first place."

"Good. Okay, Kim, I want you to stop now. The movie has ended and the drapes are closing again. The lights have come back on, but I want you to stay in the theater. Keep sitting in your seat. Take a couple of deep breaths. Feeling okay?"

"Yes."

"Now the curtains are opening again, the lights are dimming, and the same movie begins to play. I want you to describe the same scene only this time I want you to describe your reaction if you were brave. What things would you say and do as the courageous you?"

"All right. I see the same god awful storm with large waves and lightening. The brave me is standing by the helm watching it happen. Water is pouring in. The kids are crying and afraid."

I stopped here and groped to figure out what was going on inside of me. Trying to own the concept of bravery.

"What emotions are the brave you feeling?" Dave prompted.

"This is interesting. I am experiencing a surprising emotion. The brave me is angry that this is happening. I am very angry. I am thinking that this storm is not going to get the better of me, but even if it does, I'm going to fight it. So I…I leave the helm and start mopping up water with a towel. When it becomes clear that we're going to sink, I help Mike with the life raft and get everyone inside it."

"Good, do you feel anything else besides anger?"

"I feel…determined. Confident. Strong."

"Any fear at all?"

"Some. Yes, I am still afraid, but the fear has taken a back seat to my determination to fight the circumstances."

"Excellent. Take a few deep breaths. The drapes are closing. You can stand up now and leave the theater. Are you still feeling okay?"

"Yes."

"This is a very simple Neuro Linguistic Programming exercise. What I'd like you to do is to take some time this afternoon and journal about this experience. Think about some of the other things in your life that you are afraid of, a loved one dying for instance, and imagine how the brave you would respond in those circumstances. Make sure to record what you are feeling. Then call me back tomorrow with your thoughts."

That night I wrote in my journal: "What I find amazing in this simple exercise is that for so long I have considered myself a fearful person that I'd forgotten there were other ways to respond. It never occurred to me that I could be brave in that kind of situation. That it could be part of who I was. Seeing myself acting bravely on that screen reminded me that there were options. How could I have missed something so incredibly simple?"

I called Dave back the next day and told him, "I have been in the habit all these years of responding to fear as a fearful person and approaching Fear from a position of subservience. It helped a great deal to imagine myself acting as a brave person. The image is very powerful. Something switched inside my brain, yesterday. And another thing, I know the odds of us being in a storm of that caliber are slim, but the odds of losing a child to SIDS are slim as well. While I kept telling myself 'everything would be okay,' deep down I didn't believe it. I don't trust the odds anymore and my mind isn't fooled by them because if the odds happened to me once, they could happen again."

"This is why you are still struggling. Your mind cannot be fooled anymore by stats. It knows that no one can promise you that there is a 100 percent chance that you won't run into a storm, or that you won't lose another loved one. The only thing you can do is to retrain yourself in how to positively and creatively respond to that fear. Then the question is no longer "what IF something like that happens," but "WHEN something like that happens, I will respond with this positive emotion." Learn to listen to yourself. Try to distinguish that fear voice in your head and address it as if you are standing outside yourself in the third person. Coach yourself. In the coming days, record what the negative voice inside you is saying. Try to counter that voice with a positive, brave, message."

"One more thing," he said continuing. "Have you heard of Julian of Norwich?"

"Yes, but I don't know much about her. She was a Nun right? A mystic?"

"She was a hermit, an anchoress, not a nun. A mystic, yes. She devoted her life to contemplative prayer in the late 1300's. She used to say, 'All shall be well, and all shall be well, all manner of things will be well.' I think, Kim, that when you accept that despite great suffering you can survive and live fully again, only then will you be released from the bondage of fearing the unknown. You survived losing a child, yes?"

"Yes."

"Then you have already survived one of the worst things life can dish out. Release your fear of the unknown. All will eventually be well. All manner of things will be well. Trust that the God of the Universe has, ultimately, a larger agenda with our wholeness in mind."

He said it as if it solved everything. I wasn't sure it was as easy as that. I said, "Maybe it is a process?"

"Yes, yes, it is a process. A journey. One that you will likely wrestle with for the rest of your life. But, it should get easier. Like anything, you must practice to become adept."

In the following days I thought a lot about that quote from Julian of Norwich. I also noticed a real trend in my thought processes. I often responded toward problems, even small ones, with a negative, fearful, and often victimized voice, as if I was at the complete mercy of what life handed to me instead of a co-conspirator. Sometimes this attitude would emerge as a joke. I shared some of this with Mike and the kids, who took it upon themselves to check my negative responses.

While docking into a tight spot, I said sarcastically one day, "Oh great, we're gonna die!"

Lauren grabbed my arm and said, "Mom, are you hiding a negative thought pattern inside a joke? I think you are. I want to hear you say that we are absolutely NOT going to die. We are going to do a fantastic job docking. Come on, now, let me hear you say it."

I thought: 'Oh that's great, just what I need in my life, three mini would-be psychoanalysts evaluating me.' But I knew she was right. I actively listened to what I was saying both out loud and in my head. I took each event as it happened and meditated on it in the mornings. I filled the ruts formed from bad habits in my brain with what little soil remained before tromping off through the bush to form a new path.

35

While in Florida, I decided to cross the Atlantic. I decided to cross mainly because I knew that if Mike and the kids went without me, I would never be able to live with myself. I had imagined future conversations when one of the kids would say something like, "Oh! Remember that time we were in between Bermuda and the Azores and we saw that huge whale! That was so amazing!" And then the three of them would recount all of the glories of the Atlantic crossing and I would sit in silence and regret. I was fairly certain I would rather be swept overboard and die at sea than be forced into a lifetime of such moments. And there was one other reason, slight as it was. A dogged curiosity that made me both wonder what was out there and how I would respond to it that, in the end, always seemed to tip the scales in favor of exploration over fear.

Our plan was to make it to the Mediterranean. I still had a hard time focusing on the anticipation of traveling through countries like Morocco, Spain, France, and Italy, because I was so preoccupied with simply "making it" to the Pillars of Hercules. In fact, I knew that the greatest mental feat for me would be our arrival in the Azores after the longest and most dangerous crossing. After that, there were a couple shorter crossings to the mouth of the Mediterranean, but these were closer to land and in more heavily traveled waters. I knew that with the larger crossing accomplished, I could enjoy the rest of the passage more fully.

Lauren, having experienced a soul awakening, was excited to go to the Mediterranean, as were Stefan and Mike for different reasons. Stefan believed the crowning achievement would be to jump into the water midway between Bermuda and the Azores. While having coffee in the cockpit one evening, Mike confessed to me that the thought of being in the middle of the Atlantic made him a little nervous. He hadn't mentioned it before because one fearful person was enough to deal with in a relationship. He said, "I have to say that I tried that NLP exercise Dave had you do, the one where you watched yourself on the screen. It helped."

I was a little taken aback by Mike's confession of fear. It was strange, I thought, that I could live in such close proximity with Mike and still not be aware of what he was thinking. I wondered, then, how he was processing everything. I asked him, "Is this what you imagined back in university when we wrote down on our dream list 'live on a boat'?"

"It is…" he paused. "You know, for all my life I have lived for the rush of a moment. I have loved the high of adrenalin that doing wild and crazy things provided. Those fearful moments make a great story out of my life, which as you know, I use to my advantage," he smiled before going on. "Experiencing this live-aboard life, this much-quieter-than-I-had- anticipated life, is causing me to take a deep look at myself and my journey. I feel like I am coming at life from a more whole position. I accept who I am here and now, rather than placing my life on hold waiting for the next daring moment and allowing those moments to define me. All the things that matter most to me exist in the simple day to day. I am learning to value those moments. I don't think I will ever stop enjoying adventure, but that need is starting to take its proper place in my life. And I am not so sure that there isn't a fair bit of adventure in the simple things anyway. It just depends a great deal on how you look at it."

Practically speaking, there was a lot to do to prepare for the passage. I hauled out our ditch bag to re-examine its contents.

This large, yellow, nylon duffel held everything we needed in case *Chrysalis* floundered and we would have to launch the life raft and abandon ship. Its contents would allow us to survive at sea for a number of days. I was assured by all offshore cruisers that planning for this is of grave importance; a matter of life or death. I took their advice and tried to keep the picture of the "brave" me in my mind.

Rummaging through the bag's musty contents, I found a watermaker. I read the label and was told that it would take sea water and make roughly 1 liter of fresh water an hour. Not bad. In addition there were about 40 pouches of sealed fresh drinking water. The directions on the back read: "*If stranded in a life raft, make every attempt at drinking no water during the first 24 hours unless sick or injured. Thereafter, crew may be allowed 2 pouches (holding 4 ozs each) of water daily until rescued.*"

I considered that this was a cup of water a day. I got thirsty just thinking about the small portion. Digging further, I discovered several small packages of energy bars, vacuumed sealed, holding 6 bars each. "*Instructions: Eat one bar every 6 hours. Eat in small pieces to aid digestion.*" There was a fishing packet containing line, lures, and hooks; two thermal blankets, an extra inflatable lifejacket, a bailer, a radar reflector, a submersible flashlight, signal mirror, and a small parachute anchor for rough seas. Many of the items included in our ditch bag were redundant, as our life raft also contained a separate smaller ditch bag with many of the previous things including flares, repair kit, paddle, and strobe lights.

Along with a portable GPS and VHF, our EPIRB, or Emergency Position Indicating Radio Beacon, was also in this bag. Once activated, whether manually or upon contact with water, an EPIRB emits a unique distress signal. When picked up by the Coast Guard, it will not only give our location, but the make and model of our boat, its ownership, and how many crew members were aboard. Receiving your signal, the authorities could then send out a search and rescue party. As I turned the yellow EPIRB over in my hands, intent on figuring it out, I inadvertently pushed the "activate" button and the EPIRB emitted a deafening "beep," startling me so that I almost fell off the couch. I frantically looked around for the "off" switch, found it, and, panting, thought that the sound alone could be heard from miles around.

Lastly, I pulled out a book entitled, *Your Ultimate Guide to Liferaft Survival,* that warned us to be as prepared for emergencies possible, since help could be several hours or days in coming. The book urged us to think ahead by imagining what life might be like all alone on a life raft in the middle of the ocean. Try to anticipate your needs, the book said.

Thumbing through the pages, I found helpful advice and a list of many "comfort" items that were not included in either of our ditch bags, and which I subsequently added: lip balm, sunscreen, toilet paper, duct tape, Tylenol, spare batteries, hard candy, reading material, knife/scissors, seasickness meds.

Upon further reading I found this helpful tip: *if you are carrying cans of food make sure to pack a can opener as getting into a can is virtually impossible without one.* Having forgotten, I stuck one in. Keeping up morale under such conditions was vital. Anticipating our needs, I added a plastic deck of playing cards, a notebook with a pen, a book of Suduko, and a couple of Dirk Pitt novels, and a large bag of chocolate turtles. What could be better to keep up morale than chocolate?

The authors continued with something like: If you can bring a towel, sunglasses, and a spare set of clothes it would be helpful. Sounded like I was packing for a vacation. Why not add a margarita mixer and really have a party? Then this: "Take only what is necessary. Pack light but with great thought." Great advice, I thought, on abandoning ship or being born.

A few months before moving onto *Chrysalis,* the four of us had taken a first aid course, but I thought we could use a refresher. Lauren had recently completed her lifeguard training. Since it was fresh in her mind, I asked her if she would take over the medical aspect of our crossing. She pulled out our First Aid Manual and typed up a brief synopsis of each important chapter, then printed the pages and put them in a binder with labeled tabs for quick reference. She called us into the pilothouse one day to remind us of a few things. She went over the basics of CPR, what to do if someone broke an arm or a leg, and the proper care of a burn. Calling on Stefan, she demonstrated how to give someone the Heimlich Maneuver.

"Everything is here in this binder, so if I am the one that needs help, you won't have to ask me." Lauren mentioned at the end of her tutorial.

She also hauled out our large medical bag, roughly 2' x 2' x 3', and we went through its contents together. This bag contained several mini-kits inside one big bag. There was a wound care kit with sterile gloves, antibiotic ointment, gauze, bandages, wound closure strips, needle and thread, scalpel, several bags of cotton, syringes, Kelly clamps, and skin stapler. A burn care kit with gloves, aloe, medicated burn pads, and non-adhesive bandages. A large Fracture/Sprain kit contained several splints in varying sizes, elastic bandages with Velcro, and instant cold compresses. Also included was a large manual on how to do things like perform an appendectomy, remove a bullet, suture a wound, and set a fracture. It even described the proper way to remove a splinter.

Although I hoped to avoid the circumstances that would require the use of such instruction, I did appreciate the thoroughness, and was confident that if a medical emergency happened underway, we would have the necessary means to deal with most issues until help arrived. As we had decided not to carry any weapons on board, I tried not to envision a scenario when one of us might need to surgically remove a bullet.

Mike and Stefan prepared our parachute anchor. They took it out of its bag and made sure the lines weren't tangled and the hooks were in place. They secured it to two long lines that ran out each bow. They also rigged up a jackline, a long cable attached to the stanchions, running the length of the starboard rails. If weather was bad and we needed to launch the parachute anchor, you could open the pilothouse door and attach the clip on your life vest to this line and walk up to the bow secure in the knowledge that should a rogue 30-foot wave hit you, it wouldn't wash you overboard.

One afternoon, the four of us stood on the deck and Mike explained how the parachute anchor worked. "In heavy seas, you throw the bag overboard, like this," he demonstrated chucking an invisible bag overboard, "and it will open, under water, into a large parachute. This should slow *Chrysalis* down so we won't drift too far off course. It will also keep the bows into the wind and keep us from being tossed around as much."

Right after that, we went up to the flybridge, and reviewed how to launch the life raft. In case something happened to Mike or me, Lauren and Stefan individually needed to know what to do to get *Chrysalis*, or themselves, to safety. The moment was a serious one.

"Remember," I said, "the life raft is equipped with a CO2 cartridge. When the case around the raft is opened and tossed into the water, the cartridge releases the gas, blowing up the raft automatically. The raft will be tethered to the stern so that it doesn't float away while you are attempting to get into it." Then I went about reminding everyone how to remove the life raft container from its holder.

Chrysalis is made of foam-cored fiberglass. Even if holed and submerged, she is supposed to float. All of our survival guides tell us that if it becomes necessary to launch a life raft and abandon ship, we will have a much better chance of being found if the life raft can remain tethered to our boat. From a rescue plane or helicopter, it is easier to spot a yacht, even overturned, than a small life raft.

"It is important," one of our guides told us, "to make sure and have a knife handy to cut your tethered line in case the yacht begins to sink, otherwise, your life raft will go down along with your ship." This, I thought, was an important safety tip.

I found our four "man overboard" watches and made sure the batteries were working. These bulky digital watches are worn on the wrist, and on contact with water, will sound an alarm at the helm, indicating that someone had fallen overboard. The closer *Chrysalis* got to the overboard watch, the more beeps you would hear, enabling you find the person and pick them up. We had worn them a couple times when we first moved aboard and then they had disappeared into a drawer. The kids didn't particularly care for them, calling them, "dorky." I told them there wasn't going to be any fashion shows in the middle of the Atlantic, and that we were going to wear them anyway. Sensing the gravity of the situation, they complied.

Mike had been accumulating spare parts to add to his collection. He told me one day he had spare parts for the spare parts. When I asked him if he thought he had everything he needed, he replied, "While underway, I could build a full scale replica of *Chrysalis* right here in the cockpit."

As Mike foraged for parts, I planned out our meals. From past experience, I had learned that if seasick, we needed small, nutritious, easy to prepare meals. I made things ahead like chicken noodle soup and sliced cheese and sausage for crackers, as well as heartier fare like lasagna and burritos. These I froze in individual portions for quick reheating in the microwave. I bought lots of energy bars, dried fruit and bottled water in case our watermaker decided to quit. I also did research into what sort of things might be difficult to obtain in Europe. From other cruisers I learned that peanut butter, brown sugar, powdered sugar, and real maple syrup, were a challenge to track down, and expensive even when found. I went with a friend to a big box store and stocked up. I organized all this in our small pantry on board, as well as the additional storage we had for dry goods in compartments under our large settee and watch berth in the pilothouse.

In between trips to the market, I went back to our family physician. He assumed I had returned to discuss my panic attacks, but I told him that since talking with my friend, I hadn't had any more, a fact he seemed both surprised and glad to hear. I explained that plans were still underway to cross the Atlantic and I requested antibiotics, pain medicine, antihistamine, and several packages of the Transderm Scop for seasickness. As I left his office with a stack of prescriptions, he said, "I am very curious to see how you do on this crossing. I would love to follow your progress." I handed him a card.

I got us all appointments for cleanings at the dentist office. We were long overdue anyway. When our dentist heard what we were doing, she hunted around in several cupboards before finding a portable filling kit. With it, we could perform an emergency filling underway. She showed me how to mix the white paste and apply it, smoothing it over with the tool included in the kit.

"It won't be a permanent solution, but it will hold you for at least a couple of weeks until you can find a dentist," she said. She also loaded us up with a few extra toothbrushes and tubes of toothpaste.

Back on board, I consulted the websites of the countries I intended to visit to make sure we could meet their travel requirements. I made sure all of our ship's papers were in order and typed up a crew list as well as a list of provisions on board. Finally, I made copies of passports, boat insurance and registration and put everything into an organized leather attaché case.

Mike took a VHF radio course and received a license. He also found a marine weather forecaster who would update us underway of any weather changes throughout the voyage by sending a daily forecast to our satellite phone. At the end of a particularly busy day in March, Mike looked at me and said, "Well, I think we are as ready as we are ever going to be."

Then we waited.

Every morning and evening, Mike and I checked the weather for a possible window. We had ten years of past weather history of the Atlantic stored on a disc and we had studied the months of March, April, and May for trends. It was possible to get a five day window in March, but the chances increased as the months progressed. March came and went. We were docked in a marina with a large live-aboard population who were aware of our plans, and every day we met folks on the docks who were watching the weather with us.

"You're not leaving this week, are you?" one of them would ask. "The weather looks terrible the next few days. Maybe next week?"

The next week proved a mixed weather bag. We were tempted. Something happens when you are tied up at a dock and the sun blazes and the water beckons enticingly smooth. From your vantage point in a nice, calm, marina or anchorage, you begin to feel a tad invincible. You are tired of waiting. So tired. And annoyed with a weather system which, like the Stock Market, you hope to bend to your will using what little super telepathic abilities you imagine you possess. I can only guess how many sailors without the benefit of a detailed weather forecast went out to sea on a perfectly lovely day thinking, "How bad can it be?" Pretty bad, we learn from the sad outcome of many. We have good friends who have lived aboard and sailed offshore for over twenty years. They have never been in a squall dangerous enough to invoke fear, but know many who have. They told us that in ocean passagemaking of any kind it is imperative to be patient. Wait for the window. Wait for a whole season if you have to, it will eventually present itself to you.

We tried to be patient. We ticked off the slow progression of days that blended into three months. Each one began with a grain of hope that would end up dashed after checking the latest update. We busied ourselves with work, chores, school, and community. We ate all the food I had prepared for the crossing and I had to re-supply. Lauren managed to get a job at local souvenir shop. She and Stefan made several friends at the marina and the beach. When a weather window finally opened up at the beginning of June, I wondered if this would make it more difficult for them to leave, but they seemed as genuinely excited as Mike and I.

The day before we left we dressed ship. We scrubbed *Chrysalis* down and strung all of our flags. We rechecked our systems. Took *Chrysalis* out in the Intracoastal for a few hours to see how she was running. All systems were go.

For many years after college, I would sporadically dream that I had forgotten to study for an exam. In my dream, several friends would arrive at my dorm room and ask if I had been up all night studying for the final exam and I would say "What final exam?" They would look surprised and say, "The one that is worth 35 percent of your grade! The one that is today—look at your calendar. Today is the day you have circled in red marker." I would think "Oh no!" and panic and try to cram on my way to class, which everyone knows does little good. I would plea bargain with the professor, who would gaze at me through narrow eyes as if he had heard it all before. Then he would shake his head and hand me an exam and after reading through the first page, I wouldn't know the answer to a single question. At that point in the dream, I would wake up with a gasp.

The night before the beginning of our Atlantic crossing felt like the night before a final exam, only this time, it felt like I had been preparing, cramming, studying, for a very long time.

Thinking backwards, I couldn't pinpoint when I had started preparing. I thought about sitting in the cafeteria with Mike so many years ago and flippantly writing down our list of dreams with no comprehension of the significance the moment held or how that list would pursue us through our marriage, our lives. Pushing further on in my memories, I considered Bethany's death. I thought about how I was basically a kid when she died, my adult life yet to be sculpted, and how it had altered, forever, the course of my life. How it, on the one hand, challenged me to value life and to live out what was most important, while at the same time, instilling a fear of the unknown. The two battling for supremacy ever since.

And I thought all the way back to my childhood, when I had been unafraid to explore the possibilities of living large. Where do you delineate the beginnings of a dream? Do you push further? Had it been hardwired into me from Nordic sea-faring ancestors who left everything they knew to start a new life in America?

As if it were the beginning of a school term, I had circled the supposed crossing date in red on a mental calendar months, maybe even years before. I realized that the fear I had felt back then was the result of fast forwarding my past self to this moment, and my past self hadn't been ready. She lacked the research and experience. The journey up to this point in time had prepared me. I was confident in *Chrysalis*, confident that we had prepared ourselves to the very best of our abilities. I was ready.

I sought out the giant woman Fear, which I had never done before because she was always seeking me out. In my imagination, she appeared domesticated. I found her sitting in an overstuffed arm chair, eating petit fours. Her feet were up on an ottoman. She wasn't as large as I remembered and she seemed more sedate and this wasn't necessarily a bad thing.

"You've been quieter than usual," I told her, "especially considering the circumstances."

"Yes, well when you decided that you would be okay no matter what happened, I sort of lost motivation. Don't worry though, hon, I'll always be around if you need me."

Her parting comment caused me to consider the fact that being a recovering fearful person is similar in some ways to being a recovering alcoholic, or a recovering anything for that matter. There is always the temptation to give in to the idea that comfort equals safety. That escape is a good substitute for wholeness. And that change can wait until tomorrow. I knew that I would forever carry the temptation to give into Fear, into letting it tempt me back to my LazyBoy, but I now recognized those patterns in my life. That, I hoped, was something.

In the morning, the four of us met in the pilothouse. I sensed the relational undercurrent of shared experiences, both difficult and inspiring, that had forged strong ties between us. We instinctively reached for each other hands.

Mike said, "This is it, guys. This is the day we have been working toward for a long time. How is everyone feeling?"

I watched Lauren and Stefan. Under the umbrella of two parents who they knew loved them and carried the responsibility to care for them no matter what, they had the freedom to be joyous. They cheered and danced, Mike and I joining in, before we sought out each other hands again. We got quiet.

"Let's pray, eh?" Mike said.

So we bowed our heads and we prayed because that is just what you do when you are about to cross 4,000 miles of open water. I had long since given up the 'name it and claim' view of prayer. As if God was some giant genie who had nothing better to do than decide whether or not to grant my latest wish. I really wasn't sure if prayer was even about making our requests known as much as it was about turning inward in order to turn us outward again, changing our perspectives, and encouraging us to enter in to the goodness already growing in our lives. And there was something bonding, I thought, about sharing our concerns with others who were traveling a similar faith journey. For my own part, my words had less to do with twisting God's arm into allowing us safe passage, and more to do with communicating the changes that had been going on in my life. Outside of that, I wasn't sure about the ramifications of prayer, but it was instinctual for me, so I followed through despite big doubts and banked on mercy and grace no matter the outcome. This time, as we took turns talking out loud, we asked for safety, of course, and good weather. Each of us was grateful to be embarking on the journey.

When it was my turn, I said, "I don't know exactly who you are, God, or how you work, or what my life holds, but I am thankful for this day, for my life, for the lives of these three here with me. I can't imagine three people I'd rather be with. And I think that whoever you are, you must get a sense of joy watching us take on this challenge. Exploring both the world you made, and our own limits and abilities. Tell Bethany, wherever she is, that we wish she could be here with us. Maybe she already is, who knows. I do know one thing. That somewhere along the way I have come to trust, to believe that whatever happens, all manner of things *are* well, and *will* most assuredly be well."

We said Amen and hugged and then Lauren said, "Let's get on with it already!"

In the morning sunshine, we released the lines, waved to several friends who had gathered on the docks to see us off, and headed for the Ft. Worth Inlet and open water.

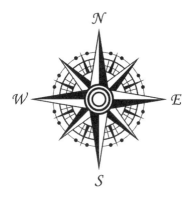

~*Part Five*~

Cast off: To loose, unfasten; to undo all mooring lines in preparation for departure.

36

Evidently fear was no longer a factor for me. At least it wasn't for the moment. I stood at the bow and watched a pod of bottlenose dolphin and scanned my soul. No fear. No heart palpitations or gripping anxiety. Days before, when we had run *Chrysalis* up and down the Intracoastal to test her out, we had come across a particularly shallow area, and instead of panicking, the picture of the brave me entered my brain without conscious effort on my part for the very first time. I had held my ground at the helm with Mike, and we had calmly discussed an alternate course together. I didn't even recognize the fact that I hadn't freaked out until Mike mentioned it afterwards.

Entering the Atlantic, there was the feeling that I was heading out into the unknown. It wasn't the final frontier and it wasn't even close to going where no one had ever gone before. Thousands had come before me. But it was the unknown for me. I felt a combination of excitement mixed with curiosity. It would have been intoxicating except for the fact that the unknown and I have had a rather rocky relationship. While I had wanted to know the future so I could manhandle it to my advantage, life, at least so far, preferred to keep me guessing. Looking out over the ocean, feeling the wind and the sunshine, I wrote in my journal:

"It is strange that I am unafraid. I keep thinking that if I can do this, cross the Atlantic Ocean, I can do anything. What could be worse, (or better?), for my control freaky self than sitting in the middle of nowhere, no land, no help, anywhere for days? I am at the mercy of the elements. The mercy of God. In a tangible sense, crossing the Atlantic is my way of saying to God: It is okay that I don't understand you; nor can I control you. Both You and life are untamable. I might lose Mike

or the kids. I might fall overboard and drown. I have released my fear of the outcome of such events. Whatever happens, all will most assuredly be well. I cannot help but think this is good for me."

When we were well into the Gulf Stream, Mike called us into the pilothouse to confirm our overnight watch schedule. Mike would be on from 6 p.m. - 9 p.m., Stefan took over from 9 p.m. - 11 p.m., Lauren from 11-2 a.m., and I opted for the early morning shift from 2-5 a.m., after which Mike could resume having had a decent 6-7 hour sleep. I was protective of Mike's sleeping routine. If something went wrong, he would be the one called on, day or night, to fix it. I liked the early morning hour watch. If I pushed myself, I could let Mike get a few more hours of sleep, and I could enjoy the sunrise.

We timed the crossing to take advantage of a nice, fat, high pressure system that had developed in between two low pressure systems. Out in front of us, the remains of Tropical Storm Barry made its way east across the Atlantic. We waited until things settled down significantly enough to make things comfortable before untying the lines and taking on fuel. *Chrysalis* carries 1500 gallons of fuel. At 9 knots, she has a 3,000 nautical mile range. At 6.5 knots, the range increases to 4,500 nm. For our crossing, we planned on traveling at 8.5 knots. At such a rate, we had plenty of room for unforeseen incidents, such as burst fuel lines, dirty fuel, and emergency course corrections.

All day long we traveled at 1400 rpm and had been making 9.8 - 10.2 knots with the Gulf Stream giving us a boost in speed. While this was great, we were pulling closer than anticipated to the residual effects of Tropical Storm Barry. With the distance made overnight, we would be about thirty miles closer than we had speculated. Seas could potentially get a little choppy. This we had to balance with our desire to reach safe harbor in Bermuda ahead of schedule.

Around eight o'clock on the evening of the first day, we called our weather forecaster, Bill, on the satellite phone. He suggested heading north in the Gulf Stream for several hours. In this way we could both take advantage of the current and possibly avoid the remnants of Barry. After talking with him, Mike and I discussed it. Heading north in the Stream would give us an extra few knots, but it would also add distance and time on the water. We were concerned about the low approaching Bermuda from the west. Since the leftover seas from Barry were only forecast to be four-to-six feet, we chose the lesser distance over the risk of running into the low creeping up behind us.

Having built *Chrysalis* ourselves, we were intimately familiar with how and where our systems were set up. The importance of this had been revealed to me by leaky plumbing and fuel lines, loose gaskets, gummed up filters, burned out solenoids, and many other problems that were guaranteed to break down in pairs when we were miles away from the nearest West Marine and very close to a reef.

Before our live aboard days, I had a rough understanding of mechanical and electrical systems. I knew the difference between alternating current and direct current. I knew that if I put my finger in a socket, or touched the prong of something that was in a socket, a connection would be made via the tip of my finger, the result of which would be quite unpleasant. I attempted to pass along my personal electrical heritage to my children.

"Remember that story I told you about the time I was seven and visiting my cousins on the farm in Iowa? And how they had me run through wet grass and then touch the electric fence that penned in the cows? Never ever do that."

In light of our extended offshore voyage, it was essential that I knew what to do should something happen to Mike while underway. When we first moved aboard, that knowledge was fresh in my mind, but since Mike tended to manage these systems, I had become a little forgetful. Before we left, we reviewed transferring fuel and basic engine and generator repair. What to do if we ran out of power and where he kept the oil in case any one of the former needed a top up. Once again, I had confidence enough in my abilities to know that I could keep things running and get us safely into port without Mike's help. I wouldn't like it, but I could do it.

It is important, when you are cruising hundreds of miles offshore, to have power. Other mid-life men might have mustangs or mistresses, but Mike had our DC generator, Big Bertha. Lucky him. I didn't begrudge him the late nights spent with her. The gifts of oil. A shiny new solenoid. The homage paid to her in the form of blessing and cursing, ranting and pleading. Even I saw the value of wooing her when we were miles away from anything. In terms of comfort, she was the gatekeeper to our happiness afloat. When running well she supplied our electricity for items like television, refrigerator, microwave, and running water. More importantly, we could keep our charts loaded on the computer and transfer fuel between our storage and day tanks. All was dependent on her generosity. I had a great affection or dislike for her, depending on the day.

"It doesn't help," I told Mike, having become frustrated with her performance several months previous, "that she is a temperamental old thing. Who can understand why one minute she is working happily and the next she grumbles to a complete halt for no reason whatsoever. She is complicated and quirky and drives me crazy! What?"

I had noticed Mike was smiling.

"What?" I asked again.

"Nothing really. It's just that Big Bertha sort of reminds me of someone else I know."

"Oh you're just a laugh a minute aren't you, funny man?"

"Let's just say this is as good a reason as any to keep polygamy illegal."

When Mike started up Big Bertha for the first time since leaving Florida, everything was working fine. About an hour later he looked at the gauge and it appeared that the generator was not charging the batteries. He checked around. Nothing seemed out of order. The charge controller seemed to be working properly and there was 28+ volts coming off the generator, but the battery bank was only at 23.5. He was finally able to trace down the problem to the On-Off switch that connected the two. He pulled off the switch and the back was completely melted. It didn't take long to replace it. If there was going to be a problem, it was nice that it was a simple one, easily solved.

As the sun went down, we put out the fishing rods. Stefan and I sat in the cockpit, and it wasn't long until both lines started whirring and we both struggled to reel in two hefty thirty pound Mahi Mahi's. Mike and Stefan filleted them and we let the lines out again. A couple hours later, Stefan and I fell asleep in the reclining lounge chairs in the cockpit. I awoke much later to a curious sound of flapping, much like a bird in rapid flight. I turned on the cockpit lights to find several flying fish thrashing around on the floor. Evidently, we were making our way through a school of them. As I looked over the edge, one flew up and over the cockpit rail, right in front of me, hitting the still sleeping Stefan in the head before falling into his lap, where it wriggled violently. Stefan never budged. Flying fish, although a bit bony, can be delicious, but since we had more than enough fish in our freezer, I grabbed the fish by the tail and tossed him overboard. Stefan, none the wiser of his interaction between himself and the deep, slept on.

We were cruising along the northern boundary of the Bermuda Triangle whose coordinates vary depending on what source you consult. Typically, the Triangle encompasses the southeastern coastline of Florida, Bermuda, Puerto Rico, and then back to southern Florida. My dad, lover of historical mysteries, asked before we left if I was worried about cruising through such fabled waters.

"After all," he said, his voice building with excitement, "there are accounts of ships disappearing, alien abductions, and the suspension of the normal laws of time and physics!"

"Dad," I had told him, "I don't need anything else to be worried about on this trip okay? But you know me, I am pretty skeptical of all that stuff. I get more nervous thinking about what would happen if we ran into a whale or a floating container that has fallen off some tanker."

"Oh," he said, disappointed. Obviously we differed in our opinions as to which were more exciting, containers and whales, or aliens and time travel. "Look," he continued, seeking to reassure me, "you're about as likely to run into a container or a whale as you would be to encounter aliens. Still, it is the Bermuda Triangle."

That's just great, I thought.

I am not a big fan of slice-and-dice horror movies, but once in awhile, I do enjoy a well thought out suspense movie with a conclusion that ends in a twist. While watching one with the rest of the family, I am inclined to believe that the main character can hear me speaking to them. With a scrunched up pillow in my grasp, I wonder aloud why they are opening the door to investigate that strange noise. Why look under the bed? Or enter that walk-in freezer? Why oh why go down that dark downtown alley in search of the shadowy figure? I say with disgust, my eyes closed tightly, that only an idiot would go looking for trouble. They are such idiots, I whisper it again and again until someone pokes me and reminds me that no one on the screen can hear me, only those in the room, and they aren't happy about it at all.

Mike told me once, "The main characters aren't idiots, they are curious. It is human nature to want to know what you are up against. Look at your own life. In the past you have been scared of living on a boat, of crossing an ocean, but here you are looking that danger full in the face. Doing just what you always tell the main characters not to. Are you saying you're an idiot?!"

Touché.

I hoped that by entering the Bermuda Triangle I hadn't gone looking for trouble. With regard to it, I was not interested in the numerous and similar tales of Joe Blow who, while cruising alone through the Bermuda Triangle, happened to see several flying saucers after recently imbibing half a bottle of Jack Daniels. I was more interested in the facts. In the last thirty years, about a hundred ships and planes and a thousand sailors and pilots have disappeared without a trace in the Bermuda Triangle. Many attempts have been made to explain this, including alien abduction and chasms in the space-time continuum. The area is one of two places in the world where a compass points to true north rather than magnetic north, suggesting a magnetic anomaly that may confuse pilots and captains. The conjecture is that this magnetism could very well interrupt their navigational and communication equipment, causing captains to become disoriented, lost. Floating in circles, they could run out of fuel, drift for days, before being lost in a storm. Even stranger was the fact that in 1968 the U.S. Navy and NASA undertook a deep-sea exploration project of the area and found no sea life between 300 and 2,200 feet. The significance of this I could not confirm, but it didn't sound good. If fish knew enough to stay away from the area, what was I doing running right through it?

I took solace in the fact that Lloyds of London, the great marine insurance company, reported that accidents in the Bermuda Triangle were no more dangerous or prevalent than in the rest of the world and did not require additional insurance when passing through its waters. Of all people, I figured, they should know.

The first night I was on watch, we were well into the Triangle. Alone, under the light of a full moon, *Chrysalis* went through patches of thick fog. For a few minutes, the dark water and a darker sky, would be clearly visible. Then we would enter the fog. The world would turn into an Edgar Allan Poe poem or a murky version of a Claude Monet painting, awash in foreboding shadows. To pass the hours, I kept myself amused by imagining that we were about to run into some prehistoric uncharted island populated with dinosaurs. I thought I could just make out a rocky shoreline. Several times, through parted fog, I thought for sure I had caught a glimpse of the ghostly, black form of the Flying Dutchman, her sails in tatters, passing about a hundred yards off our starboard bow. Just as I raised the binoculars, it would vanish into the fog. This, I thought, was the effect the Bermuda Triangle was having on me. It was a world where anything was possible. Rules and regulations meant little. We were well over a hundred miles from the nearest red tape. My mind subconsciously sensed the freedom and took full advantage of it while it could.

We continued to make 9 knots overnight and by the time I roused Mike for his turn on watch, the seas had built. As anticipated, bumpy six footers tossed us around. I had put on a transderm patch behind my ear the night before we left Florida, so I felt no seasickness. The effects of the Scop patch last about three days, after which you can put on a subsequent patch, but no more until waiting for several days. Later in the morning, when I awoke, the waves had calmed down. I was just starting to settle into my routine of reading, eating, reading, when Mike came into the pilothouse and announced that Big Bertha wouldn't start.

Mike gets very quiet and collected under pressure, which is probably one of the reasons our marriage has lasted through building three houses and a boat. He calmly told us to turn off everything that didn't need to be on, lights, television, computers, and then he disappeared into the generator compartment. He worked on Big Bertha for several hours while the kids and I took turns on watch and running small errands for him, getting tools, and keeping an eye on the electrical panel.

Around lunchtime, Mike emerged to tell me that the melted battery switch from the day before was only the tip of the iceberg. The generator controller had shorted out at some point and blown the switch. Mike and I had about five back-up plans to keep us supplied with power, so neither of us panicked. We decided to try plan B, the backup alternator on the generator, but when that failed to start, Lauren and Stefan helped him haul out our small, portable, AC generator. This initially worked fine, but stalled about an hour later.

At that point, we began to get a little nervous. Since I am queen of the worst case scenario, we had already discussed in detail what would happen should all our backup plans fail and we ran out of power. The engines could run by themselves, as they generated their own power. We could manually supply them with fuel. The engine batteries could supply us with some power. We had two handheld, battery operated GPS units, and two handheld VHF units (and about a year's supply of reserve batteries). We could mark our coordinates down on paper charts and navigate the rest of the way "by hand." The lack of running water would be an inconvenience in regards to flushing the heads. This we could do with the ample supply of bottled water we carried. Our 6' x 3' x 4' freezer was jammed full, but even without power, it would likely remain cold until we arrived in Bermuda.

"We may not be as comfortable and a little more stressed," Mike told me, "but we should make it to Bermuda."

While taking a break at one point, he tried to talk it through with me. When a resolution proved elusive, he asked if I had any ideas. Since the generator would start and then sputter, I said it sounded like a fuel problem to me. Earlier on in the day, he had checked the fuel line, but he had been working on it for several hours, running more diesel through the lines. I told him to recheck the line and the filter. Maybe we had picked up some bad diesel. He went back to Bertha's den to revisit the issue.

At the end of the day, Mike reappeared to tell me he couldn't figure out what the problem was with Bertha. He had rechecked the fuel line and the filter, but they were fine. He was able to get the backup alternator on Big Bertha working, and it began to supply us enough power to equal our consumption. He moved on to the portable generator and got that working. Using both, we would be able to keep the freezer running. It had been a long day and he was exhausted.

"We have power, for now, although I'm not entirely comfortable with the whole process. I'm heading to bed. Wake me if anything comes up."

I awoke late the next morning to calm seas. In our race across the Atlantic, Tropical Storm Barry had pulled out in front. I reheated some coffee leftover from Mike's watch earlier and sliced myself a couple of pieces of banana bread, and headed up to the flybridge. Mike was already there, enjoying the sunshine. He gave me a brief update on our power situation. Big Bertha wouldn't start, but the portable generator was holding its own. We had passed the halfway point in this first crossing, which we both agreed was good news. The hours, we thought, would tick by more quickly now.

I had been watching the radar off and on since the night we left, and there had been no ships either by sight or by radar. I found this somewhat surprising, as we were supposedly in the shipping lanes. I hadn't expected the shipping lanes to be like 6 p.m. on Hwy 401 in downtown Toronto, but seeing a couple of tankers would have gone a long way toward curbing the feeling that we were the only ones alive in the universe. Plus, there would have been some reassurance in knowing that someone else was out there should we require assistance. At night, I scanned the horizon with binoculars looking for a friendly, twinkling light; by day, I sought out the interruption of water and sky with a dark, rectangular block indicating a ship. Nothing. While watching the very small, red boat indicating

Chrysalis' position on our computer chart, I tried hard to comprehend the fact that my whole world was but a tiny fleck on that wide expanse of water.

By the end of the second day we had exhausted the new movies I had bought. We had already played several rounds of Family Feud and Password. Read until our eyes got bloodshot. We were moving en masse toward boredom. While eating a burrito on the flybridge, Lauren wondered aloud if we were bored on day three of this short crossing, how were we going to survive the nine day crossing to the Azores? After doing a few chores and laying outside in the sunshine, Lauren and Stefan decided to have a *Lord of the Rings* marathon.

Around 4:30 a.m. on the morning of day four, I had a lengthy discussion with Mike over coffee about the impending weather report we had received from Max Sea Weather via our satellite phone. The low traveling southeast across the north Atlantic states, right for Bermuda, looked to be a fast moving cell, but it was uncertain as to how it would develop or how far south it would travel. At the time, Max Sea was forecasting seas of 6-8 feet around the time of our arrival into Bermuda. Seas of this sort would not be a problem, assuming that all our systems were working, but they were not the pleasant seas we had enjoyed for the past twenty four hours. Even though it meant arriving in Bermuda in the early morning hours, we decided to keep our speed of 9 knots. Better, we reasoned, to pull in earlier, even if it meant we had to wait outside the harbor, than to risk tangling with that low pressure system for longer than necessary in open waters.

Mid morning, about 150 miles from Bermuda, it was a relief to hear voices come over the VHF. The four of us gathered around the radio and hungrily listened to a local fisherman and a cruise ship hail Hamilton Harbour. The harbormaster spoke with a distinct British accent. He wished everyone a "very good morning to you, sir." There was human life on this planet after all, and it was well mannered to boot. Switching the channel, we picked up the local weather forecast, which was slightly different from the report we had from Max Sea. Bermuda Weather called for calmer seas that night with winds from the northwest. This meant that as soon as we reached the south end of the island we would be protected from the wind and waves while we proceeded along the south eastern shore.

In spite of Mike's best coaxing efforts, Big Bertha had obstinately remained inoperable. We had been running our reserve generator continuously since day two. As long as it continued its loyal service, it would supply us with enough power to get us into Bermuda. Although we were certain our arrival into Bermuda was forthcoming, it did cast a shadow over the longer crossing to the Azores yet to come.

I awoke out of habit at 2 a.m. on day five. I climbed the steps to the pilothouse and found Stefan asleep on the settee, Lauren reading on the watch berth, and Mike at the helm. They had decided to stay awake until land was sighted. Stefan hadn't quite made it. Mike handed me the binoculars and said, "Take a look."

There, off to port, were the twinkling lights of Bermuda. One crossing down, two more, including the nine day crossing to the Azores, yet to go. About an hour later, I radioed the harbormaster to let him know of our approach. I was hoping we would cruise into the harbor just in time for a beautiful sunrise, but as the morning progressed, it became apparent that the low we had been keeping an eye on and thought we might encounter had finally made its way southeast and was approaching in grey, threatening clouds.

Even as we made our way to Town Cut, the wind began to kick up. We listened to the Bermuda weather channel on the VHF, which was predicting average seas upwards of 7 – 9 ft., winds of 30 knots with gusts well over 40, and rain later that morning. We were relieved to pull into Ordnance Island around

7:30 a.m. to check into customs. While Mike was inside the Customs House, the sun came out for awhile before clouding over again. Not long after, it began to rain. From Customs House, we were able to secure a berth at the Dinghy Club just outside of St. Georges on the northeast end of the island.

Hearing the howling wind made it feel even better than usual to be tied up to a dock. In terms of value, the phrase "safe harbor" had a new meaning for me. Mike and I sat in the galley. Although exhausted, we were too excited just yet for sleep.

He asked me, "Did you see that big cruise ship come into the harbor just as we were leaving Customs? You know, I looked up at the hundreds of passengers lined up along the sides and I am unsure of how I feel about those cushy cruisers. Part of me feels contempt because those people hardly know what it is like to be in the middle of the ocean with no generator and to be completely on your own. But the other part of me is jealous because judging from the smiles on their faces, they enjoyed the crossing with much less worry than I did."

I said, "I like a cruise ship just as much as the next girl, but honestly, would you rather have made this journey on that floating city? I can't see it. Even with the worry, you love the story. Challenging yourself."

"You're right, I suppose. But it is easy to say that now when we are safe at a marina."

After a quick bite to eat, the four of us fell to our berths and slept for most of the afternoon while the wind raged and the rain poured down. Just before falling asleep, I searched my soul for emotion. There was the relief one feels in a classroom, after the professor, who has been handing out graded midterms, finally hands you yours and low and behold, you haven't flubbed it. But your comfort is short-lived because in the next instant the prof begins to discuss the intricacies of the coming final exam. This, I had yet to accomplish, and it was worth a hearty portion of my final grade.

We woke up around four in the afternoon, and even though it was still sprinkling rain outside, we walked into town in search of a place to eat dinner. Passing by the pink, white, and occasional light blue buildings, along with all of the flowers, reminded me of spots I had visited in the Caribbean. The air was fresh, as it was back home after a hard rain, with the faint scent of flowers and saltwater.

Although it was only 5 p.m., most stores had closed for the evening. Several restaurants were open, and we quickly decided on a British pub, Tudor in style, that had a blackboard outside the door advertising "Best fish and chips on the Island."

We ordered a bottle of champagne to go along with our fish and chips. With it, we made lofty and verbose toasts to the weather, to *Chrysalis*, her Captain, First Mate and cook, resourceful and eager crewmates, and because our server told us the next day was the Queen's Birthday, we raised our glasses to the Queen.

In St. Georges, Bermuda, we began to connect the dots of history we had studied while docked in Norfolk, Virginia. While walking through Jamestown, the first permanent British settlement in America established in 1607, we had learned about Pocahontas and John Rolfe. Reading through the history of St. Georges in our travel guide, the name John Rolfe appeared again. Here in 1609, the ship he was on, *Sea Venture*, laden with settlers and supplies bound for Jamestown, Virginia, was intentionally run aground in a heavy storm. John Rolfe, future husband of Pocahontas, remained with the passengers on the island of Bermuda for ten months. During this time, unable to dislodge *SeaVenture*, they salvaged her and built two new ships, *Deliverance* and *Patience*. In these, they continued on their journey to Jamestown, arriving having used up their supplies and with little to offer the residents of the New World other than more mouths to feed.

"Oh I get it now," Stefan said as we discussed this walking

around downtown. "This is the same John Rolfe who came all the way from England, was shipwrecked here, in this very spot—maybe even walked where I am walking now, then made it to Jamestown, and met and married Pocahontas! Man, what a journey he had!"

I was thinking that Stefan, age 14, would fit the title of "old soul." When I first heard this phrase as a kid, I thought it meant "old sole" as in the sole of a shoe. Worn, comfortable, frayed around the edges, been around. It was apt either way. At the time, he was interested in theology, philosophy, and practical jokes. I told him the three fields of study were completely compatible. His wit was dry. He would state the obvious and to his surprise, we roared.

"What do you think about John Rolfe being shipwrecked here?" I asked him.

He shrugged his shoulders and said as a matter of fact, "I think he should have waited for a better weather window."

37

Two days later, we made our way through the reefs on the north side of the island and into ˙Hamilton Harbour where we anchored just across from the Royal Bermuda Yacht Club. Big Bertha began working again for reasons we could not explain. While this was good news in the short term, we needed to solve the mystery before we could continue to make our way east. While Mike considered all the ways to placate his mistress, I planned to do some provisioning.

Before we left Florida, I stacked up our large freezer with meat, sliced cheese and bread, as well as some prepared favorites like gourmet sausages, small pizzas and potstickers. In consulting other experienced Mediterranean cruisers, many told me that meat in some places could be substandard. Although we were all looking forward to experiencing the cuisine in the different countries through which we traveled, I imagined there would be something comforting in hauling out a few nice Colorado steaks for dinner. Plus, it is in my nature to be over-prepared.

What we lacked was fresh produce. When the wire fruit basket in our galley got low, I started to hear about it from the crew, and I knew it was time to hit a local market. I don't mind as I'm one of those people who actually like doing the grocery shopping. Even better, walking the aisles of a foreign country whose shelves could hold any manner of unfamiliar wonders. Still, living on a boat, particularly at anchor, my whole day could be spent just making a trip to the market.

I woke up early one morning, went online, and found two markets within walking distance. I plotted them out on my local map. When Lauren emerged from her stateroom, we each grabbed a wheelie cart which was a blue plastic cart with wheels that, when folded, looks like a cumbersome briefcase but when opened into a small crate, can haul several bags of groceries. I put the map in my backpack and as we were getting into *Crabcakes*, Mike decided to tag along in search of parts for Big Bertha.

Hamilton Harbour was busy. There were numerous ferries and small boats coming and going. It was windy and wavy so between dodging waves and water taxis we got a fair amount of spray all over us. We arrived at the dinghy dock looking a little wet and windblown. After agreeing on a meeting time, Mike took off in one direction, and Lauren and I took off in the opposite toward Pitts Bay Rd. We walked about three or four blocks, through a historic district, with government buildings, modern apartment buildings, and colonial homes. We followed the streets on my map, but found no market. After asking a gentleman carrying what looked to be a grocery bag, we made our way up a little side street and there found a discreet sign with numerous grocery carts alerting us to its presence.

Walking in, we found the store to be a similar version of boutique, gourmet grocery stores back home. It was well stocked but outrageously expensive. Lauren and I nearly fell over checking out the prices, and she reminded me that Bermudan dollars were on par with the US dollar.

"Look, Laurs," I said, "$5.80 for a box of cereal!" We gaped at each other.

At the meat counter, Lauren pointed out a roasting chicken for $25.00. I was glad I already had several in our freezer. Continuing through the meat section, I held up a pound of ground turkey so Lauren could exclaim over the $6.75. Even produce left us shaking our heads, but we needed it. We splurged on a cantaloupe for $4.99.

As to be expected, the store also carried a great many items from Britain. Things like canned curry and tikka sauces. Bangers and mash. Frozen steak and kidney pie. Jars of mincemeat. The all-important staple: shortbread. I put an overpriced but worth-every-cent box in my cart. Also needed were Wine Gums and some lovely fried, sugary donuts that looked similar to our crullers back home. Before long, our grocery cart was full. We checked out, opened up our rolling carts, stacked our groceries inside, and then happily made our way back to the dinghy, our carts "ca-clunking" over the cracks in the sidewalk.

That evening, Mike tried to start the generator and nothing happened. We ran our portable for awhile, but wanting to save its life for the crossing ahead, we resorted to turning off all our unneeded power. That night, we read by small battery operated lanterns and went to bed early. When we woke up the next morning, we were completely without power.

Since the engines started on their own, it wasn't long before we crossed the bay to the Royal Bermuda Yacht Club, where we immediately plugged into shore power to feed our hungry batteries. Mike set about finding a professional who could help him fix the generator. After consulting several locals as well as a few other Americans at the marina, he was able to track down the "best generator guy on the island." Jerry, an American ex-pat, showed up the next morning and he and Mike spent the next few hours getting to know each other and Big Bertha in tight quarters.

Later that afternoon, both Jerry and Mike emerged looking grim. The kids and I came to the galley to hear the verdict.

"I am stumped," Jerry said shaking his head. "I hate to tell you guys this, but with all these generator problems, I wouldn't put too much hope in making it to the Azores any time soon. Best thing I can suggest is to order a new generator from the States and try to cross later in the summer. Maybe fall."

We thanked him for his help, and upon seeing our long faces, he left saying we didn't owe him anything.

Nineteen years in a monogamous relationship had given me a pretty good idea of how my partner would respond in certain situations. When I heard the proclamation of "Electrician Jerry," I didn't put too much stock in it. In fact, I knew that this would only further motivate Mike to find the problem and solve it. It kills him to be confronted with a puzzle that threatens to get the better of him. When faced with defeat, he displays considerable perseverance and tenacity. I have found this to be an admirable trait, especially when we are on the same side, working towards the same goals. Not so great when we are arguing.

For the next two days, he practically moved in with Bertha. This, I thought, brought a new meaning to the phrase, "open relationship." When Mike and I happened to run into each other, we spoke in short, staccato sentences. At lunch, for instance,

"Sandwich?" I would ask when he appeared sweaty and covered with grime.

"Yup."

"Any good news?"

"Nope."

"Can I help in any way?"

"Nope."

He would disappear again only to reappear a few hours later for a duplicate conversation.

On the afternoon of day four, he called us into the pilothouse.

He said sadly, "You people know I've done everything in my power to fix this stupid generator. I have pulled the thing apart looking for the problem…."

"We know," the three of us said somberly in unison nodding our heads.

"And…" here his demeanor changed drastically before he continued, "I FIXED IT! WE CAN KEEP CROSSING!"

We all stood up, cheering, and held our very own mosh pit, slamming into each other with joy, until Stefan stumbled and almost fell down stairs, and out of habit I said, "Oh, careful, guys, careful," which, as usual, was ignored.

When things had calmed down, Mike told us, "After pulling wires, patching cable, and nearly electrocuting myself once a day, I finally figured it out. You know that song about the leg bone connected to the thigh bone, the thigh bone connected to the...whatever it is...you know that song?"

We nodded.

"Well this is how it works with a generator. The grounding wire was loose and that led to a power surge, which led to a shorting of something somewhere, which, of course, led to a draining of power everywhere. The root of it was actually very simple. There was a loose connection in the circuit board of the main control box. While crossing to Bermuda, when we leaned to port, a connection was made, when we leaned to starboard the connection was lost. Once I figured it out, all I had to do was tighten a screw, and everything worked fine."

We left the marina that afternoon and anchored out for several nights to reaffirm that Big Bertha was, indeed, like the rest of us, in better spirits. Knowing that we could cross renewed our passion to be ready when very large, very calm, weather window to the Azores might present itself. Unlike our experience waiting for weather to cross to Bermuda from Florida, this time, a window emerged almost immediately.

There are nine islands that make up the Azores archipelago which lie about 750 NM west of Portugal, 1800 NM east of Bermuda. The islands themselves make up an autonomous region of Portugal. Mike and I briefly discussed landing first on the small island of Flores, but decided in the end to push for Faial and the main town of Horta. Once there we would need to decide if we wanted to explore the Azores. All reports from fellow cruisers were that the Azores were pristine and well worth a few weeks stay. We tentatively decided to spend time on the island of Sao Miguel and Madeira before making our way to Gibraltar.

We called Forecaster Bill who confirmed our thoughts on the weather window, saying, "It looks like that Azores High is beginning to settle into the area. Things look calm in the west. I think you could go for it."

We decided to leave the following day.

38

The next morning, the skies were overcast and spitting rain; the tail end of a fast moving low pressure system. Once again, our plans were to follow it east. In order to allow it to pass further ahead of us, we waited until around noon to haul up our anchor. The waiting was painful. Everything was tied down and we were ready to go around 9 a.m. We had a leisurely breakfast of French toast and sausage, then wandered around *Chrysalis* checking and rechecking everything. Every five minutes or so one of the kids would ask if it was time to leave yet. In regards to time, I told them they were worse than I was back in the Bahamas.

"Relax," I told them, smiling, "We're on island time, mon!" For both Lauren and Stefan, waiting for this day had been a little like waiting for the end of school and the first day of summer vacation. Even more than the idea of nine days on the water, they anticipated our arrival on a different continent and the ability to say, "I have crossed the Atlantic Ocean on my own boat."

Mike seemed more skittish than usual. I thought this might be due to the fact that the weather was not going to be great for the first few hours after our departure. I asked him about it and he said, "This is the first time I have been a little nervous. I think all the problems we had on the crossing to Bermuda sort of opened to my eyes to all of the unforeseen things that can go wrong. I am trying to go over all the scenarios in my head and account for everything, but there is this nagging feeling that I'm forgetting something." I told him we had been over everything again and again and that we would be fine. He looked at me with raised eyebrows, then wandered around, displaced, for most of the morning.

For myself, I was resigned. It was the feeling you get when you have prepared and studied for the exam, and now you are sitting in the classroom at your desk, and you know that, although you have prayed for just such a thing, nothing but an earthquake or a tornado is going to keep you from having to follow through with the taking of this test, so you might as well just relax and get it over with. Do your best. Lauren, privy to my dealings with fear, had told me earlier in the morning that I was practically bordering on cheerful.

Around 11:30 a.m., we prayed together, hauled up the anchor, made our way out the Cut, and into choppy five to seven foot waves coming off the stern quarter. We even experienced some drenching rain, wind, and lightening. I would have been a little anxious about this had I not known the weather forecast. As expected, things were bumpy for the first four or five hours, but by evening, the waves began to settle down.

I awoke the second morning to sunny skies and fat, gentle, three-foot rollers coming by every now and again to remind us we are actually in the ocean and not on a lake in Northern Ontario. As I ate breakfast, Mike whacked his forehead with an open palm and said, "Oh! I wish I would have thought to bring an inner tube. The kids would have loved being able to say they tubed across the Atlantic!"

Then, once again, there was water for as far as I could see. The horizon was hypnotizing. Just when I would start to slip into the oblivion of nothingness, I would see what appeared to be the water spout of a whale, which would smack me awake again. After flowing in and out of consciousness for an hour or maybe a day, I would crave a diversion and go inside to play MarioKart with Stefan and, even though I won several races, he beat me overall for about the hundredth time. Seeking to sooth my wounded ego, I took my lunch, tabbouleh salad with hummus, and a book up to the bow and fell asleep listening to the sloshing of the water under *Chrysalis*. It was all very mundane and peaceful and helped soothe the occasional thoughts that tip-toed across my brain like, "What if..."

We had entered the Azores High. This semi-permanent high pressure zone forms across the expanse between Bermuda and the Azores, and in the summer brings hot, dry weather to the area. Once established, it can hover there for several months. I was hopeful that the weather forecast would prove accurate; fair seas and fair skies for the next four days. All our systems had been performing well. We were making better than anticipated fuel mileage and at two miles to the gallon, I jokingly told Mike that if we wanted, we could just bypass the Azores all together and go straight to Gibraltar.

"Is that a challenge?" he asked, smiling.

"Definitely not," I told him.

In the afternoon, with Stefan at the helm on watch and reading a comic book, I went toward the stern and found Mike sleeping peacefully in the cockpit. I was glad he was enjoying the fruits of his generator labor. I leaned up against the side of the barbeque and watched him for awhile. He had been reading a book on stock trading and it lay open, face down, on his chest. His beard was coming in and threads of grey were starting to erupt on his chin. Recently, I had told him I liked the stubble. His brown hair was a little tousled. Seeing him there and thinking about this journey we were on, stirred something in my soul just then.

I wondered how it was that after so many years, there were still times when he would offer a surprising response, and I would question if I really knew him at all. More often, though, the great amount of time spent in his company enabled me to predict his reactions. Well beyond finishing each other sentences, we were so familiar with the subtleties of each other's personalities, it was difficult for me to discern where the patterns of my own original thoughts ceased and Mike's began.

We were so young when we were married, with so much of our adult selves yet to be formed. When I thought back on it, I understood the caution more seasoned marriage veterans had offered when we decided to marry. Over the course of almost twenty years Mike had changed. He was not the person I imagined he would be, but then, he had said as much of me. Perhaps the greatest traits we both retained through all those years was a commitment to our friendship and the ability to change with each other's best interest in mind.

I had friends who asked me with incredulity, "How could you have only been with one man all your life? Don't you get bored?"

One dear friend, divorced years previous, had said more profoundly, "It isn't that I would get bored spending my life with one person, I would be get tired or annoyed with all the quirks. You know, like on *Seinfeld*, the way someone ate their peas, or the fact that they had man-hands, or were a close talker. I mean, think about this for a minute: years and years of someone calling you schmoopy. No thanks." To complete the thought, she said, "You know what it really boils down to? It is trying to keep your marriage alive over the course of all those years, when there are so many distractions. Not just outwards ones, either, but all the inward issues we carry with us. Don't you wish there was a manual? If you do A, B, and C you will accomplish marriage nirvana?"

All this I considered. In regards to quirks, Mike was full of them. Lucky for him, I had none, or thereabouts. Right. But quirks, I thought, were negotiable and had been in our relationship. In order to save our sanity, let alone marriage, ceasing to eat peas one by one was easy enough to change. There was, however, the question of boredom, of keeping a marriage alive. If I was honest, building and living aboard *Chrysalis* had gone a long way toward reigniting our friendship at a pivotal time in our marriage. It had connected us with our dream list and with those feelings we had when we were just beginning our journey together. Working so hard toward a shared goal, watching each other change and grow through the process, had increased our passion for life and each other. When the days got rough, when selfishness and pettiness threatened to undo us, there were all of the years of shared experiences and inside jokes hanging on the counter balance that had kept divorce at bay. We had no illusions of invincibility in this regard, which kept us on our toes, tossing the football back and forth to each other as we inched our way down the field toward the goal line. A finer teammate I could not have imagined. In many ways, in light of all the changes over the years, Mike was every bit a different partner with all the benefits of mutual history.

In the cockpit, Mike stirred, opened his eyes, and saw me watching him. He instinctively offered me a sleepy grin and stretched.

"Hey beautiful," he said in that groggy, soft voice I recognized so well. "I was just thinking. We could make our own mile high club right here. After all, we may not be a mile up in the air, but floating here, we are more than a mile above the surface of the earth."

I smiled back. Some things, I thought, never changed.

Nights on board were seductive. With *Chrysalis* on autopilot, the four of us donned inflatable lifejackets, and with a sleeping bag, went to lie down for awhile on the roof of the pilothouse. The evening was clear. The moon, full. Since we were over three hundred miles from land, there was no residual city light. After checking to see if there were any ships in the area, we turned off all our lights, including the running lights.

The sky was spattered with stars. It was as if the Divine Artist had taken a paintbrush, dipped it into white paint, and flung it onto a black canvas. Obviously the artist had gotten a little carried away. There were so many stars visible that the constellations themselves were a jumble and we struggled to identify them. After some effort and minor disagreement, we managed to find the location of the Big Dipper, which, I told them, makes up part of the Great Bear. "We know, Mom," Lauren said. After that it wasn't too difficult to find Polaris, or the North Star, and from there we could make our way to the "W" shape of Cassiopeia. As it tends to when looking at the night sky, the conversation centered for awhile on how small we were, and how in light of vastness of the universe, we could ever imagine to fully comprehend who God was. Mike mentioned that earlier in the day he had noticed we were cruising over water that was almost three miles deep. Who knew how many miles of space existed above us?

We were feeling pretty giddy and connected to each other and I figured that it was as good a time as any to ask Lauren, who had turned seventeen a month before, a question that had been on my mind for awhile. After two years living on *Chrysalis*, and at least one more yet to come in the Mediterranean, I wondered what her thoughts were.

"Laur," I asked her softly, "do you have any regrets?"

Mike and Stefan were off in their own little world joking about Uranus and some bodily function, so Lauren turned to face me. She propped her head up on her hand, became serious, and said, "You know, I feel much better than I did a year ago. And being able to get a job and have friends when we were in Florida went a long way toward satisfying the social part of me. I know there are several things I would have enjoyed about being in a typical high school, attending classes and sports activities, but I am looking forward to university because I think I will be able to experience a lot of what I missed while I'm there, so I feel good about that. When I get regretful, I think how I would have missed out on all of this," here she waved her hands at the sky before continuing, "and I have come to the realization that this is so good too. It is always a struggle in my brain."

I reached out my hand to touch her cheek and she simultaneously brought her own hand up to grasp mine, and then she pressed it against her face. Her tender reaction made tears come to my eyes because I knew that living on a boat had not always been easy for her. For any of us. And I started to say something, but before I could choke it out, she continued, "and I think I understand why you and Dad decided to do this. I understand you wanting to reconnect with us and with the world in a deliberate way. I think it was a good thing, for the most part. And I am so excited to get to the Med, you can't even imagine. And, Mom, I am so proud of us for crossing the ocean and for pushing through the fear." Then she smiled at me, patted and released my hand, and we turned to lie on our backs. It grew quiet, and for awhile the four of us lay looking up at the stars in silence and feeling the rise and fall of *Chrysalis*.

"I love you three knuckleheads," I said out loud.

"Love you, too," Mike and Lauren said at the same time.

After a slight pause, Stefan gave a dramatic sigh and said, "I love you, too, Mom, even though you SUCK at MarioKart."

39

Alone, alone, oh! all alone,
Alone on a wide, wide, sea
And never a saint took pity on
My soul in agony.
 -Coleridge, *The Rime of the Ancient Mariner*

The smallest known sailboat to cross the Atlantic was the 5 foot, 4 inch, *Fathers Day*. In 1993, her captain, Hugo Vihlen, a former airline pilot in his sixties, traveled all the way from the East Coast of the United States, to Falmouth, England, passing through the often treacherous North Atlantic. The trip took him 105 days and earned him a spot in the *Guiness Book of World Records*. Packed in tiny quarters, he brought along enough food for 85 days: 65 MRE's (meals ready to eat), two gallons of M & M's, 34 gallons of fresh water, a gallon of dried fruit, and 100 cans of Hawaiian Punch. This, he was able to stretch to accommodate his extra time on the water. In his bathtub-sized craft, he routinely traveled through waves 12-15 feet, and once over what he thought to be a wave 30-feet high. When asked what he did all day for 105 days, he told reporters he read several books including the world almanac, the dictionary, and a sailing book. More than just a boating adventure, he took the journey because of the mental challenge it proposed.

The third day out found us roughly four hundred miles east of Bermuda. It was as close to madness as I had yet come in my life, and I wasn't the only one. I passed Lauren in the galley and asked her how she was. I noticed she had a wide-eyed, crazy look, the kind Jack Nicholson's character had in the movie *The Shining* just before he chased his family around a vacant hotel and tried to murder them with an ax. Her hair was frazzled and there were stains on her shirt.

When she responded to my question, her voice was high pitched and running in fast forward. "Oh I'm fine. Why do you ask? Do I not look fine to you? Because I am fine. Really fine. Everything is just fine. Did I mention how fine I am?"

Geez, I thought. I watched her get a magazine and stretch out on the settee. She didn't seem to be actually reading it, but stared straight ahead. Every once in awhile she mechanically turned a page.

I tracked down Stefan who was playing a video game in his stateroom. I had to snap my fingers in front of his face at least three times before he slowly turned in my direction. His hair was sticking up and he was wearing the same blue t-shirt and baggie black shorts he had on the day before. There were several dishes piled up on his bed with a couple of left over bread crusts scattered on top. When our eyes met, I thought he had a glazed-over zombie look and he seemed to be staring straight through me.

"You okay?" I asked.

"Are we there yet?" he asked, his mouth forming the words slowly, his speech almost inaudible.

"No, there is still five and half more days to go," I said.

He let out a sort of primal groan, and resumed his playing. Studying him, I thought I noticed a small facial tic.

Then I went up to the pilothouse. Mike was sitting in the captain's chair, feet propped up on the helm, his head buried in a novel. He grunted at my hello. I asked him if he wanted to play cribbage, but he said he was tired of games. He was into his book. He asked to please just be left alone. It appeared that everyone was tired of playing games. Tired of traveling. Tired of trying to occupy themselves with menial labor.

So I went up to the flybridge. Seas were calm. I should have been happy about that, but all I could think of was how much water there was. For hundreds and hundreds of miles there was nothing but water and no way off this boat. Even though there was all this open space around me, I was engulfed in a wave of claustrophobia. I suddenly felt penned in, trapped. It seemed I had been floating forever and that I had never known anything else. The sun dallied, meandering from one horizon to the other. We had seeped well into boredom, past congeniality, and we weren't even half way through the journey yet. Hugo Vihlen, who somehow survived 105 days alone on the ocean, would no doubt shake his head at our unimpressive mental capacity a mere three days into our crossing.

As I considered the length of 105 days, Stefan's head erupted from the hatch in front of me.

"I'm bored," he said, "is there anything to do?"

Boredom is a state of existence that I have long been trained to avoid: idle hands are the devil's plaything. The Protestant work ethic had pulsed blood proficiently through my veins for as long as I could remember. On land, I positioned myself alongside a culture that abhors boredom of any kind and will go to great lengths to avoid it using any number of debased and profitable methods. Blaise Pascale, that seventeenth-century mathematician and scientist, believed we hate boredom because it causes us to face our own mortality. "[This] is why gaming and feminine society, war and high office are so popular. It is not that they really bring happiness, nor that anyone imagines true bliss comes from possessing the money to be won at gaming...what people want is not the easy peaceful life that allows us to think of our unhappy condition...but the agitation that takes our mind off it and diverts us. When I set to thinking about the various activities of men, I have often said that the sole cause of man's unhappiness is that he does not know how to stay quietly in his room." Here, in the middle of the Atlantic, four people were trying to "stay quietly in their own rooms" without going mad. Of course, we fought against it, but we were quickly running out of ammunition. I decided that instead of fighting it, I would rest in it.

"Stef," I said, "I've got nothing for you to do. Why don't you come up here and sit with me awhile?" I patted the seat next to mine.

He stared hard at me for a few seconds, as if checking for indications of faltering sanity, before taking a deep breath in and expelling it slowly. You would have thought I had just asked if I could pull out his toenails one by one with needlenose pliers.

"Oh all right, fine," he said as if extending me a huge portion of grace.

A few seconds later, he walked up the stairs and sat down beside me on the white vinyl settee. The first few moments of quiet between us was kind of awkward. I scanned my brain for topics of conversation, but we had already exhausted the weather, books, movies, and what was for lunch and then dinner. There seemed nothing more to say in my opinion, so I decided not to say anything and Stefan obviously felt the same because the two of us sat silently for about an hour.

During that time, the awkwardness gradually gave way to a comfortable familiarity. We settled in. In the quiet, I focused on him. I thought about what he was like as a toddler, tenderhearted, kind, and recalled the various mother-son battles we'd had over the years and eventually made peace with. At one point, about twenty minutes after he came up, I remembered an endearing moment from the year he was six, and I spontaneously reached over and without saying a word, smiled, and hugged him. When I released him, he looked at me and grinned, but neither of us said anything. Then we sat for another twenty-five minutes or so in silence and all the while I felt the acute awareness of his presence and our relationship to each other and how *Chrysalis* was carrying us both over the swells, and how good the wind felt, and how soothing it was just to exist there together without being compelled to say anything. I felt completely at ease and sensed he did to. The claustrophobia I felt earlier disappeared and a peace settled over me. From time to time I glanced over to look at Stefan and watched him study the sea. The crease in his brow had disappeared. I wondered what he was thinking. The dearness of him, his value to me and the world, came to my mind and I focused on that. I thanked God for his existence. After about an hour, he patted my knee, and without saying a word, went back down into the pilothouse. I did not feel the loss of his presence. It seemed a natural parting.

When I think about it now, I consider that hour to be one of the finest conversations I've ever had.

Good news came on day four. It was the day before Half-Way Day. Everyone's spirits were bolstered with the knowledge. There was a lot to do. I held a meeting at the galley table to discuss plans. A celebratory menu was decided upon for the following day: fresh caught fish, macaroni and cheese, salad for dinner, chocolate cake for dessert and champagne for toasts. The fresh fish was going to be a challenge. Our fishing rods had been out since we had left Bermuda but so far the sea had withheld her bounty. I was banking on Mike's love of a good challenge, but didn't tell him I had Italian sausages to grill in case our bad luck continued. We also discussed plans to jump into the water. I told the crew there was no way I was jumping into the middle of the Atlantic. If they wanted to that was fine, but crossing an ocean was enough for me. Still, they kept trying to convince me. It was a rite of passage, just like a baptism, Stefan said. Forget it, I told them. Besides, there were more important matters at hand to discuss like the "Throwing the Message in a Bottle Ceremony" and the firecracker celebration put together by Stefan.

The Half-Way Day is important on many levels. Emotionally, we knew we were heading over the mid-point with the hardest part, at least in terms of waiting, behind us. After half-way day, day five, the excitement of fulfilling this part of the journey, would multiply as we mentally checked off the remaining days. Physically it was an important day as well. Up to that point, should we have had an accident, a broken arm, appendicitis, or a mechanical problem, we would have had to make our way back to Bermuda. But from that day forward, it would be closer to head to the Azores. Sobering, though, was the fact that at this very junction we were at our most vulnerable part of the journey. Should we require help it would be awhile, maybe days, in coming from any mainland. We were truly on our own in the middle of nowhere.

To put it into perspective: on Half-Way Day the depth of the water beneath *Chrysalis* was over three miles, about 15,840 feet. The nearest land was 900 miles away.

In the morning, floating on top of three foot, glassy, rolling waves I made a chocolate bundt cake, frosted it, and wrote "Happy Half Way" in blue decorator icing. While I was doing that, Mike caught a long, slender Wahoo, so dinner was taken care of. Later on, we each wrote out a message on a piece of paper to put into our bottle. When I asked what everyone had written, Stefan adamantly said that our personal notes were like a wish and couldn't be revealed without seriously affecting the progress and safety of the bottle. Everyone else agreed. That is why, even though I am tempted, it is best I not reveal what I wrote, as we have yet to learn the bottle's whereabouts. Lauren rolled up each note and put them into an empty wine bottle that had previously held a nice cabernet from Australia. We stood in the cockpit, blessed the bottle and its travels and the person who might find it, and Stefan threw it in. Then we all stood around for awhile watching it drift farther and farther behind us until finally it disappeared altogether.

The day before, Mike and the kids had decided to form a new club: The Mid Atlantic Swim Team. Membership, they said, could only be obtained by those who swam in the Atlantic Ocean midway between Bermuda and the Azores. Lauren immediately set about designing T-shirts.

On the afternoon of Half-Way Day, we put the engines in neutral and got on our swimming suits. I had initially intended not to jump in the water until I realized I wouldn't be allowed on the Mid Atlantic Swim Team, which meant I wouldn't get a t-shirt, and that was too much to bear. The whole morning, I had been wondering what was up with this LIFE and the way it was always stretching me. Demanding things from me. Tapping me on the shoulder. Couldn't it just leave me alone in peace for once? Wasn't it enough to just be crossing the Atlantic? Must I now be required to jump into the middle of it?

But something Stefan had said about baptism made me rethink the issue. When I was sixteen, I was baptized by full dunking, wearing white, in a Protestant Church. The pastor at the time told me that it wasn't admittance into the Church or even into Christendom itself, it was public declaration of a transformed heart and life, a sign of renewed birth and faith, and an announcement of life beginning as a new creation. It included a commitment to following through within a community that would both encourage me and keep me accountable. With this in mind, and in light of all the changes in my life, I told the kids I would jump in, although I wasn't too happy about it. I was, in every way, the reluctant convert.

We threw the life ring, attached to a white line, overboard. Mike jumped in first and we all cheered. He thrashed around and yelled out "Whoo hooo Mid Atlantic Swim Team Rules!" before climbing back on board. Then Stefan jumped in, followed closely by Lauren. I was amazed at how quickly the current pulled *Chrysalis* away from them, even with the engines in neutral. As they were good swimmers, it took little effort for them to catch up to the ring. I could tell by the way they quickly swam for the life ring that they were a little nervous. We hauled them back on board.

Then, they said it was my turn. They cheered and encouraged me. I paced nervously in the cockpit, wringing my hands. I made my way slowly to the swim platform, and looked out into bluish-grey, churning water. Fear, sensing an opportunity, sprang to life and reminded me of the remains of the tuna we had caught in the Bahamas, the one whose body had been ripped off by a shark. "What was I thinking standing on the edge ready to jump in, let alone allowing my kids to?" Fear asked. I chose to ignore her. Once again, I was resigned. I was going in and there was nothing for it.

I sucked in a breath, looked back at my congregation, closed my eyes, took a small step, and over I went.

The Unknown gulped me down. In the end, the Unknown, with all its mystery, would have its way with me. I surrendered myself to its coolness. The wetness revived me, alerting all my senses to the tingly feeling of being alive. My body swayed with influence of the current. I existed there, completely immersed for a few seconds, before rising up through the surface to take a breath. I saw Mike and the kids, smiling, calling to me, and leaning over the port swim platform with their arms outstretched. An unexpected feeling of joy came over me. As I swam for the life ring, I could feel tears mingling with the salt water drops on my face. Surprised, I thought, this is who I am after all; the kind of person who jumps off a homemade boat into the middle of the Atlantic Ocean. Perhaps this baptism wasn't announcing I was a new creation as much as it was acknowledging who I was in the first place.

As Mike pulled me in, Stefan yelled, "All right Mom! Now you get a Mid Atlantic Swim Team t-shirt!"

Tongue in cheek, I replied, smiling and panting from the exertion, "Just what I always wanted." But when I thought about this later, I considered it closer to the truth then I had initially realized.

40

On day six, I walked up to the bow and found a small gray squid about the size of my hand. Wondering how it had come to be there, I instinctively checked for wings, thinking, I suppose, that I had found a species in flux. Then I realized that a gull had likely dropped it, and recently, because it was still wet. I went inside and got a paper towel, carefully scooped him up, and threw him back into the water. Later that morning I found another one. I could not account for this other than to think that the same gull was concerned about our wellbeing.

But maybe it was the sea itself that was sending its manna onto our decks because every day I found three or four flying fish near the bow. These were small, usually between eight to ten inches long, and by the time I had found them, they were nearly dehydrated and hardly worth the effort to fillet. After studying their filigree wings, I threw them back into the water, hoping some other creature could make use of nature's bounty.

That day I washed the dishes. They had been piling up in the sink. After that, I popped in a load of laundry. Although we had a washer dryer combination, it took too much power to dry laundry on a crossing, so I planned to hang it outside to dry later in the day. I took a tour of *Chrysalis*, picking up dishes and wrappers and generally tidying the place up. I reminded Stefan to pick up his socks, and asked Lauren if she would mind making sandwiches for lunch. After eating a tuna fish sandwich, I took a short nap. Got up and read a bit of *Small Wonder*, by Barbara Kingsolver, which inspired me to write until suppertime. I pulled some lasagna out of the freezer, chopped up a salad and ate dinner while trying to help Mike download our latest weather, which turned out to be a wonderfully boring rendition of the last few days.

What an odd thing, I thought, *to be doing simple daily chores eight hundred miles from anywhere.*

We each dealt with the wide expanse of time and space in our own way. Lauren couldn't sit still. It was the story of her life. Because she had experience in managing her own day, she planned ahead. She had purchased a "Teach yourself Portuguese" class on DVD. She went through it at night while on watch.

When I came up at 2 a.m. to relieve her, she said, "*Obrigado,* Mama. *Boa noite!*"

About two days into the crossing, she was reorganizing a compartment and found one of our old knot tying guides. She spent a couple afternoons practicing with lines on the cleat in the cockpit. She then proceeded to go through the manual from the Power Squadron class we took a few years previous. She wrote the tests and reviewed the charts.

Stefan had earned the nickname Rip Van Winkle. Rip for short. The sound of the engines, the motion of *Chrysalis,* and the fact that he had started growing, combined to make a sleeping elixir he found difficult to resist. As soon as we started the engines, he fell asleep. He would wake up, have breakfast, play a game or two, and then sleep again. One night he came out of his stateroom around 6:30 in the evening. I told him to grab some supper. He thought I was joking as he was sure he had slept through the night and it was the next morning. The debate continued, as only a debate can with a teenager, until I finally took him outside and pointed to the setting sun and a compass.

The mood changed on day seven. We began to get excited. All our systems continued to work well, and every afternoon we received a weather forecast that was gloriously benign right up until our arrival in Horta, only two days away. Seas were negligible. Rarely had we seen such calm conditions. The sky was the palest blue with a few scattered cirrus clouds.

As if to heighten our anticipation, we began to see more birds. I saw what appeared to be a Herring Gull with its characteristic yellow eyes and legs. Several flew across our path throughout the course of the day. I pointed out a Little Shearwater to Stefan as we sat in the cockpit reading. Smaller than other shearwaters, I watched as he circled *Chrysalis*, following us, as if curious. At one point he came close to the flybridge, and I thought he might land, but he took off again to follow behind us. I couldn't be sure, but it seemed like the same gull followed us for the remainder of our journey.

It can be lonely at sea. The loneliness is not from a lack of human companionship, but a sense that you are a very small being on a globe whose circumference you can barely comprehend, and all this is spinning in a universe whose borders have yet to be determined. As indicated, what little there is on board to distract you from this plight quickly loses its appeal, and you begin to miss the hustle and bustle offered by the cultured world you alternately love and despise. There is no Facebook, no Twitter, no up-to-the-minute breaking news. Nations could declare war, a chunk of mountain fall into the sea, the paparazzi could snap a thousand photos, and you would keep existing, none the wiser and fully functioning, in a watery world, forever floating up and down, up and down.

Under such circumstances, boredom gives way to silence and solitude, and you begin to hear yourself think. God only knows where that will lead you. Experts in silence and solitude will tell you this is the point: to meet yourself, with all your pain, shame, and glory. To stare yourself full in the face without distraction and mourn and ask forgiveness, and to accept the good, yes, the incredible thought that we are unique in a vast universe, seemingly loved and drawn to wholeness by a Being who we may never fully comprehend, in a world that both shocks and inspires. And to accept that life may very well serve us several heaping portions of suffering, and it is what we do with those portions that often determines the kind of person we become in the end. This is what we work out in silence and solitude.

And this, I decided, was one of the reasons why I decided to live on a boat and cross an ocean: because midway through my journey I didn't know who I was and wanted to find out. I was very concerned about what I might find there, inside of me, and rightly so. I encountered agony, doubt, failure, and fear, but I discovered, like so many, that when pushed into facing those things, there is something in the human spirit that rises up. I can only imagine it comes from God's own spark of cells within us, the Imago Dei, always expanding and drawing outward, then back in again, like the movement of the ocean. Which is all to say, that by turning outward into an unknown world, I was drawn inward, where I not only discovered a little more of who I was, but who God is as well. And in terms of God, the more information I gathered along the way, and the more I sought to relate to this Being, the more I found I didn't know, which was disconcerting at first, but in the end, I learned to accept, along with my own inability to manhandle my own future to the degree that I wished. And this releasing my addiction to control brought a great deal of peace as I sat on the flybridge settee in the middle of the Atlantic Ocean.

While careening through space and inching our way across 4,000 miles of Atlantic Ocean, seeing the gulls swooping off our stern was a reminder that we were not alone. The gulls brought us a message: not only are you not alone, but land is somewhere close by.

The Azores was two hours ahead of Bermuda, but we decided not to change our clocks until arriving in Horta because it would mess up our watch schedule. This meant that at 4a.m. Bermuda time, I began to see light on the horizon. I turned on

Andrea Bocelli, softly, so as not to wake the sleeping crew. Then I resumed my post, sitting in the doorway of the pilothouse sipping coffee, eating peanut butter toast, and watching the sunrise. In the realm of good things, there hasn't been much to top those early morning hours I sat quietly in the middle of the Atlantic Ocean, listening to Bocelli, the sun rising to fill the pilothouse with light.

Around noon on day eight I smelled something. It smelled sweet, flowery, like perfume. I thought Lauren had sprayed perfume all over the boat and went down to investigate.

When I found her, she said, "Hey, just so you know, you put on too much perfume. And why did you put perfume on in the middle of the Atlantic anyway?"

"What? I thought you put on perfume!" I said.

"If you didn't put any on and I didn't put any on, then what is that smell?" Lauren asked, putting her book down to look at me.

Mike, who had been listening in from the galley, called up, exuberant, "It's land!"

The island of Faial is small, roughly 13 miles by 8 miles, with a population of about 20,000. Its primary town, Horta, was our destination. The island itself had been referred to as the Ilha Azul, or Blue Island, by poet Raul Brandao because of the masses of blue hydrangeas that bloomed in spring and early summer. I wondered if we could be smelling the flowers that far offshore.

A little while later, Mike called us up to the helm, and there on the computer chart, we could see the island of Faial, and five miles beyond it, the larger island of Pico which has a volcanic mountain that rises 1400 feet in elevation. Even though we were still over a hundred miles away, I instinctively looked out the window towards the horizon, hoping to see the dark outline of Pico's mountain, but of course we were still too far away.

We received our final weather update that evening, which hadn't changed for days. Light winds, around ten knots, from the west, and sunshine. Seas 1-2 feet. The crew was in grand spirits. We decided to stay up all night to watch for land. I pulled out two store-bought pizza crusts, and the four of us made up a couple of pizzas, putting what we liked on a half a pizza each. To pass the remaining few hours we played nertz, euchre, Clue, and had a round of Mariokart, which Stefan won, again. "Maybe next time," he said, "I should play blindfolded."

In the early morning hours, with the four of us watching, the lights of Faial finally came into view. Beyond it, we could make out the dark peak of Pico rising up off the horizon. We all cheered when Mike, looking through the binoculars, said, "Land Ho!" I felt the relief of a thousand sailors and cruisers as Mike handed me the binoculars and I could distinctly make out the dark outline of Faial's coastline. Soon our feet would know the feeling of solid ground and the peace and stability it offered. I had a longing for it unlike any I had experienced before.

Around 7:00 a.m., we approached Monte de Guia on the southeastern tip of the island. We were heady with the sweet smell of the island and the successful crossing. Although we still had a smaller crossing yet to accomplish, the passage to Gibraltar, the most difficult part was over. When we pulled around Monte de Guia and the town of Horta with its wide bay and its black and white homes and terra cotta rooftops creeping up the surrounding hillside, Lauren, Stefan, and I went to the bow and put our arms around each other. Lauren looked at me with tears of joy in her eyes, and immediately my own eyes filled.

Standing on the bow, I let the tears fall down my cheeks. I wept because I cannot make sense of how there can be such overwhelming beauty and joy walking right alongside horror and agony. I wept thinking how much life changes and how it is hardly ever the way you imagine it will be. In the face of such polarization, what more can you do but stand with your arms outstretched like the sea whip coral. My arms raised partly in praise because once in awhile, life is better than anything you could have anticipated, and partly in bewilderment, as if to say, "Who can make any sense of it at all?"

For good reason, I have been taught that pride is downfall of many, but while pulling closer to Horta, I felt something that transcended the mere idea of surging emotion at accomplishing a goal. It was a power I hadn't felt before. It coursed through my whole body, making me feel invincible, as if there was now nothing I couldn't do. The giant woman Fear became the Incredible Shrinking Woman right before my eyes, until she was about four inches tall and spoke high and squeaky, like one of the animated Chipmunks on television. I didn't even recognize her, and I hardly recognized myself. Or did I, maybe for the first time? I was reminded, then, of my elderly Aunt's response, who upon listening to my description of the Internet and email, said in a shaky voice, "Well, I'll be surprised at nothing after this." I wondered if this nugget of thought was the origin of the power I was feeling.

And right alongside the power, was a flood of gratitude for the journey that led me to this very spot. But that was perplexing because I had a strong inclination that I would not be in Horta had events not happened in my life the way they did, including Bethany's death. I had a hard time coming to grips with the thought that from the devastation of her loss, I could be thankful for the good things it had so obviously brought about. It seemed almost a betrayal. But it was the questions, the struggles, and the hope that had propelled me to take risks I doubted I ever would have felt the need to take otherwise. So I was grateful for those good things and I told God. At that moment, a picture came to mind of the good, the bad, and the ugly in our lives being mashed around in a giant mortar and pestle and somehow, the taste of life was richer because of it.

"Why, Mom, why?" I hear the incessant voices of my kids when they were younger asking me.

"I do not know. Go ask your father."

Mike steered us around the breakwater and we pulled slowly into the harbor. As it was early, the marina was quiet. It appeared every berth was full. We spun around with the intent of anchoring outside the breakwater, when Stefan said, "Hey, check it out," while pointing to a man who beckoned to us from the deck of a large Swiss schooner.

"You can tie up alongside us!" he called out, his English spoken with a heavy accent.

Grateful, we adjusted fenders, pulled *Chrysalis* close, and Stefan accepted the line he threw in his direction.

"Good morning! Where are you coming from?" asked the cheerful man on the schooner.

"Bermuda!" Lauren and Stefan called out simultaneously, delighted.

While hitching a fender, I glanced around the marina and it occurred to me that we were the only foreign powerboat in a harbor full of sailboats.

"Really?" the Swiss man seemed genuinely surprised. "How long did it take you?"

"This is our ninth day," Stefan said while effortlessly cleating a line.

"That so? Then congratulations, guys! Well done. Well done! Welcome to Horta!"

At that moment, I was inadvertently watching Mike roll up a black line at the bow. As if in slow motion, he stopped what was doing and turned around to look at me, the morning sunshine and green foliage of Monte de Guia making a picturesque backdrop behind him. Our eyes locked. He smiled broadly and winked in my direction.

41

Horta was a melting pot if there ever was one. Mike and I joined the steady throng who walked the docks of the large marina attempting to fill in a mental world atlas with all of the countries represented by the flags of various boats now tied up and secure after long passages. There was a pervasive air of respect and triumph, even jubilation, when striking up conversations with other boaters, as simply getting to Horta from outside the Azores required some experience and risk. I felt the instant camaraderie of others who knew what it was like to spend days at sea looking at nothing but water. These were serious, nautical folk, and I told Mike it was hard to imagine myself a part of such company.

While walking through the marina one day, Mike and I had settled at the end of a dock on a bench to enjoy the scenery, and while doing so, a small boat entered the harbor under full sail. The wind was coming in gusts that late afternoon, and in the warm sun it was obvious that the two young guys on board were having difficulty maneuvering without the use of their engine. As they swung back and forth attempting to harness the wind without allowing it to drive them into pilings, I said to Mike, "Let's go help them out." When it became apparent where they intended to tie up, we left the bench and met them at their berth.

The two guys on board, probably in their lower twenties, looked young to me. They were wearing faded and frayed shorts and t-shirts. As they pulled closer, I could tell their beards were coming in, giving them a haggard look. While I caught a line and cleated it, I guessed their sailboat to be a little over 30 feet long.

It was an older vessel and in rough condition. Noting the US flag at the stern, I wondered that their craft could make an extended offshore voyage without splintering apart midway through the journey. As Mike asked the usual questions, I listened in. They had come straight from Halifax and shortly after they left, their engine quit, and they had to sail the remainder of the way. It took them seventeen days and during that time they went through two gales of some significance. Not long after their engine quit, their radar and GPS went out as well. I looked around for signs of a liferaft, but couldn't find one.

"So you guys came across about two thousand miles under sail with only a compass?" Mike asked.

"Not only that, but we couldn't afford any charts either. Luckily, we made it right to Horta using the bearing we looked up before we left Halifax. Otherwise, we had intended to sail up and down the coast until we found a suitable harbor."

Subsequent introductions were made, and I committed their names, Joe and Curt, both Americans from New York City, to memory. We made plans to meet later that night at a pub. While walking away, Mike leaned over to me and whispered, "OK, doing what they did, crossing with no charts, no GPS, no engine, THAT is too much adventure even for me! I can handle a few unknowns, but even I have my limits."

We met Joe and Curt for dinner at a well known pub, Peters Café Sport. Afterwards, we all took a tour of *Chrysalis* and Mike gave them some charts of Morocco, their next destination. Then they wanted to show us their sailboat and wondered if Mike could take a look at their engine, so we walked across the marina and boarded their vessel which was small, but comfortable. A decent, floating, bachelor pad.

"You should have seen the place when we left Halifax!" Joe said. "Every spare inch was packed with food and gear. There was hardly any room to sleep! Doesn't look half bad now, eh, Curt, ole buddy?"

As he said this, he nudged Curt with his elbow. Curt muttered that there would have been a lot more room if they hadn't had to take all those boxes of Hostess cherry pies Joe loved. Directly after that, Curt and Mike went below to have a look at the engine and Joe and I settled at the galley table, just big enough for two. Over coffee, we discussed future plans. Joe was Jewish. His parents had immigrated to New York from Israel many years ago. He had a lot of family back in Israel, near Natanya, and that was where they were headed. After that, who knew? He and Curt had gone to high school together and had always dreamed of sailing across the ocean. After graduation, they worked hard as waiters in a posh Italian restaurant and saved up money. With it, they purchased their sailboat and planned to travel for at least a year. Longer, if the money held out.

When he asked me where we were going, I told him we would likely get as far as Greece, maybe Turkey. He said as long as we were in the area, we should definitely visit Israel, a place that hadn't even entered my mind as an option. He told me I would love it there. Scoffing, he continued, "America has this big notion that THEY are a 'melting pot' but Israel is the quintessential melting pot. There are all these people of passion from all over the world, living in close quarters, with thousands of years of history thrown in just to make it interesting. When you get there, be sure to look me up. I'll invite you to my grandparent's house and my Bubbe will fix you the best hummus and challah in Israel."

"I love hummus," I said.

"Not 'hummus', 'HO-mmus', he corrected me with a guttural pronouncement.

"Isn't Israel kind of, you know, politically unstable at the moment?"

"When isn't it politically unstable? Stick to the tourist sights and keep a watch on the US travel advisory and you should be fine. It really is pretty safe to travel in Israel and well worth a visit. If you don't want to stay right at the big marina in Tel Aviv, there are several other nice marinas. Try Herzliya. It's new and very nice."

About that time, we heard the engine sputter to life and Joe and I cheered. Mike emerged with a smudge of grease on his cheek, smiling.

Several days later, Mike and I walked with Lauren and Stefan down the dock to say goodbye to Joe and Curt who now had a working engine, charts, and a new GPS. I handed them a plate of chocolate brownies, for which they seemed grateful, and while waving goodbye, we watched them motor out around the breakwater. When they had passed out of sight, Lauren and Stefan turned to walk out ahead, intent on the promised afternoon gelato. As Mike and I made our way toward the marina restaurant, I told him about Joe's description of Israel. For perhaps the first time, I didn't instinctually make a pro/con list in my brain including the great travel distance or the political dangers of the Middle East. I didn't look around to see what the giant woman FEAR would have to say about it. Instead, I had thoughts of the possibility of the four of us walking the streets of Jerusalem, climbing the Mount of Olives and swimming in the Dead Sea.

I leaned towards Mike and, taking his arm, said, "Huh…Israel… wouldn't that be something…"

EPILOGUE

While looking for a map to hang in our galley, I came across *Amerique Septentrionale* and instantly loved it. Drawn in 1650 by a respected French cartographer named Nicolas Sanson d' Abbeville, the map represents the extent of what was known at the time about the Americas. It lacked the fanfare and colorful vibrancy of the Dutch maps I had found of the same era being simply drawn in black ink on pale yellow parchment. In researching the map, I learned that French cartographers of the day attempted to utilize scientific proof in their mapmaking, as opposed to artistry, and focused their efforts on producing clean, geographically sound maps. I was attracted to its straightforward presentation.

On this map created almost four hundred years ago, the eastern coastline of the United States and Canada was well defined and the Caribbean was rendered in detail indicating that the islands had been explored and documented. On the lower end of the page, the tip of South America and the Lesser Antilles Islands were easily recognized, and I could make out the names of Aruba and Margarita Island. The five Great Lakes were represented although they were not completely accurate, falling further north than in actuality. The Labrador Sea was depicted, marked on the map as Mer de Canada, and also Davis Strait opening into Baffin Bay, but as the waterway snaked its way west, it opened up into nothingness, hinting that there might be a Northwest Passage.

But the best part of the map was the west coast. Delightfully out of place and situated well offshore, California had been drawn as an island. With pronounced authority, the Gulf of

California pushed its way north, leaving several islands in its wake, to open back up into the Pacific. Even better, from the Isle of California north and modern day Saskatchewan west, the whole Pacific Northwest on this particular map had been left blank, as if to say, "We, the experts, have absolutely no idea what is out there, and cannot with any accuracy even attempt a guess." Although theories surrounding the geography were plentiful, I admired the assumed humility of a professional scholar, artist and businessman who signed his name to an official chart with the inherent message: "There is still a great deal I don't know."

Corroborated by several other explorers and Jesuit missionaries who had traveled the area, the idea of California as an island was held as truth for almost a hundred years, until 1747 when an official decree was made by the King of Spain announcing reality: California was not an island. Lines were erased. Charts had to be redrawn using more accurate information. Expert mapmakers and explorers, many of whom planned dangerous expeditions lasting many years based on faulty instruction, rolled their eyes, threw up their hands and declared, "Okay! So we were wrong!"

I am fond of the metaphor, because just about the time I start to think I know how things work and begin to draw lines in the sand the tide rises higher than it has in a thousand years inching closer and closer to my lines until the water laps them up completely. In light of this, I am learning to hold onto things loosely, releasing certain beliefs, no matter how treasured, when new information presents itself. This is not to say that there is no bedrock, certain values I would fight passionately to the death for: love, peace, justice, but the bedrock in my life is much smaller than it was before I lost a child. Before I gave up everything I knew to live this crazy boating life. The more I travel, the more I find that what binds me closely with the rest of the world is that so much is unknown. All of our charts and maps are only half-filled in. And for me, being okay with that has been one of the greatest struggles. I shared these thoughts with a wise friend one day, and he said, "It seems to me that it is easier to admit there are things we don't know, than to erase the lines we have drawn with confidence over the course of a lifetime when new information presents itself. Doing so means we have to admit we were wrong in the first place."

In light of such ambiguity, I am learning to keep my heart open while at the same releasing my need for control, a tricky two-step. As the giant woman, Fear, recedes, much smaller now than before, another entity takes root and sprouts: Hope. The word is optimistically pregnant with a question mark. Will I ever know for certain that things will work out the way I plan? No. But I am learning to trust in the bigger picture. I hope that despite the suffering, all things will eventually be made well, and that I can be a part of all things becoming well, not only for myself, but for others. And this is what I had been trying to find since the death of our daughter. This is the gift her life and the journey has brought me.

Acknowledgments

I am deeply grateful to my husband Mike for reading the manuscript and offering critique at all hours of the day and night and for walking me through the wanderings (in more ways than one) of a work in progress. I would like to thank Lauren and Stefan who offered their input on numerous occasions, often filling the gaps in my memory. I owe them a great deal for simply agreeing to participate in the bigger storyline. From the time we began to talk about living on a boat, we were fortunate to be surrounded by people who believed in us and encouraged us to go after our dreams: Mark and Karen, Rick and Joan, our group of friends in Cambridge, Ontario, affectionately known as the Sojourners, including Barb Berg. The older I get the more I realize the importance these people played in helping us to accomplish our goals. I am grateful too, for our parents, Bob and Sharon Eggert and Reg and Carol Petersen, who, although nervous about our Atlantic Ocean crossing, stood by us not only through the passage, but throughout our journey.

Professionally, I would like to express my thanks to Mary Jo Cartledgehayes from Creative Nonfiction, who was the first to review part of the manuscript, as well as my editor, Susan Schwartz, whose coaching has proven to be invaluable. Lynn Price at Behler Publications has been fantastic to work with as has my publicist, Paula Margulies.

Visit Kim Petersen's website at www.chartingtheunknown.com